Biblical UFO Revelations

Did Extraterrestrial Powers Cause Ancient Miracles?

Rev. Barry H. Downing

BIBLICAL UFO REVELATIONS
By
Dr. Barry H. Downing

Published in the United States of America By
Global Communications/Conspiracy Journal
Box 753 · New Brunswick, NJ 08903

Staff Members
Timothy G. Beckley, Publisher
Carol Ann Rodriguez, Assistant to the Publisher
Sean Casteel, General Associate Editor
Tim R. Swartz, Graphics and Editorial Consultant
William Kern, Editorial and Art Consultant

Sign Up On The Web For Our Free Weekly Newsletter
and Mail Order Version of Conspiracy Journal
and Bizarre Bazaar
www.ConspiracyJournal.com

Order Hot Line: 1-732-602-3407
PayPal: MrUFO8@hotmail.com

TO ELEANOR

WHOSE FAITH AND LOVE HAVE ENCOURAGED ME.

ACKNOWLEDGEMENTS

As will quickly become clear to all who read this book, I am indebted to Richard Dolan and Bryce Zabel for their excellent book *A.D. After Disclosure: The People's Guide to Life After Contact* (2010). For more than fifty years I have been exploring the relation between our modern UFO/flying saucer mystery, biblical reports of strange objects in the sky, and biblical reports of beings called angels. My basic question takes several shapes: if our modern UFOs were to appear to biblical people, what would be their response? From another point of view, how might aliens have interacted with biblical people, or ancient people in any culture? Might aliens, both ancient, and modern, see themselves as guardians of life on earth? Would there be any significant difference between guardian angels, and guardian aliens, and if so, how would we tell the difference?

Dolan and Zabel explore the cultural stress that will come to planet earth when the day of disclosure arrives. By "disclosure," they mean the day when the governments of the world can no longer hide the truth about the extraterrestrial presence on earth. On that day there will be major shifts in belief systems in politics, science, finance, and religion. In "A.D." they explore these issues well, and in the process they have set free my own thinking about my Protestant Christian tradition, and the implications of disclosure for that tradition. I began exploring these issues in my book *The Bible and Flying Saucers* (1968), and in the following pages I weigh the issues as I now see them.

I also owe a debt of gratitude to the late Walter Andrus, Jr. He founded the Midwest UFO Network, which expanded and became the Mutual UFO Network (MUFON). In 1972 Andrus recruited me to become a consultant in religion to MUFON, and encouraged me to write for their monthly newsletter, *Skylook*, which later expanded to become *The MUFON UFO Journal.* Andrus also encouraged me to write papers, and be a speaker at several of the annual symposium meetings sponsored by MUFON. To put it mildly, traditional religious journals were not interested in printing my material. Although serving as a Presbyterian pastor was my main vocation, trying to come to grips with the religious implications of the

UFO mystery was my major avocation. I was always treated with respect by MUFON members, although most were doubtful that I was going in a direction that made sense. I treasure the contacts I had with those like Budd Hopkins, who was very skeptical of my theology, but who nevertheless listened to me with patience. Others, like Stanton Friedman, have encouraged my work even though the evidence for my point of view is far from anything like solid science at this time.

I also am in debt to James Cunningham, owner and administrator of the "Strong Delusion" website. This website deals with UFOs and related issues from an evangelical Christian point of view. In 2008, Cunningham contacted me. I was not aware of his website at the time. He explained that some conservative Christians had been saying negative things about my UFO point of view on his website, and he wondered if I would like to defend myself.

I was a little slow getting off the mark here, but Cunningham was very gracious to put online everything I sent. And most of what is printed in this book appeared on his website between 2008 and 2012. Cunningham gave me more space than I had ever had to explore the theological, political and scientific issues that we now face, and will face more directly, when disclosure happens. I have no idea when disclosure will happen. I do not see the governments of the world in any hurry at all to release their UFO information, and so far, for reasons known only to the aliens, the aliens have mostly cooperated with the UFO cover-up. Not totally, of course, or UFOs would not be the world wide mystery that they are. (MUFON usually receives reports of more than 500 sightings per month, from around the world, to their website.)

In any case, I am indebted to Richard Dolan, Bryce Zabel, Walter Andrus, Jr. and MUFON, and to James Cunningham and his "Strong Delusion" website. All of them are very much part of this book.

And finally, I am in debt to my publisher, Timothy Beckley, who somehow tracked me down forty years after we shared the stage at a UFO conference, and asked me if I had written anything since my first book. Thanks also to Sean Casteel for a good question and answer session, which became the basis for his introduction.

Barry H. Downing
Endwell, NY
September, 2017

CONTENTS

THE BIBLE AND THE UFO MYSTERY
By Timothy Green Beckley

I have to admit that I am not a true believer!

You can't include me among the flock. Some might call me a "heathen," but I wouldn't go quite that far.

I don't really want to go into my own prejudices in regards to Christianity or all other organized faiths. Some of what the ministers, rabbis and imams say may hold moral virtues that we should adopt in our daily lives, but to me it's mostly "old news," what happened 2,000 years ago, and in most cases don't see how it applies to my getting by in life. Getting on your knees never got you anywhere, I always figured.

To my way of thinking, most of religious belief is like "pie in the sky, in the great by and by."

But actually, the reason I can "get into" Reverend Barry Downing's writing is because he is into "pie" in the sky (the making of manna, for example) for real, when it comes to UFOs, angels, and other explainable miracles as written about in the Holy Biblical texts.

For Downing sees the angels as being real flesh-and-blood beings who could pilot a spacecraft following the Jews in the desert as they made their great escape. At other times, these same angels could visit ordinary people in their homes and break bread with them.

The parting of the Red Sea really happened!

Moses did speak to some "higher being"!

Ezekiel did have a close encounter with advanced beings, and saw their craft close-up.

Jesus could have been transported to his Father's Kingdom in a physical craft of some sort.

Saul heard Jesus speak to him through a blinding white light in the sky while on the road to Damascus.

It's all here in black and white, and I can't help but be impressed. Most certainly by the fact that Downing was the first minister and academic to tackle the issue of flying saucers in the Old and New Testaments. His first book was actually published in the same year as Eric von Daniken's "Chariots of the Gods?," offering proof that Downing was way ahead of the times.

Though officially retired from his ministerial duties, he does keep active by delivering an occasional sermon and fine-tuning his thinking on the UFO phenomenon, a pursuit he keeps up with most rigorously.

Whether you are an atheist, an agnostic, a true believer, or simply a "truth seeker" like yours truly, there will be much to ponder in Reverend Downing's latest offering (in this case the "collection plate" might turn into a legitimate flying saucer). So join us on our junket to the stars and into the Heavenly realms beyond.

SUGGESTED READING (Books Available From Amazon.com)

Flying Saucers In the Holy Bible: Modern, Revised Interpretations by Rev Virginia Brasington, Prof G.C. Schellhorn

Excluded Books of the Bible Revised by Sean Casteel

Signs and Symbols of the Second Coming by Sean Casteel

The Heretic's UFO Guidebook by Sean Casteel

A Lifting of the Veil by Betty Andreasson Luca and Bob Luca

SUGGESTED VIEWING

Flying Saucers In Biblical Times - Full Documentary

https://m.youtube.com/watch?v=vmDkVxyGFqI

Ezekiel And Other Biblical Mysteries Revealed

https://www.youtube.com/watch?v=8MOTHsJzSCM

SLOW TRAIN COMING:
THE STORY OF BARRY DOWNING AND HIS SECOND BOOK
By Sean Casteel

*** The Reverend Barry Downing established his UFOlogical credentials with the 1968 publication of his groundbreaking book, "The Bible and Flying Saucers." Rest assured, Downing has not been idle in the nearly 50 years since. "Biblical UFO Revelations" is the latest from the Biblical expert, who has kept abreast of and responded to the ever-changing landscape of UFO and alien-related research and how it all relates to the many ancient mysteries of the Bible.

*** Downing's research into UFOs and his Biblical interpretations of the phenomenon are routinely rejected by both liberal and conservative Christians as well as the secular, mainstream publishing community. But you've come to the right place to learn vital truths that will likely impact not only your sense of reality but perhaps your immortal soul as well.

*** Are we willing to see UFO salvation in our near future? Is the world ready to accept Barry Downing's optimistic view that the ubiquitous flying saucers are piloted and crewed by angels that serve Jesus Christ and the Heavenly Father? Reading "Biblical UFO Revelations" will bolster your belief in Biblical truth and the reality of a UFO presence that stretches back to the dawning of mankind upon this earth.

******

The Reverend Barry Downing has studied the Bible most of his life. He has also studied the UFO phenomenon closely since his teen years in the mid-1950s. The combination of both pursuits resulted in the 1968 publication of his book, "The Bible and Flying Saucers," which would lay important groundwork regarding the blending of the divine with the alien.

That idea had not yet crept into public consciousness when Downing's father brought home a library book written by Donald Keyhoe in 1955.

"I read it and became a believer," Downing said. "I have never, even to this day, seen a flying saucer myself. Although I have talked to many who have, and many of those witnesses are credible, including a cousin who had a UFO fly over her house at treetop level and at walking speed. There was no noise, only a slight hum."

Downing immediately acknowledges that with most such sightings we cannot usually "prove" what we have seen.

"But my belief in the resurrection of Jesus," he added, "is based on reports of others, not on my own sighting. So my UFO beliefs and my Christian beliefs depend on faith in some sense."

Downing began reading the Bible every day when he was in the eighth grade, and by his junior year in high school he had read both the Old and New Testaments in their entirety and was beginning a second time through. Meanwhile, he excelled in science in high school and was offered a scholarship to study physics at Hartwick College in Oneonta, New York. He simultaneously felt called to be a pastor in the Presbyterian Church, but majored in physics anyway to keep his scholarship.

He thus arrived at Princeton Seminary with a degree in physics. But he was surprised to learn that some of his professors there had abandoned belief in doctrines such as the Ascension and Resurrection of Jesus in the name of science. Gone was the faith in a "three-decker universe," with heaven above, hell below and earth in the middle.

"And so stories like the Ascension (Acts, Chapter 1) were called 'mythology,'" Downing said. "My sense was – if you did not believe in heaven and in the resurrection – you as a pastor had no chance of doing a funeral with any real hope for eternal life proclaimed in the funeral message.

"I decided that after seminary I would go to the University of Edinburgh, Scotland, and seek a Ph.D. in the area of eschatology, which would deal with questions of where does earth, and where do we, end up."

In Scotland, Downing studied under Professors John McIntyre and Thomas Torrance, both of whom shared an interest in the relation between science and the Christian faith. Downing's doctoral dissertation, completed in 1966, was called "Eschatological Implications of the Understanding of Time and Space in the Thought of Isaac Newton." That may be a little complex for the layperson to grasp, but one can still see Downing blending together his knowledge of physics and his Biblical faith.

"I was very blessed," Downing said, "to have had three years at Edinburgh."

MAKING A DEAL WITH GOD

Around October of 1965, Downing was well into writing his dissertation when he began to wonder about the Biblical doctrine of angels from a different perspective. What if the beings called angels in the Bible are now what we would call extraterrestrials, maybe beings in flying saucers or UFOs?

"I started looking at objects like the 'pillar of cloud and fire' of the Exodus," he explained, "or the 'chariot of fire' of Elijah, or the 'wheels' of Ezekiel, from a space age point of view. I thought this might be important, so I made a deal with God."

Downing asked God to wait until he had finished his Ph.D. and returned to America, at which point he would write "The Bible and Flying Saucers." Downing did indeed write the book, as he had promised God he would do.

"When I got back home in May of 1966," he said, "I set up shop in my in-laws' basement and wrote my book. In the meantime, I was looking for my first church assignment, which was not available until February 1967. I finished the book the week before I began work as an assistant pastor at Northminster Presbyterian Church, Endwell, New York."

PHYSICS COMES IN HANDY

The parting of the Red Sea as recorded in Exodus is a very significant story for Downing. It is also a story in which his knowledge of physics does much to help him interpret the events from a "real-world" perspective. For Downing, the process involved treading a fine line between the physical and the non-physical as well as between visionary prophecy and observable "miracles."

"I was looking for a 'real-world' way to understand the Bible," Downing said, "but not necessarily prophecy. For instance, the story of Doubting Thomas touching the wounds in the body of Jesus (John 20:24-29) is quite a different thing from John's visions recorded in Revelation. I believe books like Revelation are the work of the Holy Spirit, but they do not seem to take place in the physical world as I understand it.

"But things like the parting of the Red Sea and the resurrection of Jesus seem to be 'real-world' events, and the tendency of some recent scholarship is to move these events into the 'psychological realm,' along with dreams and visions. So, in general, I left Biblical prophecy alone, including the 'vision' of Ezekiel's wheels, because he was the only witness to this experience. I am not sure whether the Ezekiel experience is 'real-world' or spiritual world."

In any case, Downing's theories met with much opposition.

"The irony here," he said, "is that I used the modern UFO story, seen by many as a myth, to counter the theological mythologizing of Biblical miracles, like the parting of the Red Sea. I have been criticized for substituting technological miracles for supernatural miracles. I suppose this is a just complaint. What I would say in my defense is that 'supernatural' is not a Biblical word. In fact, the word has only been used in theology for about five hundred years."

DEFINING WHAT IS "REAL"

Do we even know what is real at all?

"'The term 'real-world,'" he said, "suggests that we know a 'real-world' [entity or event] when we see one. This is an epistemological issue, an issue of 'how do we know we what we know?' I have read credible UFO reports that suggest a clear outline of a UFO can be seen against the night sky and, at the same time, stars can be seen through the UFO. Or UFOs are reported to radically change shape in midflight. Or a UFO will split into many parts; the parts will fly away from each other; only to return and be united again. What kind of 'reality' is the basis for UFO science? How can a UFO be solid and not solid?"

Much the same issue is raised with the resurrection body of Jesus, which was apparently able to go through solid walls into a locked room (John 20:19-23) or disappear in an instant from plain view (Luke 24:31). This, according to Downing, raises the issue of ontology, or of what is real and what is the nature of being.

"Modern quantum physics has revealed a world," Downing said, "that is not full of 'solid objects' on one hand and space on the other, but rather a dynamic world in which solid objects are mostly space, with various types of quantum energy spinning away to create the illusion of solid objects. In light of the new physics, how do we know what we know? And how do we know what is real? Many are trying to deal with these issues.

"But the gap between our earthly body and our resurrected body," he continued, "may not require a 'quantum leap.' Nevertheless, at the same time, if UFOs carry the angels of Christ, their 'strange technology and behavior' may be as upsetting to our government scientists as the resurrection of Jesus was to the disciples. Their 'real-world' understanding had to expand. So must ours."

WHAT WAS IN DOWNING'S FIRST BOOK?

Returning to the discussion of Downing's first book, "The Bible and Flying Saucers," written in the basement of his in-laws' home – what was it all about?

"'The Bible and Flying Saucers' consists of six chapters," he replied, "the first dealing with our emerging concepts of the universe in our space age. The book was published just before our first moon landing. The book would explore the possibility of extraterrestrial influence in the development of the Old and New Testaments."

The second chapter dealt with the evidence for the existence of UFOs, drawing on the work of Donald Keyhoe, Frank Edwards and Jacques Vallee. The latter was just beginning what would be a series of important UFO books.

"I was in no position to say we had proof that UFOs were extraterrestrial," Downing said, "but the possibility was strong."

Chapter three dealt with UFOs in the Old Testament, with special attention being given to the Book of Exodus and the main UFO reported there, the "pillar of cloud and of fire." Downing also argued that the "burning bush" seen by Moses was the same pillar of cloud and fire except that in that moment it was on the ground and in a clump of bushes.

HARD SCIENCE ON HOW THE
PARTING OF THE RED SEA REALLY HAPPENED

Downing said that the parting of the Red Sea required about 20 pages to explain in his first book, and those same issues are summarized in the new book, "Biblical UFO Revelations."

"My argument is that the Exodus UFO, the pillar of cloud and fire, which appeared cloud-like during the day and glowed in the dark," he recounted, "used its propulsion system to split the waters of the Red Sea and save Israel from the Egyptians. The reason the parting of the Red Sea is so important is that it tells in detail the environmental impact of the UFO presence. Modern UFO researchers go to landing spots with Geiger counters and all kinds of equipment in order to study the environmental impact of a flying saucer landing. Exodus 14:19-30 is a very detailed environmental impact statement.

"The standard Biblical interpretation," Downing continued, "that a 'strong wind' parted the sea, does not 'hold water,' as I say. Water weighs 62.4 pounds per cubic foot. At a depth of ten feet, this would be 624 pounds of pressure per square foot on the bottom of the seabed. Israel was moving from west to east. An east wind strong enough to part the water would have blown Moses into the sky. Nor would a strong wind give straight walls on each side, as the Bible reports. The 'east wind' was the result of the force field pushing air out of the open end of the channel. Once the walls of water were established, some energy in the center of the channel could be phased out so as not to crush Israel when they crossed.

"And the text reports three times that Israel crossed on dry ground. The parting took place during the night, so there was no sun to dry out the seabed. Modern UFO landings sometimes seem to dry out the ground on which they land. Some type of microwave effect may be involved."

Downing goes on to say that many of the largest modern UFOs are shaped like a cigar or cylinder, look cloudlike in the day and glow at night.

"I believe that the best explanation," Downing said, "for the parting of the Red Sea at this time is that the pillar of cloud and fire was some type of spaceship, and those in charge of the spaceship planned the parting of the Red Sea well in advance, to save Israel from the Egyptians and to keep Israel from going back to

Egypt, once the Jews discovered that the whole Exodus process was not a walk in the park."

Downing said the third chapter also deals with Elijah being taken up to heaven in a chariot of fire (2 Kings 2:11) and Ezekiel's vision of a "wheel within a wheel" (Ezekiel 1:16). Chapter four moves on to discuss flying saucers in the New Testament, to include the Star of Bethlehem (Matthew chapter 2), the angels appearing to the shepherds (Luke chapter 2), the baptism of Jesus (Luke 3:21-22), the "bright cloud" over Jesus at his Transfiguration (Matthew 17:1-9), the Resurrection of Jesus (Matthew 28:1-10), and the conversion of the Apostle Paul on the road to Damascus (Acts 9:1-8, also 22:3-11 and 26:12-18.)

The question of "Where is heaven?" is discussed in chapter five, and Downing posits that it may simply be another dimension, a place Jesus calls "the kingdom of heaven," as well as being the point of origin for UFOs.

"The idea that UFOs may come to earth through 'wormholes' or some such space-bending idea has gained wider attention since my first book," Downing said, "but not because of my book. The final chapter explores the issue of the Second Coming of Christ with UFOs providing the transportation for Christ and his angels. In this chapter, I also explore the possible meaning of our own resurrection.

"My basic thesis," Downing said, "is that we need to explore the Biblical concept of angels in light of our emerging concepts of the universe and in light of modern UFO reports."

A CHILLY RECEPTION FROM HIS FELLOW BELIEVERS

When "The Bible and Flying Saucers" was first published in 1968, Downing believed the book would be better received by conservative Christians than liberal Christians.

"As it turned out," Downing said, "neither liberals nor conservatives liked my book. So, in a sense, I was treated 'fairly' by both sides."

Downing mentions in a chapter in "Biblical UFO Revelations" a 1968 review in the magazine "Christianity Today."

"The reviewer was sure," Downing remembered, "that we would all have been better off if the book had not been published. He thought it was strange that I would not have 'proof' that UFOs exist and still argue that there might be a Biblical connection. The reviewer did not seem excited at all by the possibility that the angels of Christ are flying in our skies and being chased by United States Air Force jets. Of course, from my point of view, UFOs set up a church-state conflict of a very high order. So far, the state, with its lies about the UFO presence, is winning the church-state conflict without any noise of protest from the church."

Meanwhile, the reaction from more liberal Christians was equally negative.

"Liberals mostly ignored my book," Downing said. "Or if they noticed, they put it in the same class as Erich von Daniken's 'Chariots of the Gods?,' a book that turns angels into space aliens of the type we see in movies. I appeared in several episodes of the History Channel 'Ancient Aliens' series, a program which is very much oriented toward the von Daniken point of view.

"I was not totally at ease with my role in the 'Ancient Aliens' series, but, as the saying goes, you can only dance with those that ask you to dance. Neither liberal nor conservative Christians invited me to dance. The History Channel asked me to dance, so I did. This involved four separate interviews in New York, each about two hours long. My interviews provided four of the 'buckets of paint' that the editors used to paint the story they wanted to paint.

"Neither von Daniken, nor the 'Ancient Aliens series, were much interested in the religious 'beliefs' of the ancient aliens. They focus on how heavy the rocks were that they used to build their temples, or the drawings in caves of things that may have impressed the natives, or on what type of advanced technology the aliens might have passed on to humans to speed our technological development.

"From my point of view, we now have so much technological development and so little true religion ['love your enemies,' Matthew 5:44] that we are only a super power mistake in judgment away from blowing ourselves up."

THE NEED FOR THIS SECOND BOOK

Downing's first book was published nearly 50 years ago as of this writing. He acknowledges the long gap in time between publications.

"But I was working fulltime as a pastor," he explained, "which does not leave a lot of time for book writing. At the same time, I did write a couple of book-length manuscripts which were never accepted for publication."

Nevertheless, Downing kept up with the UFO field. In 1972, he was asked by Walter Andrus, Jr., who founded the Mutual UFO Network (MUFON), to join the organization and to write articles for the organization's newsletter. This book contains a bibliography of more than 40 articles and papers Downing has had published since 1968.

"But most publishing houses," he said, "are not interested in my work. My UFO writings are too frightening and heretical for conservatives, too silly and unbelievable for liberal Christians. On the other hand, secular publishers see me as too religious, too Christian. I do not fit in the Erich von Daniken camp."

Downing was approached by James Cunningham, who operates a website called "Strong Delusion" which deals with UFOs from a conservative Christian point of view. Some conservative writers, such as Gary Bates, had written negative things about Downing, suggesting that Downing was a fraud as a Christian.

Cunningham gave Downing the chance to defend himself on the "Strong Delusion" website.

"Before long," Downing explained, "I had published several articles on his site. And then one day I had a sense that I could write a series of articles that would, in the end, be a book. Cunningham agreed to publish this 12-chapter series, which went under the title 'UFO Revelation.' When Tim Beckley learned of this, he offered to publish this online work in hardcopy, and I am very thankful that he is doing this."

All of us at Global Communications/Inner Light are thankful ourselves to be bringing the work of a pioneer UFO researcher and a devoutly Christian interpreter of the UFO phenomenon to a new audience who are likely being exposed to Reverend Barry Downing's later work for the first time. Read "Biblical UFO Revelations" for the kind of insight into the flying saucer phenomenon that only Downing can provide.

Conspiracy Journal
PRODUCTIONS

BIBLICAL UFO REVELATIONS
by Dr. Barry H. Downing

UFO REVELATION—1

One of the most respected current writers in the area of UFO research is Richard M. Dolan. Jacques Vallee produced some excellent books beginning in the 1960s, one of his best, Dimensions, was published in 1988, but his productivity has since declined. In 1972 J. Allen Hynek, who had been a U.S. Air Force scientific consultant on UFOs, published The UFO Experience. A chapter in his book was made famous in the Steven Spielberg film "Close Encounters of the Third Kind." Hynek's change from being negative about the UFO reality to positive was important in encouraging a new generation of UFO researchers. British author Timothy Good has also done some excellent work, especially in Above Top Secret: The Worldwide UFO Cover-up (1988). These and other researchers helped pave the way for Richard Dolan, who in 2000 published Volume I of a series UFOs and the National Security State: An Unclassified History covering the period 1941-1973, and followed it with Volume II in 2009, covering the period 1973-1991. He is working on Volume III, covering from 1991 to the present. He presents hundreds of documented military and civilian UFO cases, and places the UFO mystery in the context of national security issues. He has become such an established authority that no modern UFO conference wants to be without Dolan on its lecture list. (I have met Hynek, Good and Dolan at various MUFON conferences, but have never met Vallee.)

Dolan is not a scientist, but rather a trained historian, with specialized training in "U.S. cold war strategy." This has made it easy for him to think of UFOs from the point of military and scientific strategy, which in our modern age go hand in glove, like "the military-industrial complex," a danger Dwight Eisenhower warned us about.

In 2010 Dolan teamed up with Bryce Zabel to write a book called A.D. After Disclosure: The People's Guide to Life After Contact. Zabel is a media professional, having created NBC's Dark Skies series, and worked with the Spielberg-produced miniseries Taken.

The opening chapter develops a fictionalized scene in which the President of the United States, through a series of circumstances, is forced to announce that UFOs exist, and are piloted by aliens. (The announcement takes place on Friday, after the stock market has closed. Other countries around the world follow the American lead and confirm some kind of truth about UFOs.) But what kind of truth? Will it be full disclosure, partial, or false? (In a false disclosure, the government might admit that UFOs exist, but claim they are made from human technology.)

Most of the book is devoted to exploring what the consequences will be for economics, science, the media, world politics, world defense, and religion. In a sense, the whole book is "fiction," meaning there has been no "Disclosure," and therefore talking about "After Disclosure" is fictional.

At the same time, we have seen in recent years a tremendous explosion of Christian fiction about the Second Coming of Jesus and the Rapture, most notably from those like Tim LaHaye and Jerry Jenkins who wrote the Left Behind series. Stephen Yulish has written a novel dealing with the end times in light of the UFO mystery.

I find it interesting that both UFO writers and Christian writers are creating fictionalized accounts of a "disclosure" or "revelation" event. We usually talk about Divine Revelation in theology, but anyone who reads theology knows that theologians use the word "disclosure" and "revelation" interchangeably. Dr. Steven Greer, who began the "Disclosure Project," has attempted to force the government of the United States to tell the truth about UFO reality by gathering UFO testimony from military leaders and other reliable sources. He was one of the first to claim the term "disclosure" as part of UFO vocabulary. Dolan and Zabel were glad to use the word as the defining term for their book.

Revelation/Disclosure is a theological term because the ultimate reality studied by theology is God, and God is invisible. God exists behind some kind of curtain or wall. The early Genesis story says that when Adam and Eve were created, there was no wall. But they sinned, and were kicked out of the garden, and the gate to the garden was slammed shut. The biblical view is that human life now seems godless, except that God has the freedom to look over the wall, or peak out from behind the curtain, and reveal himself—not to everyone, but to select people, chosen people. Abraham, Isaac, Jacob, Joseph, Moses, Isaiah, and Ezekiel in the Old Testament experience revelation. Then in the New Testament God comes to earth disguised as a human being. The Word became Flesh. In Jesus the invisible God became visible, but in human form very few recognized him. It seemed impossible for many to believe "He who has seen me has seen the Father." (Jn. 14:9)

BIBLICAL UFO REVELATIONS

From my point of view, we are caught up in what I call God's Game, which is a faith game. I see the game idea in texts such as Deuteronomy 8:16, which says the purpose of God in the Exodus was "to humble you and test you, to do you good in the end." We have to enter into this game by faith, as Hebrews chapter 11 makes clear. Human life is some kind of test, contest, game. Our opponent is evil, the devil. Jesus, as part of his humanity, had to be tested in the wilderness. (Matt. 4:1-11) Jesus passed the test that Adam and Eve failed. I will come back to the issue of testing several times in this UFO Revelation series.

How do we recognize, identify, the work of the invisible God on earth? It is not easy. Adam and Eve ate the fruit of knowledge of good and evil, as if it were easy to tell the difference. But it is not. The most religious people in Jerusalem did not recognize Jesus for who he was. The New Testament is a warning, especially if any of us think we would do any better at recognizing God walking among us now! False prophets come in the name of Jesus. The whole world, and perhaps the church, might be caught up in a "strong delusion" if we are not on guard (2 Thess. 2:14), and even if we are on guard, if the church is in a state of spiritual corruption, it may not have the purity of faith to recognize divine signs when they are given. Jesus gave plenty of signs of his authority, but spiritual corruption often blinded those who witnessed his power.

How does Richard Dolan see the UFO world? He has talked to enough reliable UFO witnesses, including astronauts and military leaders, to be absolutely sure UFOs are real and extraterrestrial in some sense. Are they from another planet, another dimension, time travelers? He is not sure about that, but explores the possibilities in A.D. (See chapter 5, "Threat Analysis: Who Goes There and What do They Want?" p. 134 ff.)

The title A.D. was chosen deliberately to acknowledge that the coming of Jesus (A.D.—Anno Domini, in the year of the Lord) was a historical turning point. Dolan and Zabel see the announcement of UFO presence as changing history as radically as did the coming of Jesus for Western culture.

But there is another dimension to Dolan's work. Because UFO research has "top secret" status in the United States, and has had for more than 60 years, Dolan believes that a whole secret community has grown up, funded by American black budget money. This money, which goes to secret projects unknown to congress, ends up in the hands of private scientific corporations who are milking UFO technology for their own purposes, whatever these purposes may be. Dolan calls the group controlling UFO secrets a "Breakaway Civilization," which is explored in chapter 3 in A.D., "Breakaway: How Secrets Created a World Within a World." (p. 59 ff.) It is Dolan's belief that not even the current President of the United States knows the truth about UFOs, because according to rules of classified information, he does not have a "need to know" UFO truth.

Thus we find Dolan believes in two invisible kingdoms: one that is human, whose main purpose is to gain UFO secrets from the aliens, and use these secrets in a way that gives them more power to do whatever the Breakaway Group wants to do. But he also believes in the kingdom of the aliens, who come from somewhere other than earth. Notice that these two kingdoms are invisible to Dolan, but he infers their existence on the basis of eye witnesses he has come to trust, witnesses who can either explain to him how the Breakaway Civilization works, or who have seen the alien craft, and perhaps the aliens themselves.

We Christians believe in the kingdom of heaven, which is invisible to us. We do not know where heaven is, but we believe heaven is where Christ and his angels now live, although they are free to come to earth if they want to. Christians have traditionally believed that heaven is in some sense extraterrestrial. The Bible is our primary witness. On the basis of the divine Revelation/Disclosure we find in the Bible, we have come to believe in two kingdoms, earthly, and heavenly. We pray, "thy kingdom come, thy will be done, on earth, as it is in heaven." Is what Dolan sees as the UFO kingdom, and what Christians see as the heavenly kingdom, the same kingdom? If so, how would we prove it?

If not, how would we falsify it? How would we prove the UFO kingdom and heavenly kingdom are not the same? This is the issue that has troubled me for more than 40 years. I do not want to be taken in by a "strong delusion." But the parallels between the "world's quest for UFO truth," and our Christian quest for the final coming of Jesus and his kingdom, seem to me to demand our thoughtful attention.

If Dolan and Zabel had their way, a day of Disclosure would come soon. But what shape might it take? If the Day of the Lord were to come soon, how would we tell the difference between the Lord's landing, and an ET landing? Would a UFO landing be the devil disguised as an angel of light?

One possibility is that UFO sightings might become so obvious the governments of the world would not be able to lie any more. The President of the United States might hold a news conference and say something like this: "We have not told you the truth about the UFO reality because we do not know where the aliens come from, or why they are here. But so far, they do not seem to want to conquer planet earth." How would Christians react to this kind of Disclosure?

Or suppose that the President said, "We are now ready to explain the UFO situation to the American people. To help with this explanation, let me now introduce you to our new alien friend Zorg, who will tell us what he hopes will be the future of planet earth." How would Christians react to this kind of Disclosure?

Or again, suppose that a UFO landed, not on the White House lawn, but in a poor community in Mexico, and a human got out of the UFO and said, "I am Jesus. I have come to the least of you on earth. I want all who believe in me to repent, and turn to God and your neighbor for forgiveness. Very soon I will be returning with my angels in judgment. The earth, my bride, is not ready for me, but I yearn to come. Please tell the world I long to come, 'Surely I am coming soon.'" (Rev. 22:20) How would Christians react to this kind of Disclosure?

Obviously, none of the above three scenarios may happen, but I find it interesting to think about the biblical faith, which is my heritage, in light of both current UFO thinking, and current Christian eschatological thinking. In the weeks ahead, I hope to explore these and other issues, in a field I am calling UFO Revelation.

UFO REVELATION 2
THINK TANKS AND THE SECOND COMING

I want to state my view of how the United States government works. I believe our government leaders lie to the public whenever they think it is either in the best interests of the leaders themselves, (President Nixon and Watergate, or President Clinton and Monica), or when national security seems to be at stake, whether the issues be military, financial, or scientific. The fact that they operate this way does not make our country more evil than any other country. This is how "the children of darkness" have always played their power games. When Jesus was raised from the dead, and the guards told their story to the authorities, the rulers said, "Tell people, 'His disciples came by night and stole him away while we were asleep.' And if this comes to the governor's ears, we will satisfy him and keep you out of trouble." (Matt. 28:13, 14) This is how those in power work when their power is challenged— tell a lie, give out a cover story.

Just as the story of the resurrection of Jesus was a threat to those in power in Jerusalem, so our modern UFO stories are a threat to the ruling powers of the earth. Our government leaders have given out various UFO cover stories—a mirage, Venus (always a favorite), a strange cloud, even swamp gas.

Although I believe our government may lie, or at least bend the truth frequently, I do not believe our government leaders are stupid, at least not intentionally. When confronted with the truth that UFOs are some kind of extraterrestrial reality, they would seek the wisest way to handle the challenge. They would be wondering: are we going to be under extraterrestrial attack? Will there be an open landing, will they establish contact, and treat us as equals, or enslave us? What will be the consequences for religion if UFO information is released? And since Christianity has historically been the dominant religion in the United States, what will be the implications of UFO presence for the Biblical religion?

The President of the United States would not sit in his office with a couple of military advisors, and decide what to do over a cup of coffee. They would seek the best advice they could find. And if good advice was not available, they would create an agency that would research the issues faced by extraterrestrial presence.

In December of 1960, the Brookings Institute, a high level think tank founded in 1916, located in Washington, D.C., completed a study commissioned by our government, concerning the implications of human travel in space, and the consequences of our meeting an extraterrestrial civilization. The report expressed fear "of social disintegration if humanity came in contact with an extraterrestrial life form." The report pointed to earthly examples of social disintegration when a superior culture met a less advanced one (Native Americans meet whites with guns). If we were to discover extraterrestrial life, "it might be advisable to withhold this information from the public." (Dolan and Zabel, A.D., p. 59)

On June 24th, 1947, pilot Kenneth Arnold experienced a sighting of 9 disc shaped UFOs flying in formation, which led to the term "flying saucers," and only two weeks later something strange crashed near Roswell, New Mexico.

Most UFO researchers believe an extraterrestrial craft crashed, that dead alien bodies were found, and the remains of both the craft and the bodies were flown to other military bases where they would be studied. Dolan and Zabel, in their book A.D. After Disclosure, believe the evidence of a UFO crash at Roswell is beyond dispute. (p. 116 ff)

BROOKINGS AND RAND

With this kind of challenge in front of our government, a new type of institution was necessary, one that would combine military expertise, scientific exploration, space age imagination, and sociological analysis of groups and their belief systems. In light of the above Brookings paper in 1960, I think it unlikely that Brookings handled any of the UFO research that the government would require.

Their report seemed unaware of the fact that ET contact has already happened.

I do not know what "think tank" served as the major source of UFO research, but it is interesting that the RAND Corporation was formed in 1948, one year after Roswell, originating as "United States Army Air Forces Project Rand." I do not know that the RAND Corporation was formed specifically to deal with the UFO situation, but my point is that the government would either turn to, or create, a "think tank" to work through the many issues that UFOs present to human authority.

The RAND Corporation on its website lists as its mission "to help improve decision making through research and analysis." Its current CEO is Dr. James Thomson, a physicist. With headquarters in Santa Monica, California, it also has divisions in Boston, Washington, D.C., Brussels, Cambridge, England, and even in Abu Dhabi, United Arab Emirates. It has "three federally funded research and development centers that focus on national security." How much government money given to RAND is black budget funding we of course do not know. We do not have a "need to know."

An early question for a RAND style think tank would be: Should we tell the American people of the UFO presence? And if so, how much should we tell? The answer might be: "Don't tell them if you can help it, and if you have to tell, tell as little as possible."

Dolan and Zabel suggest that several types of events might force some kind of disclosure, such as a massive leak of UFO information, or a sighting so well witnessed that UFOs could no longer be denied. Lynne D. Kitei has documented a major sighting in her book The Phoenix Lights, which deals with a UFO formation seen by hundreds of witnesses on March 13, 1997 in Arizona. Among the witnesses was Arizona Governor Fife Symington III, who at the time, denied that he had seen anything, and publically ridiculed those who had seen the UFOs. But later he admitted his deception, and published a chapter "Setting the Record Straight" in Leslie Kean's book UFOs: Generals, Pilots, and Government Officials Go on the Record. (p. 247 ff) A sighting like this, in which those in authority, like Symington, decide it is time to tell the truth, rather than go along with the cover-up, could lead to disclosure. And if the aliens decided that it is time to end the government lie, they can clearly create a UFO sighting that would be beyond the ability of our government to cover-up. Then disclosure—revelation—would happen.

Dolan and Zabel explore the various types of "disclosure" that our government might carry out— radical (total), partial (controlled), or false (deceptive). (A.D., p. 18 ff) If our government is in contact with the aliens, no one in any think tank would recommend that we carry out the first day of disclosure by having our alien friend Zorg address the United Nations.

A DISCLOSURE SCENARIO

The first level of disclosure might involve the President of the United States and other leaders saying, "We believe we must now tell you that earth is being visited by one or more intelligent realities from an extraterrestrial world. Recent sightings have forced us to admit to the alien presence, but we have to say that we do not know where they come from, or why they are here. We have been silent about the alien reality, hoping to gain better scientific information for you. All we can say at this time is that the aliens seem mainly interested in observing our planet, and they do not seem to offer any immediate threat to national security." This type of response might be plausible, especially since the aliens have not landed and taken over. The only "War of the Worlds" or "Independence Day" alien invasion story has been in the movies, not in real life. True, there are the "UFO abduction" rumors, which are troubling, but maybe this is just how the aliens do their scientific study. (As long as they leave me alone, no big deal.)

Once the governments of the world make this minimal admission, many of the consequences that Dolan and Zabel list become reality. Major adjustments have to be made by the media, finance, defense, education, science and religion. My main interest is the implications of alien presence for the Christian faith. And since the United States, despite its history of separation of church and state, has been predominately Christian in orientation, one question directed at the RAND Corporation or its equivalent would be: What would be the consequences for the Christian faith, and the reaction of Christians to the news of an alien presence?

This would be a very sensitive issue. Any such study would be classified as secret or higher for two reasons. First, it would be clear to many that UFOs are religious dynamite from the point of view of biblical Christianity. Second, if the United States government were to be found handing out information that was religiously deceptive, this would represent a potential violation of the Constitution, which guarantees citizens the right to "free exercise" of their religion. If the government were to be found manipulating religious beliefs, this would be seen as a high crime. I cannot imagine any administration that could survive the firestorm that would follow "disclosure" that the United States had manipulated religious beliefs to serve its own scientific and military purposes.

UFOS AND THE SECOND COMING

What would be the reaction of Christians if the government were to announce alien presence? In 1956 Morris K. Jessup published a book entitled UFO and the Bible. This book had a very limited distribution, I did not read it until after I had published The Bible and Flying Saucers in 1968. In the early part of his book, Jessup focuses on biblical UFOs such as the "pillar of cloud and fire" of the Exodus, the "chariot of fire" of Elijah, and of course the "wheels" of Ezekiel.

But the second half of his book is devoted mainly to the so called "Little Apocalypse" in the Gospel of Mark, chapter 13. This chapter deals with Jesus telling of the end times, and the tribulation to come. Jesus warns of "false prophets," but also promises "signs and wonders, to lead astray, if possible, the elect." (v. 22)

Then in the last days, stars will "fall from heaven" and "then they will see the Son of man coming in clouds with great power and glory. And then he will send out the angels, and gather the elect from the four winds, from the ends of the earth to the ends of heaven." (v. 24-7) Thus Jessup connected UFOs to Christ and his angels, unlike later conservatives who connected UFOs to demons. Jessup saw in UFOs a link to the Second Coming, UFOs could be a sign the end was near.

Any think tank would suppose that the release of UFO information by the government would lead to a huge blend of terror and hope among Christians, especially conservative Protestants, who have always been interested in the end times and the Second Coming of Christ. Conservative Christians have written books making a case for the demonic nature of UFOs, and holding out hope for the second coming. Clifford Wilson's U.F.O.'s and Their Mission Impossible (1974) and John Weldon and Zola Levitt who published UFOs: What on Earth is Happening? (1975), saw the apocalyptic promise and danger of UFOs, as did Timothy J. Dailey in his later book, The Millennial Deception: Angels, Aliens and the Antichrist (1995).

A government think tank would go on to document that end times hopes are dangerous, and lead to disruptive behavior. (The government would have been concerned about UFO cults long before the 39 members of the Heaven's Gate group headed by Marshall Applewhite committed suicide in California during Holy Week of 1997.)

A think tank would point out that the early Christian church expected Jesus to return very soon, and in light of that expectation, the Christians in Jerusalem sold their property, and held their money in common. "Now the company of those who believed were of one heart and soul and no one said that any of the things which he possessed was his own, but they had everything in common." (Acts 4:32) It also seemed unnecessary for some to work, since they had such a pool of money, and since Jesus was returning soon. But when Jesus did not return, the Jerusalem church ran out of money, and the Apostle Paul collected money from the Gentile Churches for the Jerusalem Church. (See Romans 15:25-7)

A think tank report would suggest that if there was an outbreak of Christian expectations that the Second Coming was near, many might stop working, and there would be major economic disruptions. Parents might start keeping their children home from school—who needs education when we may soon be taken up in the Rapture?

But the think tank report would also make this observation. Most Christians believe if UFOs exist, that they are space aliens, not angels. They think of UFOs from a space age and scientific point of view. If their government says nothing about UFOs and the aliens, Christians are likely to go their own way quietly. In 1938, actor and director Orson Welles performed a radio broadcast for the Mercury Theater on the Air. The broadcast was based on the novel by H.G. Wells, The War of the Worlds, which imagines an extraterrestrial landing and invasion. This radio broadcast was so realistic that it produced panic in many places in the United States. This event became the "gold standard" to judge American lack of readiness to accept the idea of alien presence. Space travel was on our minds, and a rumor of an invasion by aliens was something that could create a panic. A think tank report to the government might suggest that if the United States kept silent about UFOs, main stream Christianity would likewise be silent. At perhaps an unconscious level, Christians would put the hope for the Second Coming of Jesus on one side of the teeter-totter, and the fear of alien invasion on the other, and the power of hope balanced against the power of fear would cancel each other out. Whatever the reason, the Christian Church in America has been "like a lamb that is led to the slaughter, and like a sheep that before its shearers is dumb," opening not its mouth to protest the UFO cover-up. (Is. 53:7)

Covering up the UFO presence seemed like a good idea in 1947 for a lot of reasons: scientific, financial and religious. If there were people within our government who said, "Religious people have a right to this information, it has consequences for their religious beliefs, the government has no right to withhold this information from them," they would be kept quiet with the promise that, "of course, we must release the truth to the American people. But we must do it carefully, we need more time to understand the alien presence before we go public." And I suspect that this argument held the day through the 1950's and 1960's. Donald Keyhoe, in his early "Flying Saucer" books, makes it clear that there was an internal battle between those in the government who thought UFO truth should be released, and those who insisted it be classified.

Those with religious convictions might be among those who most strongly advocated for "release of the truth." If there was internal religious pressure in our government for disclosure, then what would be needed by the "secret keepers" would be a religious reason to keep the truth secret. Thus I suspect that a think tank was asked "to explore the most disturbing point of view possible concerning the religious dimension of alien presence." If the first think tank report might have been called "Religion and UFOs: Report 1," which dealt with the issue of UFOs and the Christian hope for the Second Coming, "Religion and UFOs: Report 2" would be quit different. That will be the subject of our next chapter.

UFO REVELATION 3
ANGELS AND ANCIENT ALIENS

Once one becomes totally convinced of the alien presence, as Richard Dolan and Bryce Zabel are, then the issue is raised: how long have the aliens been flying in our skies, and perhaps interacting with human culture? In a universe that is 13 billion years old, who knows? How do we know there is only one universe, rather than multiple dimensions of universes? Maybe the aliens have been watching over the earth for thousands of years, as the biblical doctrine of angels suggests. In fact, maybe the aliens have created us, or even put spiritual leaders like Jesus, Mohammed or Buddha on earth. (Dolan and Zabel, A.D., p. 282)

To put it mildly, disclosure of a UFO presence raises huge questions for the biblical tradition, possibilities that go way beyond the Second Coming of Christ. In chapter 2 of their book A.D., Dolan and Zabel explore "Facts in the Air: The History of Contact Through the Ages." This chapter includes reference to the work of Eric von Daniken in Chariots of the Gods?, pointing out that von Daniken quoted the famous passage from Ezekiel concerning the "wheel within a wheel," and that NASA scientist Josef F. Blumrich's book The Spaceships of Ezekiel (1974) "recreated" Ezekiel's wheels in spaceship form.

Ezekiel's experience, which had always been seen as supernatural, could now be thought of as an encounter with some kind of advanced technology. This led von Daniken and others to suppose that primitive humans (early Hebrew culture) projected divinity, or angelology, onto ancient astronauts— saw them as gods. Thus the angels in the Bible were not angels at all, but space beings, perhaps like ourselves, but more advanced technologically.

Dolan and Zabel reference my book, The Bible and Flying Saucers (1968) in a footnote in this chapter, but do not explore my alternative view, that perhaps the angels in the Bible do represent God, but that they use technology—UFOs—for transportation. My position stands between von Daniken on one side, and Christian conservatives who see UFOs as demons on the other side. Both sides see my view as either naïve, or dangerous.

BIBLICAL UFO REVELATIONS

Although the Ezekiel issue may have been troubling to Christians, even more so were the questions von Daniken asked about angels and the destruction of Sodom, described in Genesis chapter 19. Von Daniken asks, "What actually happened at Sodom? We cannot imagine that almighty God is tied down to a timetable. Then why were his 'angels' in such a hurry? Or was the destruction of the city by some power or other fixed to the very minute? Had the countdown already begun and did the 'angels' know about it?" (p. 36, Bantam edition)

Von Daniken goes on to suggest that Sodom was destroyed by an atomic blast, and that the angels were not angels, connected to God, but rather ancient astronauts, doing some kind of population or genetic control. Needless to say, this did not go over well with conservative Christians. Clifford Wilson wrote Crash Go the Chariots (1972), condemning von Daniken's work. But the von Daniken thesis, that the aliens are space guys, not angels, would probably gain more credibility if the Dolan and Zabel version of Disclosure were to take place.

Conservative Christians have issues that need to be faced. Since they see the Bible as inspired, exactly how does the Bible see the relation between God and angels? Does this view change, or evolve, over the more than a thousand years of Bible history? Much conservative Christian piety is about "Jesus and me," and has not thoughtfully looked at angelology.

ANGELS AND THE UNITY OF GOD

The early Genesis material does not make sharp distinctions between God and angels. Furthermore, the angels seem very human in some respects. We find this account of the appearance of God to Abraham. "And the Lord appeared to him by the oaks of Mamre, as he sat at the door of his tent in the heat of the day. He lifted up his eyes and looked, and behold, three men stood in front of him." (Gen. 18:3) Abraham welcomes these strangers, and instructs his wife Sarah to prepare a meal for the guests, which she does. This incident helped inspire the New Testament warning to "not neglect to show hospitality to strangers, for thereby some have entertained angels unawares." (Heb. 13:2) What is being said about God in his "God-ness," his ultimate nature, in this story? Are there three Gods here? If so, what does this say about the "monotheism" of the Hebrew tradition? The Apostle Paul understood that the Law was given at Sinai through angels, "it was ordained by angels through an intermediary. Now an intermediary implies more than one, but God is one." (Gal. 3:19, 20) Paul saw the conflict here, and did not seem to resolve it. There was also the danger in the early church of worshiping angels, (Col. 2:18) and there has been a kind of recent cultish interest in angels in the United States, including the CBS TV series "Touched by an Angel," which ran for more than 200 episodes.

The angels in Genesis tell Abraham that Sarah will become pregnant, she laughs silently to herself, but the angels, with special powers, "hear" her laugh, but she denies laughing. She had been barren for years, the promise of pregnancy seemed absurd. But Isaac was born—and angels seemed to empower the pregnancy. The angelic/divine reality was in control of Abraham and Sarah's reproductive system. This issue of angelic/divine reproductive control carries over into the New Testament in the case of both the birth of John the Baptist (Luke 1:5-25), and Jesus (Luke 1:26-38).

Abraham is told in this angelic encounter that God plans to destroy Sodom, where Lot and his family lived. Lot was Abraham's nephew. Strangely, the Lord now becomes "two angels" who come to Sodom, go to Lot's house, and are welcomed, where they warn Lot that the city is about to be destroyed. The men of the town demand that Lot turn the strangers (angels) over to them for sexual abuse, and Lot famously offers the men of the city his daughters in place of the angels. The men of Sodom reject the offer, try to take the angels by force, and the angels use their divine power to blind the men of Sodom, so that the angels remain safe.

Important to notice here is that the angels seemed human in appearance. The men of Sodom would have behaved differently if they had known they were dealing with divine beings. It should be noticed that Jesus told his listeners it would be more tolerable for Sodom in the day of judgment than for those cities which had rejected his work and his signs. (Mt. 11:24) John the Baptist and Jesus were the new "angels" in Israel, divine representatives having angelic empowered births, but appearing very human. But the main difference between John the Baptist and Jesus on one hand, and the angels at Sodom on the other, is that John and Jesus did not use their divine power to protect themselves from the evil of human sin. John the Baptist was beheaded because he had accused Herod of sexual immorality. (Mt. 14:1-12) Jesus of course was crucified. The biblical message from Genesis to Matthew is: if angels, or divinely sent beings, walk among us, we humans lust to abuse them, or kill them. This makes me wonder if American Air Force Jets have welcomed our modern aliens in UFOs by shooting at them. It also makes me wonder if by "demonizing" the aliens, Christians encourage our government to shoot the aliens. (In light of the Sodom story, I am thinking we better be really sure of our "identification" of our modern aliens. Shooting first, and asking questions later, turned out badly for Sodom. And it may not go well for Herod in the day of judgment, or Caiaphas, or Pilate.)

The space age has created a serious crisis for conservative Protestant Christians. They believe the Bible is inerrant. That means the angels reported in Genesis are real, and they did as reported. Von Daniken then reads Genesis literally too (as do conservative Christians), and says, "This is not the work of the angels of God; this is a bunch of space aliens." Instead of using science to say the destruction never happened, it is mythology (as some Christian liberals do), von Daniken believes the destruction happened, but gives a different interpretation to the cause. The inerrancy of scripture is not a very useful defense against the von Daniken point of view.

Part of the reason for the conservative Christian crisis is that our age—what I call our godless age— does not take the God of the Bible seriously. My wife and I listen to our local Christian radio station. Almost all the preachers talk about God's love, God's forgiveness, his grace—not his judgment. God is just such a nice guy, perhaps somewhat better than the average Rotarian. What the story of Sodom says is: God can be a killer. Conservatives are in a real box here. Few are ready to preach the judgment of God as the Bible presents it, and so von Daniken has them over a barrel. And conservatives do not like me much better, because I say, yes, these are the angels of God, and yes, God can be a killer. It is exactly this killer God that scientists like Richard Dawkins mock in his book The God Delusion. (2006) Dawkins says, "The God of the Old Testament is arguably the most unpleasant character in all fiction: jealous and proud of it." (p. 31) It is no wonder that in an age such as ours, a God with real sexual standards seems to be a joke.

ANGELS AND ALIENS: CAN WE TELL THE DIFFERENCE?

Dolan and Zabel are sure beyond doubt that we have aliens flying in our skies, watching over planet earth—just as the Bible says the angels do. How do we know if the angels in the Bible, and our modern aliens, are the same reality, or not?

If the United States has my imaginary alien Zorg and his friends tucked away in Area 51, or some such place, the thing to do would be to ask Zorg directly. There have been rumors for some time that the "secret keepers" in the Breakaway Civilization have been in partnership with some aliens for several years.

Linda Moulton Howe is a UFO researcher who has specialized in cattle mutilations, but has also sought UFO evidence from those inside what Dolan calls the Breakaway Civilization. One of her inside sources made the following claim based on alleged conversations with the aliens: "The aliens claim that man is a hybrid created by them. They claim that all religion was created by them to hasten the formation of a civilized culture and to control the human race. The aliens have furnished proof of these claims and have a device that allows them to show audibly and visually any part of history that they or we wish to see . . . They have a tendency to lie." (Howe, An Alien Harvest, 1989, p. 188-9)

British UFO researcher Timothy Good, in his book Alien Contact (1991), reports that a man named Bob Lazar claimed he had seen documents saying that the aliens had created life on earth, and earthly religions. "Supposedly Jesus and two other spiritual leaders were genetically engineered, in the sense that 'they were implanted in people on Earth and their births were closely monitored.' Again, a similar claim was made (specifically about Jesus) by Richard Doty, in conversation with Linda Howe." (p. 212) These claims cannot be substantiated, of course, and Good makes reference to my book, suggesting that ideas already in the religious market place could have been adopted to create the "revelations" of Zorg and his alien friends.

Needless to say, if these claims are true, they have tremendous significance for all Christians, in fact for all religions. But how do we tell if this is the truth, or if it is a lie put out by the secret keepers; maybe Zorg was created by the secret keepers. Or if Zorg does exist, how do we know we can trust him? We can now see that the issue of UFOs and the Bible has moved to a new level of difficulty. From the perspective of the "national security state" concerns, it is bad enough to worry about panic due to the aliens, or a sudden outburst of Christian belief that Christ will return soon, but how would a President of the United States explain to the world that all religions are a kind of cosmic joke, or a form of cosmic manipulation of humans?

When Jimmy Carter was Governor of Georgia, he saw a UFO, and apparently believed it was extraterrestrial. He promised that when he became President, he would release UFO information. But when he became President, none was released. What happened? Dolan and Zabel report, "There is also a story offered by a high-level intelligence official about a UFO briefing President Carter received in June 1977. It was unknown to the source what specifics were discussed, only that when the President was seen in his office, he was sobbing, with his head in his hands, nearly on his desk." (A.D., p. 86)

I had heard from a private source about the President sobbing after his UFO briefing. I served as a pastor of Northminster Presbyterian Church in Endwell, New York, for 34 years. During that time I worked with a person who put me in contact with someone close to the Carter administration. According to this source, Carter had been told during the UFO briefing that the aliens had put Jesus on earth, to strengthen the morality of the human race. It was this information which led the President to sob, and made him decide that UFO information could not be released. Carter is a strong Christian, and still teaches Sunday School in his Baptist church.

This story is plausible in light of our modern space age thinking, and in light of the Bible itself. But at the same time, how do we know if this is the true story, or if the secret keepers have invented this story to keep high level government officials, like President Carter, from revealing UFO truth? After all, the CIA can lie just as well as Zorg, if Zorg exists. And if Zorg does not exist, the secret keepers might invent him, to give them something like "extraterrestrial authority" when challenged by those like President Carter.

THINK TANK: REPORT 2

"Think Tank: Report 2" would move beyond the Second Coming of Jesus, and include the issues we have seen at this point: the ancient astronaut theory—angels were perhaps space aliens; possibly space aliens have created the religions of the world, or even life on earth itself. Even if the government had no Zorg as a source, a think tank could create a scenario like the above. How would the secret keepers use this interpretation of religion?

Perhaps government secret keepers took lessons from cult leaders like the French race car driver Claude Vorihon Rael. He is author of the book, The Message Given to Me By Extra-terrestrials: They took me to their Planet (1986), translated from the French by his cult followers, the Raelians. Rael claims that on December 13th, 1973, he went to visit some volcanoes in France, where he encountered a flying saucer. "I was not afraid, but rather filled with joy to be living such a moment." (p. 5) He was taken by the aliens, and given information about the history of the earth, much of it related to the Bible. He was given the true understanding of the flood, Sodom and Gomorrah, Moses, and "The Usefulness of Christ." (p. 72 f)

When someone makes claims of semi-divine encounters, it gives that person authority over anyone who will believe their story. Did the secret keepers create a "Zorg myth" in order to control President Carter, and any other Christians who might want to release UFO information? Both von Daniken's book and mine were published in English in 1968—someone with imagination could use the information in our books to invent "Zorg" or his alien equivalent, to form a religious cult, or to fool a president.

THE BLIND SPOT IN THE ANCIENT ALIEN THEORY

Should we read the Bible from a UFO/space age point of view, whether Zorg exists or not? My own faith is that angels are real, they have the Holy Spirit in a way that we humans by and large do not. And I believe the angels use technology for their travels throughout this universe, and other universes, if other or parallel universes exist.

The views of Erich von Daniken have been made clear through many television broadcasts, the most recent a series called "Ancient Aliens" shown on the History Channel. Von Daniken himself was filmed for this series, as was I. I was filmed in New York City at New York University. The interview lasted an hour and a half. It was clear that none of those involved in the interview had any clue about my work, nor had they read my book.

I explained my view that the angels use technology, that they were involved in bringing about the Exodus, meeting Moses at the burning bush, causing the plagues, including killing off the first-born of Egypt on Passover night. The "pillar of cloud and fire" was the main Exodus UFO. (Ex. 13:21,22) I argued that the Exodus UFO parted the Red Sea, dropped manna from the sky, the wilderness was the laboratory where the Jewish religion developed. In a term borrowed from Richard Dolan, the angels made the Jews a "Breakaway Civilization." The Jews were given hundreds of commandments related to worship and ethics, which became the core of their religious practice. One of the commandments forbid making graven images. (Ex. 20:4) The lesson taught was that God is not physical, God is not nature, like wood or stone, rather God is spiritual, a different kind of reality, as Jesus made clear. "God is spirit, and those who worship him must worship him in spirit and in truth." (Jn. 4:24)

Of my hour and a half interview, how much made it into the History Channel series? Maybe 30 seconds, at least as of this writing. They keep the interview in some kind of video bank, and can dip into it whenever they want. There is a major flaw in the von Daniken thesis. His argument is that religion is a result of a mistaken identity by ancient people. They were too primitive not to be in awe of alien technology, so they worshiped the aliens, rather than realizing they were just a bunch of space guys.

But look at the central focus of "the space guys" in Exodus. The aliens are not busy giving the Jews a lot of new technology. They give the Jews commandments about ethics, justice, mercy, worship, love, forgiveness. A strong relation between love and sacrifice is established in Jewish worship. Even if we suppose that the "angels" are really space aliens, how does von Daniken, or the History Channel, explain the focus of the Exodus revelation on proper worship, and proper morality? Even if we suppose Jesus is a "space alien," why is his focus on prayer, "Our Father, who art in heaven," and on ethics (the Sermon on the Mount, Matthew 5-7)? Jesus does not get rid of God, or religion. He forms a church. The Ancient Alien theory, at least in its History Channel form, is blind to this truth about the Bible. The Ancient Aliens series argues that the von Daniken view means the end of the church. I expect our UFO reality to bring about a new Reformation, but not to destroy the church. (See my article "UFOs and Meta-narrative Reformation," at the Strong Delusion archives.)

None of these issues are faced by von Daniken, or the History Channel. We still have far to travel in our UFO REVELATION series. For those who have not read my book, I want to provide next a detailed explanation of the Parting of the Red Sea. Even though I believe von Daniken and the ancient astronaut group has gotten a lot wrong, I still believe we need to read the Bible through space age eyes. After all, this is our age. UFO REVELATION 4 will deal with the Red Sea.

BIBLICAL UFO REVELATIONS

UFO REVELATION 4
RED SEA PARTING

Richard Dolan and Bryce Zabel, in their book, A.D. After Disclosure, do not spend a lot of time explaining UFO technology. But concerning UFO propulsion systems they say: "Apparent negation of gravitational effects, possibly by creation of gravitational fields, making them independent of the need for energy as we define it." (p. 162) The idea that UFOs operate by anti-gravitational power has been with us since Donald Keyhoe wrote about flying saucers in the 1950's, and it is what I assume is the kind of power that parted the Red Sea.

Following is a summary of my understanding of the Parting of the Red Sea as I have explained in detail in chapter 3 of my book The Bible and Flying Saucers. (J.B. Lippincott, 1968; Avon Books, 1970; Sphere Books, 1973 (London), Berkley Books, 1989, Marlowe & Co, 1997). I have prepared this summary version since copies of my book are not always easily available.

The Exodus begins with an encounter between Moses and the angel of God at the burning bush. This was also a "talking bush," (See Exodus chapter 3). I believe some type of UFO was in a thicket, or clump of bushes, causing it to appear to burn, but not be "consumed." Modern UFOs often glow or give off light. A series of plagues were understood to have been caused by the "angel of God" that met Moses in the bush, including the killing of the Egyptian first-born on Passover night (Exodus 12).

In Exodus 13:21-22, we discover that the Exodus is being led by a strange UFO. "And the Lord went before them by day in a pillar of cloud to lead them along the way, and by night in a pillar of fire to give them light, that they might travel by day and by night; the pillar of cloud by day and the pillar of fire by night did not depart from before the people." Moses was understood to be in voice contact with the Lord in the Exodus UFO throughout the 40 year journey. The text says that the Exodus UFO (the Lord) led the Jews up to the Red Sea deliberately (Ex. 13:21-22), probably because the UFO had the technology to cause the parting of the sea.

BIBLICAL UFO REVELATIONS

THE RED SEA BIBLICAL TEXT IS AS FOLLOWS

(Revised Standard Version)

19 "Then the angel of God who went before the host of Israel moved and went behind them; and the pillar of cloud moved from before them and stood behind them, 20 coming between the host of Egypt and the host of Israel. And there was the cloud and darkness; and the night passed without one coming near the other all night.

21 Then Moses stretched out his hand over the sea; and the Lord drove the sea back by a strong east wind all night, and made the sea dry land, and the waters were divided. 22 And the people of Israel went into the midst of the sea on dry ground, the waters being a wall to them on their right hand and on their left. 23 The Egyptians pursued, and went in after them into the midst of the sea, all Pharaoh's horses, his chariots and his horsemen. 24 And in the morning watch the Lord in the pillar of fire and of cloud looked down up n the host of the Egyptians, and discomfited the host of the Egyptians, 25 clogging+ their chariot wheels so that they drove heavily; and the Egyptians said, 'Let us flee from before Israel; for the Lord fights for them against the Egyptians.'

26 Then the Lord said to Moses, 'Stretch out your hand over the sea, that the water may come back upon the Egyptians, upon their chariots, and upon their horsemen.' 27 So Moses stretched forth his hand over the sea, and the sea returned to its wonted flow when the morning appeared; and the Egyptians fled into it, and the Lord routed the Egyptians in the midst of the sea. 28 The waters returned and covered the chariots and the horsemen and all the host of Pharaoh that had followed them into the sea; not so much as one of them remained. 29 But the people of Israel walked on dry ground through the sea, the waters being a wall to them on their right hand and on their left." (Ex. 14:19-29, Revised Standard Version)

Before looking at details in the text, notice what the text does not say. The text does not say, "This was a supernatural event." Supernatural is not a biblical word. Nor does the text say, "This is a mythological story." Whenever we say that the Red Sea story is either "supernatural" or "mythological," we are imposing our interpretation on the text. We have a right to do this—the question is, which interpretation is correct? Or is it possible neither interpretation is correct? What I am doing is offering my interpretation of the parting of the Red Sea in light of modern UFO information. I do not believe the pillar of cloud and fire was God. Rather it was a mediator of God's reality, an angel, that becomes visible on behalf of the invisible Everywhere God. It may be that some of the Jews following the Exodus UFO believed the hovering object was God, but by New Testament times it was understood to be an angelic manifestation. (Acts 7:53) Thus the hymn, which I love, "Guide Me O Thou Great Jehovah," is a bit of a theological overstatement, if it means the pillar of cloud and fire was the essence of Yahweh. But the Exodus UFO does represent the "presence" of Yahweh. (Ex. 33:14) In any case, I believe "After Disclosure" Christian theology will have to discuss from our space age point of view the meaning of the angelic, and the role of the angelic in Exodus.

FEATURES TO NOTICE:

1) Modern UFOs are sometimes cylindrical in shape, as was the Exodus UFO. Also, when we think of a pillar supporting a building, we think of it as solid, hard. Cylindrical modern UFOs are sometimes called "cloud cigars," and can glow in the dark, as well as look cloud-like during the day. Some have been reported to be up to a mile long, and among UFO researchers, are presumed to be "star ships," as opposed to the flying saucer "scout ships" which tend to be smaller.

2) The first phase involved the Exodus UFO leading Israel up to the Red Sea, and then going behind the army of Israel to keep Egypt away until dark.

3) In the "morning watch," the pillar of cloud and fire was directly above the open sea channel (vs. 24). When did the UFO move from a position on the ground between the two armies, to a position directly above the open sea channel? The text does not say. I infer that the UFO moved unseen, under cover of darkness, before the sea began to part. Why didn't the "pillar of fire" glow on this night? I don't know.

4) During the night the Lord "drove the sea back by a strong East wind all night." I believe there was an East wind, but it was an effect of some kind of force field, the UFO propulsion system, that caused the sea to part. The UFO hovered above the sea and turned on a special power. One of the side effects would be that air would be drawn down into the open channel, and would blow out the open end. The Jews were on the western shore, the wind blew in their face from the East. (I believe if the Jews had been on the eastern shore, the wind would have blown out the other end of the channel, and the Bible would have reported a West wind.)

5) Obviously the two walls of water seemed strange, which is why they are reported. Wind would not give two smooth walls, but some type of directed force field probably would.

6) There was no wind reported during the crossing. If wind created the walls of water, why wasn't wind needed to keep them in place? A 60 mile an hour wind (as some have suggested) would have blown Moses back to Egypt.

7) The text stresses that Israel crossed on dry ground. This was just as strange as the walls of water. Why wasn't the bottom of the sea bed muddy? Modern UFOs often bake the ground hard when they land. Some speculate there is some kind of microwave dimension to UFO propulsion. Likewise, the "wind" side effect would

help in drying.

8) After Israel crossed, the chariots of Egypt followed. They seemed to be doing fine until something strange happened. It is at this point that the text brings the Exodus UFO back into the story. "The Lord in the pillar of fire and of cloud looked down upon the host of the Egyptians, and discomfited the host of the Egyptians, clogging+ their chariot wheels so that they drove heavily." An invisible force (stunning glance) came down from above, and caused the chariots to "drive heavily." Part of my theory is that in order for Israel to cross under the Exodus UFO, part of the "power beam" would have to be phased out in the center, otherwise Israel would have been knocked flat. If two walls of power were left on each side, that would keep the walls of water in place. What seems to happen in vs. 24 and 25 is that the power beam is again turned on in the center, knocking the Egyptians flat, perhaps paralyzing the horses, and doing something to the chariot wheels.

9) There is an asterisk (+) after the word "clogging," because the RSV has a "q" after the word, and in a footnote says that the actual Hebrew word reports that the Lord's "look down" "removed" or broke off the Egyptian chariot wheels; an alternative reading is that the wheels were "bound" or "locked up." The RSV translators could not imagine any force that would remove or break the wheels, or cause them to be "locked up," so they invented "clogging" as if there were mud in the sea bed, which the text stresses was not the case. One Jewish translation of the Torah, published in 1962, reads "he locked the wheels of their chariots so they moved with difficulty." This raises the possibility that some type of beam technology was focused on the hubs and axles of the chariots, causing heat expansion which locked the chariot wheels so they would not rotate.

10) This part of the text is very key. Some textual theory sees the Red Sea story as transmitted orally for many generations before being written. This may be true. Or the story is seen as pure mythology. But as mythology, notice how "unnecessary" vs. 24 and 25 are. Why not skip all this, and just drown the Egyptians? Most people who know the Red Sea story quite well do not remember this part of the story without looking at the text. What we have here is a very important detail that I think can only be understood from a space age point of view.

11) Moses raised his hands , all the power was turned off, the walls of water collapsed.

AFTER THE RED SEA

The Exodus UFO led Israel into the wilderness, apparently dropped manna from the sky to feed Israel (Ex. 16), as well as providing quail. Eventually in the wilderness of Sinai Moses was given the Ten Commandments, as well as instructions for the Tabernacle, and the work of the priesthood. After a long time (the text suggests 40 years), Israel came to the Jordan River, and moved from the leadership of Moses to Joshua, moved from wilderness to promised land. After the Tabernacle was built, the pillar of cloud hovered over it. "For throughout all their journeys the cloud of the Lord was upon the tabernacle by day, and fire was in it by night, in the sight of all the house of Israel." (Ex. 40:38)

From the point of view of Dolan and Zabel, after disclosure, I would expect the above explanation of the parting of the Red Sea to begin to receive serious exegetical attention from the Christian Church. After Disclosure, we will know a very real extraterrestrial power exists, which could have caused the parting. The "supernatural" explanation will be seen as unnecessary to those outside the church, which will be troubling to conservative Christians, both Protestant and Roman Catholic. At the same time, liberals and atheists, who have assumed that the Red Sea story is myth, that it never happened, will be deeply troubled. Liberal Episcopal Bishop John Shelby Spong, in his book Why Christianity Must Change or Die (HarperCollins, 1999) supposes it is absurd, and morally wrong to talk about a God who "split the Red Sea to allow the chosen ones to walk through on dry land." (p. 9) The essence of liberal thinking is that "we are makers of our own beliefs, and our own destiny." The main crisis after disclosure for liberals and skeptics (i.e. the unspoken world view of almost every secular university in the United States) is this: it appears that an extraterrestrial power may have guided our spiritual history. We did not just make our religious beliefs up out of our human imagination. We now have to take the basic biblical message seriously again, and that message is, we have been created by a Higher Power to serve the purpose of that Power. That purpose is spelled out in the Bible, especially in the account of the life, death and resurrection of Jesus. The ground work for the meaning of Jesus is to be found in the Jewish Exodus. The first Passover sets the stage for the Passover of Jesus, sets the stage for the Lamb of God who takes away the sins of the world. Jesus, in his death and resurrection, leads those who have been slaves, not to Pharaoh, but to sin, on a new Exodus journey, to a new Promised Land. An eternal Promised Land. We are called to a trial in which we are to follow Christ in seeking the Holy Spirit to rule the darker side of our fallen human nature. God's faith game is still on.

BIBLICAL UFO REVELATIONS

UFO REVELATION 5
SCIENTISTS AND UFO SECRECY

One hearsay memo discovered by Dolan and Zabel involved a conversation between Winston Churchill and Dwight Eisenhower. An RAF pilot had been paced on his way back to England by a flying metallic object. After discussing the UFO sighting, Churchill "said the report should be immediately classified because it would 'create mass panic amongst the general population and destroy one's belief in the Church.'" (A.D. After Disclosure, p. 107; also see my review of the Dolan and Zabel book in the May 2011 edition of The MUFON UFO Journal, p. 3, 18, 19.)

I would call this a reasonable reaction by Churchill, and probably representative of the instant reaction of any authority in Western culture at that time. It seems likely that Eisenhower agreed to the UFO secrecy that Truman had put in place in 1947, but by the time Eisenhower retired as President in 1960, he understood that UFO secrecy, with its black budget billions, would lead to a dangerous "militaryindustrial complex." Dolan and Zabel believe the danger has arrived.

The more billions—or maybe trillions—of dollars poured into secret UFO research, the more comfortable everyone would be, especially everyone on the inside of Dolan's "Breakaway Civilization," the new "chosen people" whose manna dropped not from the sky, but from U.S. taxpayers, whose elected leaders did not even have the "need to know" what was going on.

In some ways keeping UFO secrets has been difficult, but in other ways, fairly easy. For one thing, the aliens cooperate. They do not land on the While House lawn and say, "Take me to your leader." Even with a mass sighting, as in Phoenix, Arizona, in 1997, with the Governor falsely making fun of those who saw the UFOs, the UFO water is very muddy, and confusion wins. (Governor Fife Symington III did not admit until years later that he had seen the UFO which he had publically ridiculed.) The media is especially good at making fun of real UFOs, while making science fiction space films that gross millions.

But one concern of the secret keepers would be that scientists are by nature curious creatures. Donald Keyhoe had been arguing since the 1950's that flying saucers were real, and the government was covering up this truth. The Air Force did have Project Blue Book, which received UFO reports. Some scientists might suspect that where there is smoke there is fire. (J. Allen Hynek, for 20 years a Blue Book consultant, would eventually admit that the best UFO reports did not come to Blue Book, but were sent to a higher level.)

If the government had a crashed UFO and some dead alien bodies, and had formed the MJ-12 group to manage the UFO challenge (Richard Dolan, UFOs and the National Security State, Vol. I, p. 82ff), then the very existence of Project Blue Book was against the best interests of the secret keepers. The less publicity about UFOs the better. The secret keepers needed scientific cover to get the Air Force out of the UFO business.

What was needed was the help of scientists who would say, "UFOs are not a serious scientific issue." What this means is the secret keepers would need scientists who would, either knowingly or unknowingly, help with the UFO cover-up. Who are these scientists? We can only guess, but there are some good candidates.

PAGE, CONDON, SAGAN AND MENZEL:
THE UFO DEBUNKING 'A' TEAM

Thorton Page, Edward Condon, Carl Sagan and Donald Menzel are all deceased, but each was a scientist with a high reputation who was involved in the public discussion of UFOs. Each contributed to keeping UFOs scientifically and publically under wraps.

Page is perhaps the least known of the four, but he was a member of the CIA formed and resourced "Robertson Panel" who met in January of 1953 and recommended that the government carry out a "debunking" program of UFOs, explaining them not as spaceships, but as weather balloons, birds, Venus, or cloud formations. Making fun of those who report UFOs, getting UFOs out of the news, was the Robertson Panel's recommended goal. (Dolan, Ibid, p. 194 ff) Taken together, Page, Condon, Sagan and Menzel represent America's "UFO Debunking 'A' Team."

Page was professor of astronomy at Wesleyan University, and a research associate at the NASA Manned Spacecraft Center in Houston. He had a security clearance, and was trusted by the CIA, which confirms his political loyalties. Those like Apollo 14 Astronaut Edgar Mitchell are convinced some UFOs are extraterrestrial. Did Page with his NASA contacts secretly share Mitchell's view?

With one or more flying saucers tucked away in underground laboratories, along perhaps with dead alien bodies, the government did not need civilians calling their local Air Force base to report a flying saucer sighting. Some people saw the existence of Project Blue Book as "proof" flying saucers were real. The Air

Force gave a contract to the University of Colorado to get them out of the flying saucer business. The contract came to Colorado because of the connections of Professor Edward Condon to the University.

Condon was a physicist who pioneered in the field of quantum mechanics, and had helped develop nuclear weapons during World War II. This means he well understood the need to keep state secrets that were scientific in nature. At one time Carl Sagan was a student of Condon's.

The Colorado study was controversial, some members of the staff charged the project was a cover-up, and so when the Scientific Study of Unidentified Flying Objects was published in 1969, it was received with skepticism.

In his "Summary of the Study," Condon said that there are some who believe the government is involved in secret UFO studies. "Some have gone so far as to assert that the government has actually captured extraterrestrial flying saucers and has their crews in secret captivity, if not in the Pentagon, at some secret military base. We believe that such teachings are fantastic nonsense, that it would be impossible to keep a secret of such enormity over two decades, and that no useful purpose would be served by engaging in such an alleged conspiracy of silence." (Condon, p. 14-15)

Any UFO researcher would ask a series of questions concerning Condon's statement. How many restricted military facilities have you visited? Have you been given unrestricted access to private research corporations such as Lockheed's "Skunk Works," and are the employees permitted to answer questions without a "censor" being in the room? If the government did have a crashed UFO, wouldn't the government want to keep the advanced technology a secret? In terms of keeping secrets, how long were our Stealth Aircraft kept secret from the public? They were built in America, and flown by Americans, but the press did not acknowledge their existence. From the point of view of many UFO researchers, the Condon report was presented as a "scientific smoke screen," a cover-up for the scientific reality known to the secret keepers, the "Breakaway Civilization." From the point of view of Dolan and Zabel, Condon clearly named what is being covered up— crashed UFOs, and aliens. Did Condon know he was part of the cover-up? Or was he too dumb to know he was being used? Many would have trouble believing the "dumb" explanation.

The Condon report recommended that the Air Force discontinue Project Blue Book on the grounds that nothing of scientific importance was being found. This is what the Air Force wanted, and Blue Book was discontinued. Now out of a job, J. Allen Hynek began to show another side to the UFO challenge than what came from the Condon report. He and Dr. James McDonald were giving scientific respectability to UFO studies.

BIBLICAL UFO REVELATIONS

What was needed was a "scientific debate," between scientists who believe UFO reports were of scientific significance, and those who did not. In one way this was legitimate. In the eye of the public, there was not really "proof" of the ET hypothesis. Even now, Leslie Kean in her carefully written book, UFOs: Generals, Pilots, and Government Officials Go on the Record (2010) does not say that the ET hypothesis is proven, only that it is a good hypothesis, not yet proven. In a scientific sense, if I do not have a crashed flying saucer in my basement, I do not have "scientific proof." This is the doubting Thomas test. (John 20:19-29) As far as Dolan and Zabel are concerned, the "Breakaway Civilization" is way beyond the doubting Thomas test, but the Day of Disclosure has yet to happen.

In any case, a decision was made to delay a scientific symposium on UFOs until after the Condon report was released. The "symposium on Unidentified Flying Objects, sponsored by the American Association for the Advancement of Science, was held in Boston, Massachusetts, on December 26 and 27, 1969." [UFO's: A Scientific Debate, ed. Carl Sagan and Thornton Page (Ithaca: Cornell University Press, 1972), p. ix] Carl Sagan, Condon's former student, took a lead role in organizing the event, together with Thornton Page, formerly of the CIA Robertson Panel of 1953. They then published the results of the symposium in the above cited book.

WAS CARL SAGAN A SECRET KEEPER?

Dolan and Zabel devote a substantial section of After Disclosure to the question of whether or not Carl Sagan was in on the secret of the Breakaway Civilization, but silenced by a non-disclosure agreement. Their chapter subheading is: "Carl Sagan: They're Everywhere But Here."

Zabel was in a position to evaluate the possibility Sagan knew more about UFOs than he admitted. "As an investigative reporter for PBS, specializing in space science, Bryce Zabel met Carl Sagan several times in 1981. Cosmos was still airing on the network, and the unmanned Voyager spacecraft was approaching the planet Saturn." (p. 269) Zabel had a private parking lot conversation with Sagan, and posed the UFO question. Sagan stood strongly with his public position, that most UFOs can be explained as natural phenomena (birds, clouds, ball lightning, military air craft).

But Dolan and Zabel suspect that someone like Sagan might be given a choice—you will not be allowed to know the UFO secrets, or if you are allowed to know, then you must help provide the scientific smoke screen to keep other scientists from wondering about the truth. Dolan and Zabel do not prove, of course, that Sagan was a secret keeper. But they see him as an excellent candidate.

They suggest that "Just as Harvard astronomer Donald Menzel had done before him in the 1950's and 1960's, he would have to deflect people from the truth. Or he could insist on his right to speak freely—but then the real truth would be withheld from him." (p. 271) Dolan and Zabel believe that "a major portion of the scientific community has known about these things [UFO reality] all along. It is just that their work was classified for decades. And the rest of the scientific establishment bought into the 'deny and ridicule' concept so deeply that they were forced to simply ignore inconvenient facts for fear of losing grants, prestige and promotion." (p. 268)

We need to forget the romantic notion we have that scientists are "pure souls in search of the truth." The major governments of the world have long known that it is science that gives them the technological power to rule their world. Our modern scientists, especially in regard to UFO technology, are very much like Pharaoh's magicians, who try to imitate the rod of Moses. (Ex. 7:8-13) If our scientists work for our modern Pharaohs, they may lie for the sake of "the national security state." In the choice between the Truth (Jesus) and Caesar, they may choose Caesar.

SAGAN AND MENZEL: UFOS ARE RELIGION, NOT SCIENCE

If Dolan and Zabel are right, then Sagan was perhaps the heir to Donald Menzel's chairmanship of "UFO disinformation." Menzel, who died December 14, 1976, was author of UFO books that "debunked UFOs" as a modern myth. Sagan and Page summarize Menzel's position as "that all of the UFO reports can be understood in terms of misapprehended natural phenomena." (Sagan and Page, p. xvii) Menzel's books include Flying Saucers: Myth—Truth—History (1953) and The World of Flying Saucers: Examination of a Major Myth of the Space Age (1963).

There is of course a major mythological dimension to UFOs. In my UFO travels I have come across a few people who seemed to be caught up in some kind of UFO mythology. (I am sure to some I am seen as one of the myth makers.) The noted Swiss psychologist C.G. Jung had published Flying Saucers: A Modern Myth of Things Seen in the Skies (1958). Jung suspected that in our scientific age, space aliens have replaced angels as our means of connecting with some kind of ultimate reality. In his book Jung explored UFOs in dreams, and studied UFO "prophets" like Orfeo M. Angelucci. (Jung, MJF edition, 1978, p. 112 ff.) In a letter to Donald Keyhoe, Jung stated that UFOs were of interest to him as a psychologist whether they exist or not. Jung also said, "I follow with my greatest sympathy your exploits and your endeavours to establish the truth about the Ufos." (Ibid, p. 138)

The book, UFO's: A Scientific Debate, covers a wide range of issues ranging from public education and UFOs to UFO photos, radar echoes, and a major section on "Social and Psychological Aspects."

Two presentations gave a "hard science" point of view, "Twenty-one Years of UFO Reports," in which

J. Allen Hynek surveyed the Blue Book cases he had seen, and "Science in

BIBLICAL UFO REVELATIONS

Default: Twenty-two Years of Inadequate UFO Investigations," by James E. McDonald, professor of atmospheric physics at the University of Arizona. (McDonald died of suicide June 13, 1971, before the Sagan/Page volume was published.) Two presentations gave a "mythological" point of view. "UFOs—the Modern Myth," by Donald H. Menzel, and "UFO's: The Extraterrestrial and other Hypotheses," by Carl Sagan.

What Sagan did in his presentation, after citing statistics about the possibility of life on other planets, was to suggest the modern UFO mystery is a new form of religion. "As Darwinian evolutionary views became popular and mechanistic interpretations of the origin of the solar system and of cosmology became widely disseminated, part of the traditional domain of religion contracted, whether for good or for ill. At the same time, traditional forms of religion have been a very firm portion of nearly every culture of mankind; it is unlikely that the needs for belief in the gods, whether valid or not, can be destroyed so easily. In a scientific age what is a more reasonable and acceptable disguise for the classic religious mythos than the idea that we are being visited by messengers of a powerful, wise, and benign advanced civilization?" (Sagan and Page, p. 272)

I find this point of view from Sagan very reasonable, as I am sure did most of those scientists at the Boston conference. But if Sagan was in fact one of the "secret keepers," then it is very interesting to see how he is framing the cover-up. He is saying to any scientists who will listen, "UFOs are not really about science, they are about religion, about our need to keep believing in the religious myth of angels."

It is interesting to see how religion keeps showing up in our quest for UFO truth.

Early UFO sightings would have made government leaders (like Churchill) worry about loss of religious faith, or about an outbreak of end of the world and Second Coming fanaticism. But if we have crashed UFOs, and aliens, a story that the aliens put Jesus on earth could be used to shut the mouth of a President who wanted to expose UFO truth. At the same time, if you are trying to tell scientists who might be curious about UFOs to forget it, shame scientists by telling them "UFOs are really religion, not science, don't ruin science by mixing it with UFO religious fanaticism."

MENZEL, UFOS AND THE BIBLE

In his presentation, "UFO'S—The Modern Myth," Menzel presented several UFO cases, and interpreted the reported objects as natural phenomena in various ways. But interestingly from my point of view, the final section of his paper was entitled, "Flying Saucers in the Bible."

He begins by saying that he opened "Pandora's box" when he brought up

Ezekiel in one of his books. "I pointed out that two famous visions of the prophet Ezekiel, recounted by him in chapters 1 and 10 of Ezekiel, were in fact singularly accurate descriptions, albeit in symbolic and picturesque language, of a phenomenon well known to meteorologists, technically called 'parhelia.'" (Sagan and Page, p. 177) Parhelia he explains is seen when there is a ring around the sun. A double ring caused the "wheel within a wheel" appearance that Ezekiel reports. Menzel says he has only seen two examples in his life, and it is no wonder that uninformed people throughout the ages "have regarded them with superstitious awe, as portents of some dreadful event." (p. 178) What Menzel does not explain, of course, is the "voice" that Ezekiel hears coming from the "wheel within a wheel" directed to him. From Menzel's point of view, explaining the voice was unnecessary—no wise scientific person these days would believe Ezekiel heard a voice. Nor would anyone believe that Ezekiel was taken for a ride in this "parhelia," as Ezekiel reports. "The Spirit lifted me up, and brought me to the east gate of the house of the Lord, which faces east." (Ez. 11:1) Nor would Menzel believe that Elijah was taken up into the sky in a chariot of fire. (2 Kings 2:11)

Menzel then moves on to the story of Moses and the burning bush in Exodus. He quotes directly, "And the angel of the Lord appeared unto him in a flame of fire out of the midst of a bush: and he looked, and behold, the bush burned with fire, and the bush was not consumed." (Ex. 3:2) Menzel goes on to suggest this was an example of "St. Elmo's fire," caused by an occasional electric discharge from a tree. (p. 179)

What Menzel does not do of course is explain that this is not just a burning bush, it is a talking bush. Moses hears a voice coming from the bush, a voice speaking in the name of the God of Abraham, Isaac and Jacob. (In The Bible and Flying Saucers, I suggest that the burning bush may have been caused by the pillar of cloud and fire, or a similar UFO, landing in a clump of bushes, causing them to glow, but not burn up. Had Menzel read my book, published 4 years before this article by Menzel? Was Menzel's article meant to distract scientists and Christians from asking important questions about the burning bush text?)

Menzel even goes on to imply a connection between the Star of Bethlehem, UFOs and Venus. Then he discusses the parting of the Red Sea. "Another account that appears to require a temporary suspension of the laws of nature appears in Exodus, chapter 15, the parting of the waters of the Red Sea, allowing the Israelites to pass through on dry ground. And then the waters returned to entrap the pursuing Egyptians." (p. 180) According to Menzel, the parting of the Red Sea was a mirage. The Egyptians saw what looked like a body of water in front of them, thought the army of Israel had drowned, Israel looked back, and thought the Egyptians had drowned.

BIBLICAL UFO REVELATIONS

Maybe Menzel really believed his interpretations. Or maybe not: was he just blowing scientific smoke to protect government secrets? One of the most interesting things about Menzel's Red Sea analysis is that he cites the wrong chapter. Chapter 15 of Exodus is not the Red Sea narrative, rather it is a song of celebration for the Red Sea victory. The narrative is in chapter 14, as I have shown in UFO REVELATION 4. Chapter 15 begins with the words, "Then Moses and the people of Israel sang a song to the Lord." (Ex. 15:1) The song celebrated the Red Sea victory. Then Miriam, the sister of Moses, led the Jewish women in a victory dance.

How did Menzel manage to list the wrong chapter? Because he was a dumb scientist who did not know his Bible? Or was this a deliberate work of scientific and religious "disinformation," blessed by the CIA, or the "Breakaway Civilization?" By not referring to chapter 14, Menzel avoids the problem of explaining the "pillar of cloud and of fire," which is the main UFO of the Exodus. It seems strange that in an article on "Flying Saucers in the Bible," Menzel, this careful scientist from Harvard, would make this kind of error.

Had Menzel read my book? If the "Breakaway Civilization" was doing its work, they would have agents reading every book published that might threaten the "secrets of the national security state." To connect UFOs to the Exodus, and the parting of the Red Sea, could have been seen as potentially dangerous to keeping UFOs secret, especially if Christians began to ask questions. If Menzel did not find my book on his own, the secret keepers would make sure he saw the book, if Menzel is, as Dolan and Zabel suspect, one of the main voices of "disinformation" to an all too credulous scientific and religious community. (When I read this article by Menzel, I responded as a theological consultant to MUFON by writing the paper, "Some Questions Concerning Dr. Menzel's Biblical Exegesis," 1973 MUFON Symposium Proceeding, Kansas City, Missouri.)

If Dolan and Zabel are right, then scientists like Sagan and Menzel used religion as a smokescreen to cover up UFO truth. If Dolan and Zabel are not right, I apologize for disparaging the memory of Thorton Page, Edward Condon, Carl Sagan, and Donald Menzel. But from my point of view they appear to be very good candidates for the position of "America's UFO Debunking 'A' Team." And up to this point, Christians march on, not as soldiers, but as the people of God who are mostly blind to the truth that "the children of darkness" have worked very hard to keep under cover. But some Christians have wondered about those strange lights in our modern skies. Not everyone trusts what our modern Pharaohs have said about UFOs. Next we will examine how various Christian groups have responded to the UFO mystery.

UFO REVELATION 6
UFOS AND THE ROMAN CATHOLIC CHURCH

Dolan and Zabel, in their book A.D. After Disclosure, have a chapter sub-heading entitled, "The Vatican Moves Toward Disclosure." They say that "The world's largest church seems to be positioning itself to be the world's most open religious institution, at least regarding life elsewhere in the universe." (p. 253) Dolan and Zabel point to the Vatican's interest in astronomy, as well as to persons close to the Vatican, like the late Msgr. Corrado Balducci, who has spoken openly about his belief UFOs are real and extraterrestrial. [I found no reference in Dolan and Zabel to the Eastern Orthodox tradition and UFOs; an internet search for "Eastern Orthodox Church and UFOs" yielded little.]

No Protestant denomination has anything like the Vatican. Vatican City is a sovereign state within the city of Rome, Italy. Within its walls are a little over one hundred acres, established as independent from Italy in 1929. Public safety in the Vatican is maintained by the Pontifical Swiss Guard. Regulations for the Vatican are usually published in Italian, while regulations for the Holy See, the Roman Catholic world wide church government, are usually published in Latin. The Pope, however is head, as a monarch, of both the Vatican and the Holy See.

Interestingly, it is the Holy See that conducts diplomatic relations with the nations of the world, not the Vatican. Catholic diplomats are called nuncios, and go through special training before being assigned.

The Vatican is sometimes seen as a place of intrigue, as in the film "Angels and Demons" (2009), staring Tom Hanks, and based on the book by Dan Brown. In the film Hanks stars as a symbologist who has specialized in the "Illuminati," a secret group that has for centuries tried, in the name of science, to avenge the crimes of the Roman Church against science. In some ways the film is just another terrorist bombing story, but it does give an inside view of how the Vatican works.

I want to talk about what I would do about UFOs if I were the Pope. (I do not think this fantasy is based on Protestant envy, but I cannot be sure.) I would ask my ambassadors (nuncios) to enquire of other nations concerning their views of the UFO situation. Are they extraterrestrial? What is their threat assessment? What is their origin, and purpose?

We do not know what the responses might be, but I would guess that the U.S. Ambassador would say that "UFOs are a highly classified subject, and I do not even have access to this information myself." But according to the rules of diplomacy, the Vatican would not even be able to make this statement public. We have seen the storm caused when Wikileaks started releasing classified diplomatic documents. The Holy See has to play by the world's rules in regard to diplomatic secrecy, otherwise it will not be given confidential information.

But if a Catholic nuncio to France were to ask about UFOs, he would probably be handed the French COMETA report, which states very directly the UFOs are real and extraterrestrial. If the nuncio asked for specific examples, he might be told of the French Air Force pilot, who with his wife, witnessed a UFO landing, on December 9, 1979, a little over 200 yards from their home. They said it was about 65 feet in diameter, and "the object looked like two reversed saucers pressed against each other, with a precise contour, a gray metal color on the top and dark blue below, with no lights or portholes." (Maj. Gen. Denis Letty, "The Birth of COMETA," chapter 13 in Leslie Kean's book UFOs: Generals, Pilots, and Government Officials Go on the Record, 2010, p. 124)

MSGR. CORRADO BALDUCCI—THE CATHOLIC UFO AUTHORITY

As the diplomatic reports come in, as Pope I would appoint someone to coordinate the information, and recommend both a private and public position for the church. Msgr. Corrado Balducci seems to have carried out this role for the Pope. Balducci was trained in the theology of the demonic, but became well known for TV appearances in which he spoke of the reality of UFOs, and held the position that they were extraterrestrial, and from the "natural world," not the "supernatural world." Balducci would conclude, after hearing many stories of how the UFOs appeared to be solid, and metallic, that we are dealing not with the supernatural, but rather with an advanced technology. I question the Balducci position, that UFOs are neither angels nor demons. Biblical people saw UFOs, and met "angelic beings," but these primitive people would not be in a position to distinguish between the "supernatural" and the "super-technological." We need to remember "supernatural" is not a biblical word. (See my article "The Balducci Interview and Religious Certainty," at Strong Delusion Archives, and in the MUFON UFO Journal, September 1998, p. 16 ff; also see my article "Biblical Miracles as Super-Technology," in The Encyclopedia of Extraterrestrial Encounters, 2001, p. 111 ff.; also see Whitley Strieber, Confirmation, 1998, "Extraterrestrials and Christianity," interview with Corrado Balducci, conducted by Michael Hesemann, p. 265-274.)

Balducci was also trained in the Vatican to be a nuncio. Whether he served as an ambassador who sought UFO information from other countries is not public information, and by the rules of diplomacy, could not be. If Balducci learned that the United States is in possession of crashed UFOs, and dead (or alive) aliens, this is not information he could disclose.

But the Catholic Church, in the eyes of Dolan and Zabel, is in a sense "out front" in regard to extraterrestrial contact, compared with other branches of Christianity. So far as I know, the Pope has said nothing about UFOs—this protects the credibility of the Pope, in case his nuncios have been given misleading information. But at the same time, if the Day of Disclosure comes, Catholic leaders will be able to say, "We told you so."

Dolan and Zabel point out that the Vatican's astronomer, Guy Consolmagno, has spoken openly about the possibility of life on other planets, and he gained some media attention when he said that he would offer baptism to aliens. AOL News contacted me for a response to the Consolmagno baptism idea, and I asked "why would we suppose that they [aliens] would not already have the Holy Spirit, and not need to be baptized by the Church?" (AOL News, September 24, 2010)

I do not think we should suppose that the Universal Christ has been confined to our planet, and our historical time, in a universe that is 13 billion years old. We do not know what Jesus meant when he said, "And I have other sheep, that are not of this fold." (Jn 10:16; maybe he meant the Gentiles, or maybe he meant beyond this world.)

The people of God have frequently supposed they have the right to restrain, or put boundaries on, the Spirit of God, and by implication, to limit the love of God. If God is love (1 Jn. 4:8), the church makes a bad witness whenever we imply we control the love of God. Consolmagno's offer of baptism appears generous, and positive, but it represents a kind of arrogance that the church should avoid, but rarely does. The Bible reports an Exodus experience when God was going to pour his Spirit in a special way on the 70 ruling elders of Israel. They were all called to the Tent of Meeting for an early Holy Spirit baptism, but two did not come. There was some surprise when the two who "remained in the camp" received the spirit (Num. 11:16-35). When the Holy Spirit was given at Pentecost, it fell on all nations and tribes (Acts 2).

The Holy Spirit even came on Gentiles who had not been baptized, in response to Peter's preaching, much to the surprise of Christian leaders (Acts 10:44-48). Baptism was administered after the Holy Spirit was given, as a kind of quick follow up to what God had done without church permission. But I think it is better hospitality to offer baptism to UFO strangers (Heb. 13:2), than to condemn them as demons, as conservative Christians like Gary Bates does in his book Alien Intrusion (2004). Bates condemns me as a believer who has been "deceived and fallen away." (p. 327) He condemns me and my book without quoting a single sentence from it. Maybe I am deceived, but I think the Sodom story, not to mention the demonizing of Jesus by religious leaders, ought to make all Christians be very careful about how we demonize strangers.

THE FATIMA STORY—
CATHOLIC MIRACLE, UFO EXPERIENCE, OR BOTH?

Although I believe there are weaknesses in the current Roman Catholic position in regard to UFOs, I prefer it to the frequent Protestant position that UFOs are demons. One problem Catholics will face when Disclosure comes is identifying the difference between a UFO sighting, and an official Catholic miracle. The story of the miracle of Fatima, Portugal, in 1917 is a good example. The miracle was preceded with reports from three children that they were having occasional visitations from the Virgin Mary, while tending their sheep.

On October 13, 1917, a huge crowd, perhaps 50,000 people, saw a strange large sliver aerial disk in the sky, which went through an unusual series of motions. The light from this UFO was as bright as the sun, but the witnesses could stare at it without eye strain. The challenge here is though this is seen as a miracle by the Catholic Church, from the point of view of UFO researchers, it sounds like a somewhat standard UFO report, with some strange "paranormal" fallout. The Catholic Church claims this as a miracle. UFO researchers see it as typical of a flying saucer sighting. How do we tell the difference? Is there a difference? In what sense is this a supernatural event, as opposed to a display of advanced technology? (See Ann Druffel's article, "Fatima," in The Encyclopedia of Extraterrestrial Encounters, p. 188 ff.) At the end of UFO REVELATION 1, I put forward the hypothetical scenario: what if a UFO landed "in a poor community in Mexico, and a human got out of the UFO and said, 'I am Jesus, I am come to the least of you on earth. I want all who believe in me to repent, and turn to God and your neighbor for forgiveness. Very soon I will be returning with my angels in judgment. The earth, my bride, is not ready for me, but I yearn to come. Please tell the world I long to come, 'Surely I am coming soon.'"

I then ask, how would Christians react to this kind of Disclosure? The Roman Catholic Church would investigate this. The Fatima story, with its focus first on the children, on "the least of us," fits the divine pattern. Jesus landing, not on the White House lawn, or at the Vatican, but in a poor town in Mexico, fits the gospel priorities we all know. It would surprise the Catholic investigation team that Jesus got out of the flying saucer, not the Virgin Mary. They would question the witnesses, they would be slow to call this an official miracle. But they would take the report seriously.

Protestant liberals would ignore this all together. They believe in neither miracles, nor UFOs. This would be just another religious myth, they would stand firmly in the skeptical tradition of scientists like Donald Menzel and Carl Sagan.

Protestant conservatives would say this is just typical Catholic superstition, which the Reformation got rid of with it doctrine of "scripture alone" as the rule of faith and practice. If Jesus stands in front of us, and says hello, this is "experience," not scripture, and counts for nothing. Others, like Gary Bates, would say that the Mexico UFO story is a further example of demonic deception.

Not long ago I gave my standard UFOs and the Bible talk to a local group, with a strong emphasis on the Exodus UFO. After the presentation, a woman spoke to me, saying she was Roman Catholic, and she appreciated my presentation. I said, "Catholics seem to handle my biblical interpretation better than Protestants." She asked, "Why is that?" I said "Because you Catholics believe miracles can happen any time." She said, "That's right, we have visions of Mary all the time. In fact, Mary spoke to me when I was in Guadalupe." I have to confess that my Protestant mind froze at that point, and I did not ask the obvious question, "What did Mary say?"

During 1984 I conducted a survey of theological seminaries in the United States, sending out four questions to one hundred seminaries. One response I received was from the very Rev. J. Edgar Bruns, from the Roman Catholic Archdiocese of New Orleans, dated December 20, 1984. He did not just answer my questions, he wrote a letter saying, "I strongly suspect that many UFO sightings are authentic, i.e., not hallucinations or misperceptions of ordinary phenomena or of military experiments. It would be my assumption that any genuine UFO was controlled by intelligent beings from another world." He went on to say that our salvation in Christ is not threatened by an alien presence, and referred to the C.S. Lewis' trilogy dealing with outer space concepts ("Out of the Silent Planet" etc.) "If intelligent life exists elsewhere and has not fallen from Grace, I would consider such creatures equivalent to the biblical angels." (Letter in my possession.)

Both based on the public positions taken by Roman Catholics, apparently with Vatican approval, as well as my direct experience in discussions with Catholics, I believe they are much better positioned than Protestants, either liberal or conservative, to deal with UFO disclosure. Dolan and Zabel are right to say that Roman Catholics are best positioned among Christians to deal with Disclosure when it comes. Conservative Protestants are caught up in their fear of deception and demons, which I admit is no small issue. But liberal Protestants are clueless, and I will try to explain why in UFO REVELATION 7.

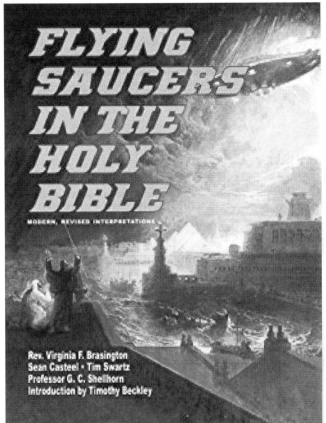

UFO REVELATION 7
UFOS AND LIBERAL PROTESTANTISM

The position of liberal Protestantism in relation to UFOs can best be described as the sound of one hand clapping. Liberal Protestants are mostly unaware that UFOs raise issues for Christian faith. This makes it a challenge to write a whole chapter explaining where liberal Protestants stand in relation to UFOs. I plan to explore the scientific and biblical nature of evil in UFO REVELATION 8, in order to lay the groundwork to evaluate the conservative Protestant position.

There are liberal Roman Catholics, and conservative Roman Catholics, but they do not get separate chapters. Why is that? Roman Catholics have a Pope who by his authority is able to discipline the extremes of left and right in the Catholic Church. Protestants have no such mediating and powerful centering force. The political split in Protestantism is obvious to all careful observers. Many liberal Protestants are Democrats, many conservative Protestants Republicans; liberals are pro-abortion, pro-gay rights, pro-Palestinian rights. Conservatives are anti-abortion, anti-gay rights, and pro-Israel. We now have blue Protestant churches and red Protestant churches. The way in which Protestantism has divided has been well documented in James Davison Hunter's 2010 book, To Change the World. Hunter explains how as liberal and conservative Christians split over political issues, they have each had less and less influence in American culture as a whole. Religion is now viewed as something like art, religion seems to add something to some people's lives, but has little to do with the way the world works. Hunter also argues, as a sociologist, that cultural change comes from the top down, not the bottom up, as many religious leaders suppose.

When Luther and Calvin brought about the Reformation, they needed an authority to match the authority of the Pope, and the authority of the Bible was the only serious choice available. Using the Bible to challenge the authority of the Pope in regard to indulgences, as Luther did, was powerful, and to some extent successful, although there were political issues between Italy and Germany that set the direction of the Reformation as well. The Roman Catholic Church claimed infallible authority for the Pope, many Protestants claimed infallible authority for the Bible. In some ways it was a stand off.

But in the mean time, science was challenging the authority of both the Pope and the Bible. This was the case with the cosmology of Copernicus, as well as Galileo with his telescope, in regard to the authority of the Catholic Church; Darwin's theories of evolution, from 1859 forward, posed a powerful challenge to the Protestant theory of biblical infallibility, especially in regard to Genesis. Some conservative Protestants are still fighting the teaching of evolution in public schools. But even more important from James Davison Hunter's point of view, is that science has created institutions with great power—our high tech industries, our research universities, our instant communication and media centers—that control attitudes and beliefs which Christianity has not successfully challenged, especially the issues of greed, justice, honesty and ecology in relation to money and markets. To understand the direction of modern culture, we need only notice how many colleges and universities in the United States were founded by Christian churches, and in the past fifty years, have rejected any Christian connection.

THE GOD OF THE BIBLE

The most basic difference between liberal and conservative Protestants is that conservatives cling to belief in the infallibility or inerrancy of Scripture, while liberals gave up that belief, although the degrees of "giving up" varied. Some liberals might say the Bible was inspired by God but is not infallible; other liberals might go so far as to see the Bible as simply a human document, with no more authority for them than the Koran or the Book of Mormon. For the most extreme liberals, religion is what the human mind creates—we create our own values, they are not God given. From the conservative point of view, some liberal Protestants have gone totally away from the God of the Bible.

This is my understanding of the God of the Bible. There are two major dimensions to the divine revelation; Jesus unifies these dimensions. The first dimension of God, the primary one, is that God is imminent. Imminent is not a word I like, so I prefer to say God is Everywhere and Invisible. "Whither shall I go from thy Spirit? Or whither shall I flee from thy presence? If I ascend to heaven, thou art there! If I make my bed in Sheol, thou art there." (Ps. 139:7, 8) The Apostle Paul spoke of the Everywhere God when he said of God to the people of Athens, "In him we live and move and have our being." (Acts 17:28) It is to the Everywhere God that Jesus prays, "Our Father." It is the Everywhere God of whom Jesus says, "God is spirit." (Jn. 4:24)

But it is not the Everywhere God that makes the Bible famous. The God that made the Bible famous is the God who killed the first-born of Egypt on Passover night, parted the Red Sea, landed on Mt. Sinai in sight of everyone and gave commandments for the Jewish faith. The actions of the Exodus UFO explained in UFO REVELATION 4 are what define the God of the Old Testament, not his Everywhereness. In the Old Testament, the claim is made that the Everywhere God has the freedom to become visible, either as "fire" perhaps, at the burning bush, or even more, as a voice that is heard, also at the burning bush. The Everywhere God can suddenly show up in a particular place, and speak to chosen people. In other words, there are special times of "revelation," when the Everywhere God somehow becomes visible in our world. Theology calls these times of God's self disclosure. Likewise the New Testament story of Jesus, crucified, and raised from the dead, is what defines the God of the New Covenant, not God's Everywhereness. But the Christian doctrine of the Incarnation says that in Jesus, the Everywhere God became human, became flesh. Jesus claimed a special relation of unity with the Everywhere God, whom he called Father. This led one of his disciples, Philip, to say, "Lord, show us the Father, and we shall be satisfied." (Jn. 14:8) Part of the response of Jesus to Philip is, "Believe me that I am in the Father, and the Father is in me, or else believe me for the sake of the works themselves." (Jn. 14:11) Thus what we might call the personality of the Everywhere God is made perfectly clear in the human person of Jesus. In Jesus the Everywhereness of God takes human form and lives among us, the ultimate form of "revelation" or "divine disclosure." When Jesus says "I am in the Father, and the Father is in me," he is explaining what we might call the "metaphysics" of how the Everywhere God can also be somewhere, such as in Jerusalem on May 3rd, A.D. 30, or whatever calendar we use to identify the historical Jesus. Although Jesus perfectly represents the Everywhere God, we need to remember that the angelic order was, and still is, the means by which the Everywhere God breaks out of his spiritual dimension, and enters our dimension of space and time.

After the Ascension of Jesus, the Holy Spirit is given at Pentecost. Now some of the Everywhereness of God, the God who is Spirit, enters into humans who believe in Jesus. How are we to understand what it means that "the Word became flesh" (Jn. 1:14) in Jesus, or that Spirit enters into flesh in God's Church?

Liberal and conservative Protestants went at these questions from different points of view. The best summary of these differences may come from the Apostle Paul himself who described the difference between the Jewish view of God and the Gentile view of God. Paul said "For Jews demand signs, and Greeks seek wisdom, but we preach Christ crucified, a stumbling block to Jews, and folly to Gentiles." (1 Cor. 1:22,23) What this means is for Jews, God is to be found in special signs of power, such as the Passover miracle, or the parting of the Red Sea, the Exodus revelation. The Gentiles—Greeks in particular, think of Plato and Aristotle—seek God in a rational understanding of life and the universe. Greeks lean more toward what would eventually become science, and an invisible Everywhere God suites their rationalism. What Jesus seemed to say to Philip was, if he could not understand the "metaphysics" of his unity with the Everywhere God, which would be a "Greek" thing to do, then he should believe in Jesus because of his "works," his miracles, which would be a "Jewish" thing to do.

What I have been doing for more than 40 years is exploring the possibility that UFOs provide a way to reconcile the split between the Bible and science, between Jewish "signs" and Greek "wisdom."

Thus, when the Protestant boat came crashing up against the rocks of modern science in the past 400 years, the boat split apart. Conservatives stuck to their infallible Bible, because they wanted to keep the signs, the miracles, which were essential to the God in whom they believed. But liberals took the rationality of modern science seriously, and given a choice between what their science told them, and what the Bible said, they went with science, if there was a conflict. By faith they trusted in an Invisible Everywhere God, but not the God of signs, the God who parted the Red Sea, or raised Jesus from the dead.

PRINCETON THEOLOGICAL SEMINARY 1960

I arrived on the campus of Princeton Theological Seminary in September of 1960, a bachelor's degree in physics in one hand, the Bible in the other. I arrived knowing there was some kind of conflict between science and the Bible, but with really no understanding of the historical dynamics behind the struggle. I soon learned there had been a historic faith struggle in the seminary, and in my denomination, about the authority of Scripture. I was to find some at the seminary who believed in the infallibility of Scripture, while there were others who thought any kind of human infallibility, either of the Pope or the Bible, was not only dangerous but heretical, a denial of our humanity.

Princeton Seminary sits more or less at the corner of Alexander and Mercer Streets in Princeton, New Jersey. Albert Einstein lived on Mercer St., just a few doors down from the seminary, when he worked at Princeton's Institute for Advanced Studies. The seminary is on the south side of Alexander, the University on the north side of Alexander. The seminary was administratively and financially separate from the University, but was very much in its intellectual shadow. Princeton is famous for its Ivy League University, not its seminary.

I did not know it at the time, but as I arrived in Princeton, Paul Ramsey, professor of religion not at the seminary, but at the university, was writing the Preface to a book written by Gabriel Vahanian entitled The Death of God: The Culture of Our Post-Christian Era. Ramsey would date his Preface as Christmas 1960. The seminary staff would know about this book, and others like it, but the seminary itself was committed to the neo-orthodoxy of Karl Barth, not to the emerging death of God theology. The most exciting event while I was at Princeton was Barth's Princeton lectures, delivered in the University Chapel.

The Vahanian book in its way saw the clear path of decline for what used to be our Christian culture, and the negative implications for my Presbyterian church. (When I was ordained in 1967, the Southern and Northern branches of my church had a combined membership of about 5 million. Now in a merged church, they have about 2 million members.) In his Preface Ramsey said, "Ours is the first attempt in recorded history to build a culture upon the premise that God is dead." (xiii) Our emerging scientific world view has eroded confidence in the supernatural almost to extinction, except among fundamentalists, according to Ramsey. Liberal Protestantism saw in science at first an optimism that science would be the means for bringing in the kingdom of God. When the nuclear age arrived, suddenly science did not seem like much of a savior, going very quickly from "the wheel to the whoosh." (p. xxiv) But science having turned demonic did not restore the supernatural. It just left despair, godlessness.

Ramsey senses that "it is still the case that the premise of contemporary culture (except in the sphere of autonomous science) is not merely the absence of theistic presuppositions, but the real absence of a God who formerly lived and had his dealings with men. It means 'the death of God' still present." (xxv)

The God who died is the God of Abraham, Isaac and Jacob who speaks to Moses, who somehow overcomes being the God of Everywhere, and becomes God in a particular place and time. Some liberal theology clung to the idea of an Everywhere God, perhaps as the "ground of being" as Paul Tillich suggested, or as the ultimate source of existence. But liberal theologians began writing articles that pondered "theology without revelation," meaning God without angelic intervention, without God breaking into our world from his Everywhereness.

I began to see the problem more clearly my senior year at Princeton, when one of my professors, in a class on doctrine discussing the Apostles' Creed, said, "No one today believes in the Ascension [of Jesus] do they? And if Jesus did not ascend, where is his body? We may only suppose his bones lie buried somewhere in the Middle East." The professor went on to explain that the Copernican revolution destroyed the ancient three decker universe, with heaven above, earth in the middle, and hell below. He suggested we now needed to see much of the supernatural dimension of the Bible as mythology, not as historical fact.

Christianity without the Resurrection and Ascension is now the "orthodox" view of liberal Christianity. One of the most respected liberal Old Testament scholars of our time is Walter Brueggemann. I have attended some of his lectures on the Psalms. What does he say about the Ascension? "The ascension refers to the poetic, imaginative claim of the church that the risen Jesus has 'gone up' to share power and honor and glory and majesty with God. It is a claim made in our creed that 'he ascended into heaven and sitteth on the right hand of God the father almighty.'"

Brueggemann goes on to say, "Now if you want to, you can vex about this prescientific formulation all you want. But you can also, as I do, take the claim as a majestic poetic affirmation that makes a claim for Jesus, that Jesus now is 'high and lifted up' in majesty, that the one crucified and risen is now the one who shares God's power and rules over all the earth. This prescientific formulation of the matter is important, because it gives us imagery of a quite concrete kind to imagine Jesus receiving power." (Brueggemann, Mandate to Difference, 2007, p. 1-2) Brueggemann understands that liberals do not "want to sound like silly supernaturalists." (p. 197)

Notice what Brueggemann does here. He turns narrative into poetry, history into make believe. The Ascension story in Luke reads as much like history as do the crucifixion and resurrection narratives. Jesus warns the disciples it is not for them to know about the end times, about God's plans for the future. Their call is to be faithful witnesses. "And when he had said this, as they were looking on, he was lifted up, and a cloud took him out of their sight."

Then two men "in white robes" said to them, "Men of Galilee, why do you stand looking into heaven? This Jesus, who was taken up from you into heaven, will come in the same way as you saw him go into heaven." (Acts 1:6-11) The Bible seems to be telling us what the biblical people saw when Jesus ascended, but in reality, for Brueggemann and many liberals, it is only what they imagined. In terms of the damage to our Christian hope of life after death, consider this analogy. A travel company runs a contest. Enter the contest and you win a free trip to Europe. You enter the contest, and are told you are a winner. You are also told there is no real trip to Europe, only a poetic one, an imaginary one. Since you are a winner, feel free to imagine your trip to Europe. It will not be long before millions of people decide not to enter the contest.

I believe we need to see the Ascension of Jesus as a UFO event, similar to the ascension of Elijah in a chariot of fire, and connected to the "pillar of cloud" tradition of Moses. By the time we get to the New Testament, "clouds" are a code term, like UFOs are a code term for us, for a heavenly transportation system. Jesus does return very soon, but not to stay, in a bright light that meets Saul/Paul on the road to Damascus. (Acts 9, 22, 26) The conversion of Paul is also part of the biblical UFO tradition, and should not be read as poetry.

Christianity which rejected the Ascension of Jesus, and the eschatology of the New Testament was a shock to my faith. I understood that if you eliminated the Resurrection and Ascension of Jesus we had no hope of life beyond death, no hope for justice in the next world.

[With no hope for justice in the next world, Protestant liberalism turned to the Marxist ideology of a classless society as its source of an earthly utopian hope in place of a heavenly one. As Dennis O'Brien has observed, "Marx was opposed to Christianity because he saw it as a distraction from history, as pie in the sky by and by." (Christian Century, May 3, 2011, p. 47) Since Protestant liberals had lost their hope of "pie in the sky by and by," Marxism's rejection of the eschatology of Jesus was no problem at all—liberal Protestants didn't believe it anyway. Liberation theology borrowed the oppressor/oppressed dialectic from Marxism as its main yardstick of political analysis, gaining special fame when Barach Obama's pastor, Jeremiah Wright, trained in the black liberation theology of James H. Cone, condemned America as an oppressive nation in such clear terms that Obama had to discontinue his relation with Wright. In the liberation theology of Jeremiah Wright, as President of the United States, Obama would become the head oppressor! It is no small irony that President Obama gave the order which led to the death of Osama bin Laden! With little difficulty liberation theology has morphed into its current secular form, which we usually call political correctness. Conservative Protestants have often tried to develop an anti-liberation politics of the right to counter the Christian political left, which has led to the situation decried by Brueggemann that we now "enlist as red or blue ministers in red or blue churches." (p. 201) I will deal with political division in church and society in more detail in UFO REVELATION 8.]

I was in a faith crisis. How could I promise life after death at a Christian funeral, if the resurrection is seen as mythology? I decided to do graduate work at the University of Edinburgh, Scotland, in the area of science and Christian eschatology. In a way, I was like the woman in search of a lost coin, the coin being eschatology, our Christian hope that Christ now rules in heaven, and our salvation will be living eternally in heaven with him. I went to Edinburgh after graduating from Princeton in 1963. My Ph.D. dissertation at Edinburgh, Eschatological Implications of the Understanding of Time and Space in the Thought of Isaac Newton, was approved in May of 1966, and I returned to the United States.

My Newton studies did not solve my faith crisis, but UFOs seemed to offer a possibility. During the Fall of 1965 I began to explore the Bible from a space age point of view, partly in regard to biblical angels, but also in regard to what appeared to be biblical UFOs—the pillar of cloud of the Exodus, the chariot of fire of Elijah, the wheels of Ezekiel. When I returned from Edinburgh, I set up a study in the basement of my in-laws home, where I waited for a pastoral position, and wrote The Bible and Flying Saucers, which was published in 1968.

BIBLICAL UFO REVELATIONS

THE WORLD WELCOMES MY BOOK (Don't I Wish!)

The book was welcomed with a few favorable reviews, such as in the Los Angeles Times, which recommended not missing "this mind stretching reading," but by and large the positive reviews were not from theologically trained reviewers. I had asked publisher J.B. Lippincott to send a copy of my book to Dr. James I. McCord, President of Princeton Seminary. He was President while I was a student there. I respected him very much, and he made financial decisions which gave Princeton a solid economic base which few seminaries enjoy today.

McCord acknowledged my book in a letter dated February 3, 1969. In my book, I had taken clear aim at the "death of God theologians," and he said "I enjoyed the cleaning you gave them."

At the same time, he had doubts about UFOs. "On the other hand, I lack sufficient imagination to have proper respect for UFOs. As a matter of fact, I still think airplanes are 'against nature.'" I appreciated the fact that he took the time to read my book, but his response illustrates where "centrist" theology was, caught between a dogmatic and narrow commitment to the Bible no matter what on the right, and "there is nothing in the Bible that is believable" on the far left. The American government UFO cover-up was more than enough to put off moderate theologians like McCord. They understood that the loss of the supernatural to scientific skepticism was a serious crisis for the church, but bringing in UFOs, which might not even exist, seemed to be no real solution.

Not everyone was as kind as President McCord. In a review of my book, Lester Kinsolving, an Episcopal priest who also practiced religious journalism, said the publishers of the book needed forgiveness for printing the book. How could the "publisher of this pseudo-theological travesty, J.B. Lippincott & Company" advertise itself as a publisher of good books? I was seen in league with "frothing Fundamentalism, " and Kinsolving was distraught that "this kind of thing is expected from assorted Bibliolatrists but hardly from Edinburgh PhDs."

By and large, I had a better welcome from Catholics than Protestants. Father Luke Farley, a priest of the Archdiocese of Boston, reviewed my book in the August 17, 1968 issue of The Pilot. After referring to other books, such as that by Morris Jessup dealing with UFOs and the Bible, Farley said, "This new treatment by Barry H. Downing, even if it is theologically 'far out,' is by far the best of the lot."

REJECTION AND THE LIBERAL THEOLOGICAL PRESS

I understood the rejection of my work on the grounds that, "UFOs don't exist, do they?" As Dolan and Zabel would say, the secret keepers with their "deny and ridicule" policy in regard to UFOs, had done a good job of making my book seem too impossible to believe. Even with proof UFOs are real, there are serious

47

challenges involved in making connections between UFO aliens and angels. I had supposed that "eventually the truth would out," as Dolan and Zabel suppose, but here I am, more than 40 years after publication of my book, and still no Disclosure.

In 1984 I sent a survey to 100 Protestant and Roman Catholic seminaries, addressed to the President of the institutions. I obtained my mailing list from Patterson's American Education. I had 26 survey forms returned to me. I asked 4 questions in the survey:

Do you believe it is possible some UFOs carry an intelligent reality from another world?

If some UFOs do carry an intelligent reality from another world, what might be some consequences for Christian theology?

Have there been any formal studies of the relation between UFOs and Christian theology in your seminary classes? (For instance, has there ever been a suggested connection between UFOs and the biblical doctrine of angels?)

Using the Freedom of Information Act, Lawrence Fawcett and Barry J. Greenwood, in their book Clear Intent: The Government Coverup of the UFO Experience, have published formerly secret CIA, FBI, and other Government UFO documents. Courts have blocked the release of hundreds of pages of UFO documents in the name of national security. Can you think of any negative consequences for Christian theology of a Government policy of UFO secrecy?

There were some interesting responses, that kind of followed liberal/conservative lines. In regard to connecting angels and UFOs in class, one conservative President wrote, "I hope not." Liberals were somewhat concerned that there might be a coverup, and thought we should know the truth; conservatives tended to suppose that if the there is a government coverup, the government is just doing its duty.

I then wrote an article based on the results of the survey, using the title, "UFOs: Four Questions for Theological Seminaries." I sent copies of the article to the following journals, with rejection coming from all of them: Union Seminary Quarterly Review, Theology Today, Perspectives on Science and Christian Faith, Pacific Theological Review, Interpretation, and Theological Studies. Finally, I sent the article to MUFON, which published the article in the 1988 edition of the MUFON Symposium Proceedings.

By and large, the survey indicated that neither liberal nor conservative theology had serious interest in looking into the UFO mystery. Eventually a significant interest would form among Christian conservatives, but this has yet to happen among Christian liberals.

BIBLICAL UFO REVELATIONS

TED PETERS—ONE LIBERAL PROTESTANT HAND CLAPPING

The most substantial liberal Protestant response to UFO theology has come from Ted Peters, a Lutheran theologian who published UFOs—God's Chariots? Flying Saucers in Politics, Science and Religion (1977). Peters traces the mythological impact of UFOs on science, politics and religion. Peters, like myself, has long been a MUFON consultant in theology, teaches at the Pacific Lutheran Theological Seminary in California, and is editor of the journal Theology and Science.

Peters takes a psychological approach to UFOs. He takes no position on the physical reality of UFOs, dealing only with their psychological power as does C.G. Jung in his book Flying Saucers: A Modern Myth of Things Seen in the Skies. Peters says, "UFOs have a way of drawing out our religious sensibilities in disguised form, even when we believe ourselves to be no longer religious. Each one of us has a deep inner need to be at one with our creator and source of life." (p. 9) In other words, we think UFOs are about science, but they are really a "disguised form of religion." (Like the Ascension of Jesus for Walter Brueggemann, UFO stories appeal to our poetic imagination. Liberals are very comfortable with the idea that religion is something we make up because we need it.)

When Peters finally gets to chapter 6, "Toward a UFO Theology," we find that he treats three authors: Eric von Daniken (Chariots of the Gods? 1968), R.L. Dione (God Drives a Flying Saucer, 1969, and Is God Supernatural? The 4000-Year Misunderstanding, 1976) and my own book (The Bible and Flying Saucers, 1968), as a unit, which makes categorical sense, but the three of us have major differences.

Von Daniken separates the angels in the Bible from God, saying the angels are really ancient astronauts, who were worshiped by mistake as "gods" by the biblical people. What we find in von Daniken is that he says he believes in God, by which he means the "Everywhere God," but he does not believe the angels in the Bible have any connection to this Everywhere God. They are just a bunch of "ancient astronauts." From the point of view of Peters, in our scientific age, we "need" to turn the angels into astronauts, which is why von Daniken has been so popular.

Dione, on the other hand, seems to get rid of the "Everywhere God," and turn him into an astronaut who flies his own flying saucer. For Dione, all the miracles in the Bible can be explained as the result of some advanced technology, not the supernatural. He too suggests the Red Sea was parted by technology, as I do, but suggests two "pillars of cloud," side by side, parted the Sea. Dione seems unaware of my book, or my different interpretation of the parting of the Red Sea. (Dione, Is God Supernatural? p. 63) This leads Peters understandably to complain that UFO theology seems to "trivialize God." (Peters, p. 115)

BIBLICAL UFO REVELATIONS

Peters does a good job of reviewing my work on the Exodus, as well as the implications of UFOs for the New Testament, and he discusses my work after reviewing von Daniken and Dione, calling my work a "more cautious and more sophisticated defense of a von Daniken-Dione type theology." (Ibid, p. 110) But in the end of the day, my "sophistication" does not save UFO theology. "What is startling about the claims of von Daniken and other would-be UFO theologians is that they actually humanize and trivialize God. They make natural what we believe to be supernatural. They make physical what we accept as spiritual. They say what we once thought to be extraordinary is really ordinary." (Ibid, p. 115)

What we find in the Peters' critique, as well as in the work of von Daniken and Dione, is that they do not understand the Dual Nature of God, first as the Everywhere God, but also as the God who can appear in angelic form, or even human form (Jesus). Peters does not say to the UFO theologians, in the words of Philip, "Show us the Father." Rather Peters says, "You have humanized and trivialized" the Father.

Peters should not blame UFO theology for this problem, he should blame the Bible. After all, from the point of view of many Jews and Muslims, they do not believe in the incarnation of Jesus, they do not believe that if you have seen Jesus you have seen the Father, because that "humanizes and trivializes God."

But because we live in a scientific age, the only God science seems to allow is the Everywhere God. At the same time, the Everywhere God is restricted by modern science, and by liberal theologians, from entering into our space-time. Revelation is not allowed. Angels are mythological, as are events might have been caused by angels, like the parting of the Red Sea. Thus, although God may be safe in his Everywhereness, he cannot get to us by the rules of modern science and liberal theology. Peters does not seem to have a working angelology, and does not explore how UFOs may be part of biblical angelology. The difficulty for liberals is, if UFOs are real, biblical revelation is back in business. Liberals find it within their comfort zone to have religion be something we create with our minds, not something given to us by a Higher Power. It seems strange that Peters would blame UFO theologians for making "natural what we believe to be supernatural." After all, liberal theology got rid of the supernatural before those of us doing UFO theology said to the "death of God theologians," take another look: it is not unscientific to say the Red Sea parted, Jesus rose from the dead, the angels of God are still with us. My position is that the biblical religion is not mythology, but some of the miracles may not be supernatural either. Whatever supernatural is, Peters does not explain, nor do my conservative critics.

The angels in the Bible are reported to be able to eat food, as did Jesus after his resurrection.

BIBLICAL UFO REVELATIONS

Do we suppose the bodies of angels, and of the resurrected Jesus, are supernatural? They seem natural in many ways. Perhaps what we have with the biblical angels, and with the resurrected Jesus, is that they come from a universe where the laws of physics are different, but not necessarily supernatural. (We will explore advanced physics and biblical interpretation in UFO REVELATION 11.)

From the point of view of Peters, it is my hope that "Science and religion can now become friends, according to UFO theology." (p. 115) I would plead guilty to this charge. I do not accept the liberal dualism that science deals with reality, while the biblical religion deals with mythology (and poetry). I realize there are many forms of religious mythology: the mistake of Christian liberals is to be way too quick to assume the angels, and the God of the Bible, are as "make believe" as the ancient gods of Greece and Rome.

An excellent book from the "religious studies" point of view, rather than a theological point of view, was written by Brenda Denzler, The Lure of the Edge: Scientific Passions, Religious Beliefs, and the Pursuit of UFOs (2001). Denzler earned her Ph.D. in religious studies at Duke University. Her opening chapter, "A Short History of the UFO Myth," establishes her point of view. The question is not, if UFOs exist, what does this mean for religion? Rather her question is, if people believe UFOs exist, what happens to their religion? Both Peters and Denzler would be very comfortable with the arguments of Carl Sagan and Donald Menzel that UFOs are a modern religious myth. Denzler refers to my work, as well as that of Peters. She sees my belief that UFOs carry the angels of God as the strongest argument for an "optimistic hermeneutic." (p. 128). She is comfortable with the way Ted Peters rejects the theological implications of UFOs. (p. 152, 157) If Dolan and Zabel are right, that Disclosure Day may come upon us, then liberal religious writers like Peters and Denzler will have to answer the question: Why did you allow yourself to be taken in by our modern Pharaohs, and their lies? Msgr. Corrado Balducci took the common sense view that thousands of eyewitness UFO reports should not be rejected out of hand, any more than we should reject the eyewitness reports of the resurrection of Jesus in the New Testament. But Peters and Denzler seem comfortable questioning UFO theologians, while not questioning the government.

In 1972, Walter Andrus, Jr., invited me to become a theological consultant to MUFON, and asked me to send articles that could be published either in MUFON's newsletter, or in the annual conference proceedings, and I began publishing frequently with MUFON. MUFON consisted of many people with a scientific orientation, but who suspected the government was lying to us. Some members, such as Andrus, had seen UFOs with their own eyes, they knew the cover-up was on. For people who were sure UFOs were real, The Bible and Flying Saucers was not so far out. I was glad to have an organization that accepted my work, and valued it.

While liberals either ignored my work, or saw it as space age religious myth making, conservative Protestants worried that I am being deceived, that UFOs are leading me down the road to some kind of "strong delusion." In order to weigh the conservative point of view, we need to explore the biblical understanding of evil. We will do that in UFO REVELATION 8.

UFO REVELATION 8
BIOLOGY, DOMINANCE, CHRIST, ANTICHRIST

Sociobiology is the relatively new science that studies the genetic consequences of the social behavior of a species. It relies on the data collected from the study of animal social behavior, especially of mammals, a science called ethology. What is clear throughout all species is that there is a system of dominance in every species, those at the top of the society are called Alpha, those at the bottom Omega. (Useful books in the field include: Edward O. Wilson, Sociobiology: The New Synthesis, 1975; Richard Dawkins, The Selfish Gene, 1976; Konrad Lorenz, On Aggression, 1966; Robert Ardrey, The Territorial Imperative, 1966; The Social Contract, 1970.)

Gaining dominance has rewards related to both food and sex. The dominant males and females usually have first choice of the food that is available, and in some cases, the dominant female will protect food for her offspring from other adults of the species. Among most species, a struggle for food means a struggle for territory, and therefore there are often "turf wars" within species to control what Robert Ardrey calls The Territorial Imperative.

Among most species, females do not have to compete for sex, but the males do.

"The maturing male of whatever species does not have it good. The sexually maturing male elephant must leave his mother and join the male band, with rank order already established, where he will find himself omega." (Ardrey, The Social Contract, 1974, p. 141) Most males as they mature will have to find a way to gain dominance within their social group in order to have sexual access to females. Usually this involves some kind of violence, head butting, clawing, biting, or goring with horns. Death is sometimes the reward for the losers in this struggle.

The sociobiological explanation for this behavior is that the weak males are weeded out through this process, and only the most fit males—fit to survive— become sexually active. It is their genes that get passed on to the females. Thus violence is one of the main means by which nature controls the quality of the genes that pass from generation to generation. Violence within a species, directed at its own kind, is common, and is related to the dietary advantage that comes with controlling territory, and the sexual advantage that comes usually to the dominant male.

It is interesting to look at the parable of the Wheat and Tares as a creation parable. Jesus tells of a man who sows good seed in his field, as we would expect God to do, "but while men were sleeping, his enemy came and sowed weeds among the wheat, and went away." (Mt. 13:25) Thus life as we find it is a mix of good and evil. If we think of the sleeping men as angels, the implication is that angels were present at creation, and it was their job to defend the earth, and help care for "God's farm." The enemy sowing his seed by night in another man's field is the classic image of adultery. But unlike the serpent seducing Eve in the Garden, there seems to be no seduction here. The "enemy" just plants his evil seed by night. When the discovery is made that wheat and weeds are growing together, it is found there is no way to pull up the weeds without hurting the wheat in the process. (vs. 29) The solution is to let both grow until harvest, until judgment day. The parable implies that we humans have good and evil in us, in our very biology. It is mixed in our very roots. This does not mean our bodies are "all bad." But it does mean our biological nature is corrupted, we have a dark side, a Satanic side, which we could say in scientific terms is planted in our DNA. If we were hopelessly bad, like Sodom, we would have been destroyed by God. But we have good in us, along with the bad, and the gospel is Christ has come to redeem the good in us, by putting his Holy Spirit in us. Our calling as Christians is to have the Holy Spirit in us rule over the Satanic laws of dominance in us. Christ will lead us on a new Exodus, not from Egyptian slavery, but from slavery to our corrupted biology, which is controlled by a spirit of domination.

What about women and the struggle for power? In the animal world, females struggle for dominance too, but the stakes are somewhat less high. Females usually do not have to compete for sex. In a flock of chickens, the females will establish a "pecking order." The dominant chicken will be able to peck all the hens below her in the order, and none will peck her back. She is Alpha. The Beta chicken will peck all below her, but not peck Alpha. The Omega chicken gets pecked by all, and can peck none back. I have seen the Omega chicken in a flock, and often it is not a pretty sight. Many feathers are missing, there are often open sores, this is the most likely chicken in the flock to die first.

Maturing males of a species will look for ways to displace the dominant males. Ardrey makes the comment, "But if the maturing male does not know as much as he thinks he knows, the established male may not either. As ignorance is the property of the young, habituation is the property of the adult." (Ibid, p. 156)

BIBLICAL UFO REVELATIONS

As we think of the recent revolutions in Egypt and Libya, we have witnessed the long established adult male leader being overthrown by the young. While most agree that the "aging leader" in each case is "oppressive," there is anxiety that the "new order" may not know what it is doing. But the message from ethology is the political struggle for power and dominance is all very natural.

From a political point of view, conservatives are those who now hold power, liberals are the ones wanting to be in power, but are not. Among humans money is one of our most basic forms of power: George Soros, Donald Trump and Warren Buffett are famous for having money. The poor are famous for not having money, and for "always being with us" as Jesus said. (Mt. 26:11)

Technology is a special source of human power, rather than horns, teeth and claws. Guns and nuclear weapons give power to those who have these weapons, humans will be in a position to dominate those who have no weapons, or who have technologically less powerful weapons. In so far as science helps build more successful weapons, science too is a form of power which enables one country to dominate another, and technological success in the market place helps one company dominate "market share" over another.

Something like "arena behavior" can be observed among certain species. The arena serves as a breeding ground, and dominant males hold territory in the arena, and only those males holding territory in the arena have sexual access to females. Females will ignore those males outside the arena who cannot control territory in the arena. Human sports frequently occur in an arena. Sports are the human ritualization of nature's biological drive to dominate. The biggest day in American television each year is Super Bowl Sunday, the day the teams with the Alpha Males of football face off to see who is the champion, the dominate team. The winners gain money, and if the rumors are to be believed, sexual access to females.

Bulls have their strength in their "bull neck;" NFL linemen usually have a bull neck; defensive linemen may make a "bull rush" on the quarterback. We worship "dominance," we worship winners, not losers.

THE ALPHA GOD

"'I am the Alpha and the Omega,' says the Lord God, who is and who was and who is to come, the Almighty." (Rev. 1:8) The God of the Bible is a strange God. He is almighty, he is the God who can dominate, and demands to be Alpha. But at the same time, this Alpha God can choose to be Omega, can choose to be dominated, as we see in the cross of Christ. Jesus loves the losers, the blind, the lame, the lepers, those who would never make an NFL roster. Jesus was sent to the losers, to the lost sheep of the house of Israel. (Mt. 10:6)

The power of God is sounded at the beginning of the Apostles' Creed: "I believe in God the Father almighty, maker of heaven and earth." Genesis speaks the opening word of our dominant God, "In the beginning God created the heavens and the earth." (Gen. 1:1) The Gospel of John makes the same claim for Jesus, "without him was not anything made that was made." (Jn. 1:3)

The God of the Exodus insists, "You shall have no other gods before me." (Ex. 20:3) Furthermore, this God is not nature, not something you can turn into an idol of stone or wood. "You shall not make for yourself any graven image." (Ex. 20: 4) Religions that worship nature are false religions. The God of the Jews is Spirit, which created nature.

In fact, the God of Moses issues commandments that counteract the drives we find in nature—killing is forbidden; killing is very natural, killing is the ultimate sign of victory in nature's dominance game. The one who lives is the winner, number one, Alpha. Adultery is forbidden, taking another man's wife, or stealing, or using deception to gain advantage (bearing false witness), the many tricks that are found throughout the animal kingdom as techniques for gaining territorial and sexual advantage, are forbidden in the commandments.

But the Alphaness of the God of the Exodus is shown in language that Pharaoh could understand. Pharaoh had ordered the killing of Hebrew male children at their birth. Moses had escaped, thanks to being hidden in the bulrushes along the shore of the Nile, only to be rescued by Pharaoh's daughter. Years later, when Moses demanded freedom for Israel in the name of God, plagues came upon the defiant Pharaoh—flies, frogs, locusts—until finally came the big hammer blow. The first-born male Egyptian children were killed on Passover night, and the Hebrew males were spared. The God of Moses could out kill Pharaoh. At the Red Sea, the pillar of cloud and fire defeated the chariots of Pharaoh. Egypt got the message, "Let us flee from before Israel, for the Lord fights for them against the Egyptians." (Ex. 14:25) This led to what modern America sees as the very politically incorrect view that the Jews were God's chosen people, a religious idea many in our generation find revolting.

Jesus never killed anyone, but he in some ways was like the young males of a species who challenge the establishment leaders, in his case, the Scribes and Pharisees. He gathered a band of disciples who became his followers, and he attracted crowds that could number in the thousands. He could heal the blind, the lame, the deaf, he could drive out demons. Thus he exhibited an Alphaness over nature, and over the destructive spiritual powers that could overtake the human mind. He was eventually seen as a threat to the Roman power structure in Jerusalem, mainly because he seemed to upset the Jewish religious and political power structure.

He sent his disciples out to preach that the kingdom of God was near. This was a strange message, which still causes debate among Christian scholars. But finally he was crucified by the Roman authorities. From the point of view of the God of Moses, Jesus seemed to be a failure. Surely if Jesus were as he claimed, the Son of God, then he should have been saved from the cross. The God who killed the first-born of Egypt, and parted the Red Sea, certainly had the power to protect Jesus. But he did not. Jesus died, but then on the third day was raised. This is strange. In Jesus we see that God is more than power, more than Alpha. In Jesus, the weakness of God, the Omega side of God, is exposed.

THE OMEGA GOD

The Apostle Paul caught the paradox of the Omega God, the God who loses in the dominance game that Jesus fought with Caiaphas and Pilate. "For Jews demand signs and Greeks seek wisdom, but we preach Christ crucified, a stumbling block to Jews and folly to Gentiles, but to those who are called, both Jews and Greeks, Christ the power of God and the wisdom of God. For the foolishness of God is wiser than men, and the weakness of God is stronger than men." (1 Cor. 1:22-25)

The essence of the spiritual battle that we find in Jesus is that he is in a battle against the desires of his own biology, his desire for food, power, success, survival. Over against that, he is seeking the power of God to heal the sick, the blind, the lame, demand that the rich show compassion toward the poor, and ordain followers who will maintain his tradition after his death and resurrection.

Immediately after his baptism, he is "led by the Spirit" into the wilderness to be tempted by the devil. The first temptation is to turn stones to bread, to use his divine power to meet the hunger of his flesh. Jesus turned down the offer with the words, "Man does not live by bread alone, but by every word that proceeds from the mouth of God." (Mt. 4:4) The lesson here is that the word of God, and will of God, must always take priority over the hungers of the flesh (for food, sex, status etc.)

The third temptation is to bow down and worship the devil, and Jesus would be given the kingdoms of the world. Jesus responded that we are to worship God alone. What was at stake here? I believe that if Jesus had used his divine power the way the rulers of this world operate, by fear, taxes, armies, and oppression, he could have ruled the world.

In a debate with his opponents Jesus said, "You are of your father the devil, and your will is to do your father's desires. He was a murderer from the beginning, and has nothing to do with the truth, because there is no truth in him. When he lies, he speaks according to his own nature, for he is a liar and the father of lies." (Jn. 8:44) Throughout the animal kingdom, deception is a strategy for dominance and success. Sometimes, murder of ones own species is part of that strategy. Jesus identified all these forms of power seeking as the work of the devil.

It is worth noting that the crowd, when given a choice between the release of Jesus, and Barabbas, elected Barabbas who "had been thrown into prison for insurrection and murder." (Lk. 23:25) The crowd preferred a "liberationist" to Christ. The crowd of Jews loved the man who wanted to throw the oppressive Romans out of Jerusalem. Jesus was not that man.

But what we also need to face here is that in the Exodus, God used the power of killing, and domination, to defeat Pharaoh. In Jesus we have a rejection of that kind of power, because it is in a sense the way of the flesh, the way of the world. This is why the New Testament really is a New Covenant. The New Covenant was not established by God out killing his enemies. In the New Testament, the son of God is killed by his enemies. I do not find it surprising that many Jews found the God Jesus preached at odds with the God of Moses. In the Old Testament, the power of God overshadowed his love. In the New Testament, the love of God overshadows his power, although in the empty tomb, we see God's power is still part of our faith reality. [In The Bible and Flying Saucers, I make the observation in regard to UFOs that "we never find the fantastic display of power in the New Testament that we found in the Old Testament in front of thousands of witnesses." (p. 159)]

The Apostle Paul understood that we who are in Christ have a Spirit that is at odds with the desire of the flesh, including our drive to dominate. This point of view is expressed clearly in Romans 8:1-17, as well as in Galatians, where he says, "Now the works of the flesh are plain:

Fornication, impurity, licentiousness, idolatry, sorcery, enmity, strife, jealousy, anger, selfishness, dissension, party spirit, envy, drunkenness, carousing and the like." (Gal. 5:19-21) In contrast the fruit of the Spirit "is love, joy, peace, patience, kindness, goodness, faithfulness, gentleness, self-control." (5:22,23) Christians are those who have "crucified the flesh with its passions and desires." (Gal. 5:24) We find Jesus speaking directly to our need to be "born again," because flesh is flesh, and spirit is spirit. (Jn. 3:3)

The biblical people saw the injustice of the strong dominating the weak, both in the animal world, and its parallel in the human world. The prophet Ezekiel used images from the shepherd experience to proclaim the will of God. "Therefore, thus says the Lord God to them: Behold, I, I myself will judge between the fat sheep and the lean sheep. Because you push with side and shoulder, and thrust at all the weak with your horns, till you have scattered them abroad.

I will save my flock, they shall no longer be a prey, and I will judge between sheep and sheep." (Ez.: 34:20-22)

When Jesus heals the sick and the lame, when he calls on the rich to share with the poor, when he condemns the scribes who "devour widows' houses," (Mk. 12:40, not unlike modern Wall Street Bankers), Jesus is very much acting the role of the Good Shepherd. (Jn. 10:11)

Jesus made the distinction between his kingdom, and the kingdoms of this world, very clear. On one occasion the mother of James and John came to Jesus, asking that one sit on his right hand, and one on his left, when Jesus came into his kingdom. This was worldly politics, in which the winners expect to share the rewards. Jesus said, "You know that the rulers of the Gentiles lord it over them, and their great men exercise authority over them. It shall not be so among you; but whoever would be great among you must be your servant, and whoever would be first among you must be your slave; even as the Son of man came not to be served but to serve, and to give his life as a ransom for many." (Mt. 20:25-28)

In other words, worldly politics is very much the Alpha Game, in which, driven by the lusts of the flesh, rulers of this world rise to the top of the pecking order. Jesus calls us not to play Alpha, but rather to play Omega, to seek not to be at the top of the pecking order, but rather at the bottom. Jesus is a contradiction in terms, a servant Lord, and we are called to join him.

Notice Jesus does not preach a Marxist style "classless society" as some liberal Christians suppose. True, Jesus has no great love for the oppressive ruling class at the top of the human pecking order, whether it be political power in the secular world, or preachers living in houses with gold faucets. Jesus did not preach a health and wealth gospel. But at the same time, Jesus does not call for a revolution to overthrow the oppressors, to bring in a society of equality, as is often typical of modern liberation theology. Jesus does not call his followers to a classless society of equality, rather we are called to join the servant class, the bottom class. That is the class in which the Holy Spirit of gentleness, kindness and meekness dwells. Most liberation movements are fueled by envy, "they have what we should have and it is only just that we take it."

In so far as modern Protestantism has split between liberals and conservatives, liberals have tended to be guilty of envy, conservatives of greed, of wanting to hold on to what they have. Both envy and greed are very natural. But they are not godly motives. There are two major sins in the Bible: rebellion and oppression. Rebellion is the basic sin of Adam and Eve in the garden. Oppression is the sin of Pharaoh as he mistreats the slave nation Israel. Liberals tend to be guilty of the sin of rebellion; conservatives of the sin of oppression. Each is usually able to see the sin in the other side, but not their own. Thus when conservatives hold fast to their money, their positions of power in the world, or the church, they are playing Alpha, in worldly terms. When liberals, like young males in the animal world, attack conservatives who hold power, they are acting out of rebellion and envy. Liberals are not Alpha, but want to be. But usually liberals put on the moral white suit of "justice" to cover their biologically motivated drive for power. Conservatives usually protect their territory by saying, "It is the law." They deny freedom to others in the name of the law. The extreme forms of both liberals and conservatives are very much caught up in the world's power game, they are not interested in hearing the call of Christ to join the servant class. As I see it, in so far as they are at war with each other, liberal and conservative Christians have really joined "the children of darkness."

There are some parables of Jesus that suggest the heavenly ideal may be a classless society, such as the parable of the workers in the vineyard, who at the end of the day receive the same pay, no matter how long or how little they worked. (Mt. 20:1-18) But the workers are paid in the opposite order in which they were hired. As Jesus explains, "So the last will be first; and the first last." (20:18)

What Jesus is preaching here is an eschatology—our future life in heaven—in which we will experience not classlessness, but class reversal. Ordinarily, those who work longest would be paid most, and be the richest. In this parable those "least deserving" from the world's point of view are most deserving from God's point of view. The story of Lazarus and the rich man in Luke makes the same point, that in the life to come, there will be class reversal, Lazarus will be rewarded. The pecking order of the world will be reversed. In the resurrection, Spirit will win out over flesh. (Lk. 16:19-31)

The distinction between liberal and conservative is strikingly clear in the parable of the Prodigal Son in Luke 15. The younger son is the liberal in rebellion. By the custom of the day, the oldest son in the family would inherit the major part of the estate. This is why Jacob, the second born twin, was so intent on stealing his brother Esau's birth right. (Gen. 25:19-34) The younger son would be in the position of natural envy of his older brother. A liberation theologian would tell the younger brother that he is the victim of an oppressive inheritance system, and he should rebel against it.

Since he has little investment in the future of the family estate, the prodigal asks for his share of the inheritance, cashes it in, and heads for a far country where he wastes his money on wild living, especially sexual promiscuity. The sin of the prodigal is the sin of rebellion, like Adam and Eve. The younger brother has a fairly typical liberal profile: he rejects the established order (home), and has little regard for sexual or financial responsibility.

The older brother represents a fairly typical conservative profile. He is hard working and obedient. "Lo, these many years I have served you, and I never disobeyed your command." (Lk. 15:29) But at the same time, there is a sense of resentment about his obedience, he has not obeyed joyfully, and notes that his father has not even killed a kid so that he could party with his friends. The older brother comes off as responsible, but hard hearted, a frequent conservative profile. He believes in crime and punishment, not crime and forgiveness. His sin is the sin of oppression, like Pharaoh in Egypt. Conservatives tend to believe because they "stayed home with father," they have the right to condemn the unfaithful brother, or as I have experienced, condemn anyone who disagrees with them. In the parable, there is a happy ending for the prodigal, but not for the older brother. But the older brother could have had a happy ending if he had repented of his hard heartedness. The two brothers together, the younger acting out rebellion, and the older oppression, represent the two sides of the war of the flesh at work, the biological struggle for dominance. But neither the liberal nor the conservative brother has the heart of the father, and therefore, they do not have the heart of Christ, who is one with the Father. (Jn. 17:22)

The gospel is that both liberals and conservatives have to repent. Liberals have to repent of their sin, or they are as good as dead. (Lk. 15:24) Conservatives have to repent of their hard hearts, or they will exclude themselves from the joy of the Father's kingdom. (Lk. 15:28)

CHRIST AND ANTICHRIST

It does not appear that Jesus supposed that his coming would bring to an end the power politics of the world, that the "laws of the flesh" would suddenly disappear. Rather, justice for those who took on the Servanthood of Christ, who lived in his Spirit, would be rewarded not in this world, but in the world to come. This is why the loss of eschatology, which I found in my studies at Princeton Seminary, meant that there was no motivation now to obey the ethics of Jesus. That is why a Marxist eschatology replaced the eschatology of Jesus in liberation theology. And perhaps why some conservatives, who supposedly believed in heaven, so easily bought the false "prosperity" gospel of modern media preachers.

Jesus said as he neared the end of his earthly ministry, "In the world you have tribulation; but be of good cheer, I have overcome the world." (Jn. 16:33) Many will come in the name of Christ, we must be careful not to be led astray. There will be wars and rumors of wars, the flesh will still rule this world. "For nation will rise against nation, and kingdom against kingdom, and there will be famines and earthquakes in various places; all this is but the beginning of the birth-pangs." (Mt. 24:7, 8)

And "wickedness will multiply." I take this warning to be inclusive, not only of wickedness in the world of politics, but also in the church, "most men's love will grow cold." (Mt. 24:12) Dolan and Zabel believe, as do I, that the government of the United States has been keeping UFO information secret for more than 60 years, and that billions, perhaps trillions of dollars in secret funds, black budget money, has gone into research regarding UFO technology. We face the possibility that a Breakaway Civilization, not our elected officials, now rule the United States. This secret group has unbelievable power to "multiply wickedness." And I fear that the love of Christ in the church has grown so cold that no Christian voice of protest speaks against this wickedness. Dolan and Zabel are doing what I believe the church of Christ should be doing, and is not. A Website like Strong Delusion is doing its best, but in the modern world of media overload, Strong Delusion has a fairly quiet voice.

What is the UFO reality? Is it demonic? Do UFOs carry fallen angels? These are the views of some conservative Christians. My view, that UFOs may carry the angels of God has almost no support, from either conservative or liberal Protestant Christians.

Should I worry about being taken in by a "strong delusion?" (2 Thes. 2:11) If so, what is the delusion, that UFOs might carry the angels of God? (Is it wicked of me to hope UFOs are a sign the angels of God are guarding the earth?) This is hardly a "strong" delusion, since I am one of the few raising this possibility. Or could it be a strong delusion that UFOs are demons?

Or a strong delusion that UFOs are just space guys, here to help give us new technology?

Paul raises the possibility that "the lawless one will be revealed." This will be by the activity of Satan and "will be with all power and with pretended signs and wonders." (2 Thes. 2:9) John sees the coming of the antichrist. "Children, it is the last hour; and as you have heard that antichrist is coming, so now many antichrists have come; therefore we know that it is the last hour." (1 Jn. 2:18) Satan, as we see in the temptations of Jesus, is very much on the side of the flesh, and its laws of domination. In a sense, the laws of the flesh, the lust to dominate, the lust for sex and power, for position and prestige, to be at the top of the pecking order, are very much Satanic characteristics. Therefore they are Anti-Christ. They are very much part of our current political order, and in no small part, visible in a corrupt church, worried about its status in the world. In modern Protestantism, with its liberal and conservative divisions, with each side saying, "We speak for the truth of Christ," both sides are taking an Anti-Christ role. By taking sides with either the prodigal brother, or the elder brother, modern Protestants fail to speak for the heart of the Father. I do not believe that modern divided Protestantism has the theological faithfulness to deal with the UFO evidence.

And we do have to worry that some extraterrestrial power might convince us that they have a god-like status in relation to us, causing us to worship them, rather than the God of Jesus Christ. If those in charge of UFO secrets are talking with Zorg (if Zorg exists), is Zorg the Antichrist? Or a false Christ? One of the questions we need to ask is: Do UFOs seek to dominate us, as we might expect Satan to do, following the laws of the flesh? Or do UFOs seem to be carrying out a servant role in relation to planet earth, which is the Christ role? Are modern UFOs, like the angels, trying to save us from ourselves? Or are they trying to enslave us? And how do we weigh the evidence? How do we get our modern Pharaohs to release the evidence? Or do we count on God to expose the lies of our modern Pharaohs with a modern UFO Passover? These are the issues that face us as we consider our next UFO REVELATION, UFOs and Conservative Protestantism.

UFO REVELATION 9
UFOS AND CONSERVATIVE PROTESTANTISM: PART I

If the position of liberal Protestantism in relation to UFOs could be described as the sound of one hand clapping, conservative Protestantism can be described as clapping with both hands, but without enthusiasm, on a limited basis. I listen a lot to Christian radio, I hear many conservative voices, and UFOs are rarely mentioned. But there are conservative Protestant Christians who know UFOs represent a serious challenge to us. Exactly how to understand the challenge is another matter, and this is not surprising. The UFOs have not shown themselves openly to us, the governments of the world have lied to us, for our own good of course, and so it is hard to get solid information.

My starting position is this: Whatever UFOs are, they are under the Lordship of Christ, either directly, or they will be in God's good time. John's Gospel says clearly of Jesus "He was in the beginning with God; all things were made through him, and without him was not anything made that was made." (Jn. 1:2) In some sense, UFOs are part of Christ's creation. UFOs might carry the angels of God, who are directly obedient to Christ; or they might be, as some writers suggest, demons. But Jesus was victorious over the demons whenever he confronted them in his ministry. If demons are "loose" in our skies now, Christ can tame them. UFOs might carry "fallen angels" as some have suggested. They may be like humanity, sinful, but in due time will face Christ in judgment. Or UFOs may be Satanic, agents of God (as in the case of Satan with Job) whose task is to test humanity, to test our faithfulness. Or they might be some life form from another planet, or universe, who may or may not know Christ. Perhaps the missionary commandment (Mt. 28:19) extends beyond planet earth, as the Pope's astronomer suggests. Guy Consolmagno has speculated that if we meet aliens, we might offer them baptism. (Lee Speigel, AOL News, September 24, 2010) But in the end, Christ will rule all, including the UFOs, whatever they are. "The Lord said to my Lord, Sit at my right hand, till I make thy enemies a stool for thy feet." (Acts 2:34,35)

My second conviction is that Christ is fair. That means he will not condemn us for not knowing things we cannot know, such as the time of his second coming. Jesus said neither he nor the angels know of the time of his coming. (Mt. 24:36) Obviously, Jesus is not going to condemn us for not knowing what he himself does not know. The Apostles warned of false prophets to come, many in the name of Jesus, or falsely proclaiming the end times, and the Rapture. A USA Today newspaper headline said, "Minister not seen after doomsday fails."

The story told of Minister Harold Camping, founder of the Family Radio network, who had been predicting the Rapture would begin Saturday, May 21st, 2011. It did not. On Sunday, Camping was no where to be found. There is danger we will fall under a "strong delusion" (2 Thes. 2:11) at the hands of Satan, and sometimes Satan speaks through the mouth of Christians, Peter being exhibit "A" (Mt. 16:23), the latest Satanic Christian voice being Minister Camping. Some people see my voice as Satanic when I wonder if UFOs carry the angels of God. I hope everyone understands that wondering about God's possibilities is not the same as being certain about them.

When Christians claim to be certain about things we have no right to be certain about it is a serious issue, and one way to avoid being deluded is to admit that we may not really know everything (really!). This takes humility. My experience with conservative Christians is that they want to know the truth, and sometimes say they believe things with total conviction that are not well supported by evidence, either biblical or scientific. If we say to Christ and each other, "we do not have enough evidence," we avoid some of the dangers of being deluded.

At the same time I do not think we need to be shy about calling the church to pay attention to the UFO mystery. UFOs may be some kind of sign from God, to the church, or to the whole world, or not. But the whole body of Christ needs to pray and wonder about the challenge before us.

The Bible does not tell us how many galaxies are in the universe; how many planets are in each galaxy; whether or not there is life on other planets. Christ is a fair judge. Christ does not expect us to know what is not in the Bible. But if science can figure some of these answers out, fine. And in regard to the situation we now face, there is nothing in the New Testament that says the year 2011 would arrive, or that in 2011 Jesus would not yet have returned. Nor does the Bible say that in 2011 many people would believe the United States and other governments are hiding secret information about UFOs.

What this means is, Christ expects us to go on faith, to deal with the UFO situation as faithfully as we can, knowing that, like Abraham, we cannot be sure where it is we are to go. (Heb. 11:8) This is what faith is—a journey with God where the path is not clear. Faith is living with the ambiguity that we face, with many choices about what UFOs may be. Abraham did not have a Bible to guide him, and the Bible does not give us clear guidance to the UFO challenge at the present time. The church by and large is blind to the issue of UFOs. There are a few of us traveling this UFO road, and some of us have been called "kooks" and "heretics" more than once. But I think that somewhere in the future, especially if what Dolan and Zabel call the "Day of Disclosure" comes, church leaders will be embarrassed that they did not ask a lot of questions sooner about what UFOs might have to do with Christ. If we are faithful maidens of Christ, with oil still in our lamps, we should be asking.

CHRISTIANITY TODAY REVIEWS MY BOOK

Christianity Today published a review of my book by Albert L. Hedrich, in the June 21, 1968 issue, under the heading, "Flying Saucers in the Bible?" Hedrich was credited with being "assistant director of research for Page Communication Engineers" in Washington, D.C. Hedrich said, "The Bible and Flying Saucers could be judged worthless but harmless were it not for the distortions it contains and the credentials of the author. He holds a doctorate in theology from the University of Edinburgh." Hedrich suggested it was wrong for me to connect UFOs to the Bible when I admitted I did not have 100% proof that flying saucers existed. From the point of view of many, we still do not have proof. But for people like Dolan and Zabel, the evidence of a mammoth cover-up is beyond dispute. Indeed, the size and nature of the cover-up is much more clear now than in 1968. Many conservative authors such as Clifford Wilson, John Weldon, Timothy Dailey and Gary Bates understand that, although they might not agree with my view on what is being covered up.

But even in 1968, it was widely rumored that there was a cover-up. The Condon Committee at the University of Colorado had not yet released their "Scientific Study," so that one would suppose I would have the right to "wonder" if UFOs were real, and if so, how they might relate to the Bible, and to Christ. Christianity is about faith, science is about proof. It seemed strange to me that the reviewer did not seem to understand that "faith is the conviction of things not seen." (Heb. 11:1) And if what Dolan and Zabel call the "Day of Disclosure" comes, we may not have a clear idea of UFO purpose even then. It seems clear in light of events like the Phoenix 1997 sightings that UFOs can show themselves powerfully if they want to, without landing and making open contact. If UFOs want to "prove themselves" to us they can, and still leave a lot of mystery about origin and purpose. Waiting until UFOs land on the White House lawn before wondering what they mean for Christians is like waiting for the Second Coming of Jesus to see if we really want to believe in him. Waiting to touch the wounds in his hands may be scientifically sound, but it is not justification by faith. The issue of UFO reality of course also concerned President McCord of Princeton Seminary. The lack of UFO proof has been the basic "excuse" for the church to look the other way.

There is much more in the book review I could complain about, but I do not want to spend the space here. The key thing that struck me was that nowhere in the review did Hedrich use the word angel, or discuss how the angels of God might relate to us in our modern times. If UFOs do not carry the angels of God, how do we tell the difference between UFOs and angels?

I wrote a letter to the editor, Dr. Carl F. H. Henry, dated July 3, 1968, stating that I thought the review failed in many ways, but especially in regard to not even mentioning the biblical doctrine of angels. I enclosed an article entitled "Angels and UFOs," requesting that it be considered for publication. The opening sentence of the article was, "Perhaps at no time in the history of the church has the Biblical doctrine of angels been more neglected than during the twentieth century." The article dealt with the role of angels in biblical revelation, the relation between angels and the Holy Spirit, modern UFO reports, and how all these might be connected.

I received a letter from Janet Rohler, editorial assistant, dated July 18, 1968, which said, "Our editorial committee has read your manuscript, 'Angels and UFOs.' Since the committee is divided about its use in Christianity Today, we should like to delay the final decision until fall when Dr. Lindsell and other new staff members will come." Many months later, I received a standard rejection letter, without comment.

One of my observations in my book was "that Jesus is portrayed in the Bible in much the same way as our modern-day 'spy' stories. Jesus came from a foreign world into our world and started to gather together a small band of people who would owe their allegiance to his world (heaven). Jesus is really an 'undercover agent.'" (The Bible and Flying Saucers, p. 145-6)

I make this reference because after the Christianity Today rejection of my article, I wondered how the "unpublished" editorial discussion of my book, and the rejected article went. I knew that Billy Graham was closely connected to Christianity Today, and I found it interesting that in 1975 he published a book with the title: Angels: God's Secret Agents.

It has been more than 40 years since my book was published. The United States government still denies that UFOs exist. And by and large, "respected" religious journals continue to publish with almost no reference to UFOs. It seems to be a pleasing arrangement to almost everyone.

But if UFOs are a gift from God to the church as a sign of God's presence and faithfulness, then we are expected to respond. Our response might very much be like Peter at Pentecost saying, "these men are not drunk, as you suppose," (Acts 2:15) except perhaps we are supposed to say in Peter's place, "these are not space aliens as you suppose, but rather they are the angels of God, and of his Christ." If that is how we are supposed to respond, then Christ may not be pleased with how "respected" Christian publications and leaders have responded to the UFO situation. In fact, I suspect that if the signs that have been given to our generation had been given to Sodom, Sodom would have repented. (Mt. 11:23)

The most basic conservative response to UFOs has been negative, either to say they have no connection to our biblical faith, or that they are demons or fallen angels. I would add on the negative side the Satanic. We will now explore these theories.

THE DEMONIC THEORY OF UFOS

There are several books that present the demonic theory of UFOs from a Christian point of view. I will consider three of them: Close Encounters: A Better Explanation (1978), by Clifford Wilson and John Weldon, The Millennial Deception: Angels, Aliens and the Antichrist (1995), by Timothy J. Dailey, and Alien Intrusion: UFOs and the Evolution Connection (2004), by Gary Bates.

(Also see my article, "Demonic Theory of UFOs," The Encyclopedia of Extraterrestrial Encounters, 2001, p. 155-7.) Clifford Wilson had previously published UFOs and Their Mission Impossible (1975), and John Weldon had published UFO's: What on Earth is Happening? (1976). Their basic thesis is that "demonic powers vary in their capacities. Some are extremely intelligent entities that are nonphysical in nature but have a capacity to assume a physical shape and to undertake certain physical activities." (p. 35)

They rely heavily on the research of John Keel, author of books such as UFO's: Operation Trojan Horse (1970), as well as The Mothman Prophecies (1975). Keel is aware that many UFO close encounters, especially involving cars, often involve children. People often have frightening dreams after a UFO encounter, and start getting strange phone calls. Keel's argument is not that UFOs come from another planet, but rather they come from another dimension, and they seem to play tricks on humans for entertainment. Wilson and Weldon say that Keel "warns strongly against youth involvement with UFO's." Keel goes on to suggest that poltergeists operate in the presence of children. (p. 77) Thus Wilson and Weldon connect the world of the paranormal with UFOs, and this is a legitimate connection in some UFO cases. Their book has an excellent bibliography, and as part of the bibliography they have a section devoted to "Occult Literature," including books dealing with "Astral Doorways," "I Talked with Spirits," and "Amazing Secrets of the Psychic World."

There are books published since the work of Wilson and Weldon which strengthen their argument, such as George P. Hansen's book The Trickster and the Paranormal (2001), including the chapter "Government Disinformation." The chapter begins with a quote from President Bill Clinton to Webb Hubbell, "If I put you at Justice, I want you to find the answers to two questions for me. One, Who killed JFK? And two, Are there UFOs?" (p. 219) Likewise the book Hunt for the Skinwalker (2005) by Colm A. Kelleher and George Knapp, tells the story of a scientific attempt to nail down the truth about UFO sightings at a ranch in Utah, an attempt which fails due to what seem to be paranormal tricks by an unknown entity.

Wilson and Weldon conclude their book with Appendix C, "The Bible and Flying Saucers."

Here they review three books in order: R.L. Dione's God Drives a Flying Saucer (1973), my own book, The Bible and Flying Saucers (1968), and Joseph Blumrich's The Spaceships of Ezekiel (1974). They are opposed to connecting UFOs as any form of spaceships with anything that is in the Bible. In particular, they do not want technological power substituted for "supernatural" power. Having read Dione's book (as well as Blumrich's), I understand how these books read more like a science text than a book full of the Holy Spirit, and seem to have lost a sense of God at work. In regard to my book Wilson and Weldon say, "We must again face the anti-supernatural bias." (p. 331) I would in my defense ask Protestants who claim they are guided by scripture to point to where the word "supernatural" appears in the Bible. It is a derived theological concept, which may have some validity, but its roots have to be reexamined.

Wilson and Weldon complain, in regard to my argument that a UFO parted the Red Sea (see UFO REVELATION 4) that the Bible states clearly that "God directly parted the sea" (p. 331), and of course the Bible does not say God "directly" parted the sea anywhere, but the Bible does say the angel of God was present at the Red Sea, and the Lord was present in this angelic form. (Ex. 14:19-30) The Everywhereness of our invisible God becomes visible only through some angelic form, and finally through Christ, who is the visible image of the invisible God. (Col. 1:15) When Christ performs miracles, it is God performing miracles. When angels carry out God's work, it is God's work. One of the basic problems is that we do not have a clear understanding of how the Everywhere God connects to his angels, to Christ, and finally to the church. Thus Eric von Daniken assumes he can just "disconnect" the angels in the Bible from God, and make them secular astronauts. Likewise, those like Wilson and Weldon assume that if the angels of God used technology, rather than the "supernatural," to part the Red Sea, they are thereby disconnected from God. If I fly in a plane it does not disconnect me from the Everywhere God, or from the Holy Spirit. My major complaint, as I made it to the editors of Christianity Today, is that most Protestants do not really allow for the work of the angels in their theology, and we see this clearly in the way Wilson and

Weldon do their analysis. Also they place way too much importance on the concept of the supernatural which is not directly a biblical idea. Nevertheless, Wilson and Weldon have made a good summary of some of the negative and troubling dimensions of the UFO mystery. It may be that some UFOs are demonic, or something like it. I will make further comments after reviewing the other two books.

FROM DEMONS TO THE ANTICHRIST

Timothy J. Dailey connects UFOs, demons, Satan and the Antichrist in his book, The Millennial Deception. At the time the book was written, Dailey was "senior editor of Chuck Colson's nationally syndicated Break-Point radio program."

It is somewhat surprising to find the opening chapter of Dailey's book deals not with UFO sightings, but rather with Betty Eadie's popular book Embraced by the Light, which tells of her near death experience. In her book Eadie meets Jesus, and angels, which might be a good thing to some, but from Dailey's point of view, her experience points to her false Mormon beliefs about Jesus and angels, and thus her story is one of spiritual deception.

Dailey says, "Betty Eadie's visit to the spiritual realm, though ultimately misleading, appears to have been for her a positive, uplifting experience. But such agreeable counterfeits are overlaid with anti-Christian teachings that lead many astray. And there is a dark side to the deception in which men, women and children report horrific experiences of being carried away in sheer terror by dreadful spirit beings." (p. 43)

Dailey then moves on to the story Whitley Strieber tells in his popular book Communion. In this book Strieber tells of some type of physical presence coming into his home, and into his bedroom, and "communing" with him in a largely nonverbal way.

Dailey then asks, "Do demonic forces actually exist and are they able to manifest their presence under certain limited circumstances? The Bible clearly says yes." (p. 45) Dailey then goes on to mention the "Gerasene madman" (Mark 5:1-17), as well as other cases where Jesus drove out demons.

Did Strieber's encounter really happen? Dailey is not sure, but believes it could have happened. "Researchers into the occult are well aware of manifold ways by which demonic beings attempt first to seduce, then to corrupt and finally to terrorize and destroy souls." (p. 45)

Dailey also draws on the work of Raymond Fowler, who has written extensively about the Betty Andreasson abduction case, published in The Andreasson Affair (1980), and various sequels. The basic story is that Betty was in her home with her children when a UFO landed in her back yard, all in the family saw it, and beings came through the door of her home without opening it, taking Betty to the UFO, where she goes through a long process, including hearing the voice of God.

During the abduction, one of Betty's daughters witnesses the abduction, while the rest of the children are "turned off." Betty believes she is dealing with the angels of God. Dailey believes she is dealing with deceptive demons.

People like Betty will lead us astray. Dailey worries, "One day the world at large may indeed witness a mind-boggling public manifestation of UFOs and their alien occupants. If and when such an event occurs, there will be little doubt as to the message they will bring. Undoubtedly many nominal Christians will attempt to view such an unsettling event in religious terms. Not a few will follow abductee Betty Andreasson in believing that this is what is meant by the Second Coming of Christ." (p. 97)

Indeed, "nominal Christians" such as myself made this argument in my book in chapter 6, "Flying Saucers and the Future." (p. 191 ff.) Interestingly, while Wilson, Weldon, and Bates all condemn me openly, Dailey never mentions me or my book. (Whether this represents poor research on Dailey's part, or wise editing, I do not know.)

We have many problems here. Exactly how are we to tell the difference between a sudden mass sighting of UFOs, and the Second Coming of Christ? But also, how are we to evaluate the testimony of those who say they have had a divine or angelic encounter in an "abduction" experience? If Elijah, after he was taken up in a chariot of fire (2 Kings 2:11), were to come back to earth and tell his story, would people have said "He has a demon?" Both Jesus and John the Baptist were accused of being demon possessed of course. (Mt. 11:18; Jn. 7:20)

Or what do we make of this statement from Paul? "I know a man in Christ who fourteen years ago was caught up to the third heaven—whether in the body or out of the body I do not know, God knows." (2 Cor. 12:2) Was this an out of the body experience, like Betty Eadie, or an abduction experience like that of Betty Andreasson? And if we follow Dailey and condemn both Eadie and Andreasson as dealing with demons, on what basis do we decide their experience is demonic, but Paul's "occult" experience was angelic or divine? If God wanted to break through to our evil and adulterous generation with a sign, how could God do it, without such a revelation being condemned by Dailey as demonic?

Part 2 of Dailey's book is entitled "Antichrist Past and Present," and here the biblical concept of the antichrist is introduced, with images from the books of Daniel and Revelation. He explores the possibility that secret organizations "like the Council on Foreign Relation, the Trilateral Commission and the Bilderburger Society" (p. 109) may be related to the Antichrist, but Dailey does not really accept these possibilities; he knows that some have wondered if the Antichrist might be Judas Iscariot raised from the dead (p. 127), but Dailey doubts it. Some of course thought Nero was the Antichrist (p. 135), but although there have been many candidates to wear the title "Beast" from the book of Revelation (p. 149 ff), no one can really claim the title without dispute.

In Part 3, "How Shall We Then Live?" Dailey returns to Betty Andreasson, making her the model of Christian deception. Betty claims to be a Christian, tells others she was taken to be a witness to the world, but Dailey is sure she is deceived. Dailey quotes an alien speaking to Betty saying that man is now in "Separation, duality. He has formed that other side. He has made it to happen. It was all good at one time. Even his choice was good at one time. He has separated it. In love there is no separation." (p. 191-2)

Dailey then goes on to comment, "Salvation, according to Eastern thought, has nothing to do with biblical teaching about sin and redemption. Rather, man is inherently divine and has somehow become separated from Brahma, the impersonal force from which the universe has arisen." (p. 192)

I guess Dailey is "free" to interpret the alien statement to Betty Andreasson this way, if that is how he sees it. But why not see the biblical imagery here? After Adam and Eve sin, God drives them out of the Garden. Humanity is now separated from God, and so the process of God bringing us back to himself is the story of Abraham, Isaac and Jacob , the God of Moses, the God of Jesus Christ. We are in a duality, what is flesh is flesh, what is spirit is spirit. Jesus says so. (Jn. 3:6) That which is born of the flesh is self seeking (seeking domination, see UFO REVELATION 8), that which is born of the Spirit is self giving. When we are redeemed in Christ, we love God, and our neighbor as ourselves, and thereby we become one with God and each other. "In love there is no separation." Dailey sees the message from the alien as "proof" that Betty is caught up in some kind of Eastern mysticism. I don't see it. I think Dailey has gone looking for evil in the Betty Andreasson story, as the Pharisees looked for a legal pretext to destroy Jesus. God calls us to "repent," like the Prodigal Son, and "come to ourselves" (Luke 15:17), the Son returned to his Father, the one I call our Everywhere God. When the son returns, the duality, the division, is gone. When we are united with Christ, our redemption is won, our separation is over.

I do not have "proof" that Betty Andreasson experienced an angelic encounter. I do not have proof that her encounter is not demonic, or Satanic, as Dailey argues. But what I would say is this. I think Dailey has gone way beyond what the evidence, either biblical, or scientific, should allow him to say. Dailey is worried about deception. I am worried that many Christians who are shouting "don't be deceived" may be among the loudest deceivers. Why can't Dailey just say the modern UFO experience raises many questions for Christians, some hopeful, some dark and dangerous? Why not say we need the whole body of Christ to wake up to this challenge, and pray for the guidance of the Holy Spirit in discerning the truth?

BIBLICAL UFO REVELATIONS

I have met Betty Andreasson, we were both speakers at the same conference in Connecticut several years ago. I think she is a beautiful child of Jesus Christ. What a price people like Dailey have made her pay for her experience.

ALIENS, DEMONS AND EVOLUTION

Gary Bates comes at the UFO issue with a special set of glasses. His book title, Alien Intrusion: UFOs and the Evolution Connection gives a clue to his real major concern, which is to protect the Genesis story of creation from the unbiblical doctrine of evolution. Groups like Creation Ministries International distribute this book. Bates says that by using the Bible, and making "simple calculations," we can estimate that "the time of creation, as recorded in the Scriptures, was only about 6,000 years ago." (p. 345) Thus Bates rejects modern scientific evidence even more radically than do the conservative voices advocating creation by "intelligent design" like Phillip Johnson (Darwin on Trial, 1993), Michael Behe (Darwin's Black Box, 1996), or William Dembski (The Design Inference: Eliminating Chance Through Small Probabilities, 1998).

The Bates position on creation which holds to a literal Genesis is seen as a joke in our wider culture. The Sunday, July 10, 2011 edition of my "Sunday Comics" featured the following "Doonesbury" cartoon by Garry Trudeau. In the first panel, a science teacher is saying to his class, "So all the evidence massively supports a theory of evolution that knits together everything we know about biology."

In the second panel, the teacher says, "However, as high school science students in the State of Louisiana, you are entitled to learn an alternative theory supported by no scientific evidence whatsoever!"

The teacher continues, "It goes like this. 5,700 years ago, a male deity created the heavens and the earth and all life on it in six days. . . .unfortunately, he didn't like his own handiwork, so God created genocide and drowned everyone on earth except the family of Noah, a 600-year-old man who was charged with saving animals."

In the fifth panel, a student interrupts, "Mr. Stiller?" The teacher responds, "Yes?"

In the final panel, the student says, "Please stop. I'd like to get into a good college." The teacher responds, "Almost done. So Noah took two of everything including microbes, but forgot the dinosaurs..."

One of the interesting features of UFO disclosure, as Richard Dolan and Bryce Zabel envision it, is that if the world were to know UFOs are real, not only does the literal Genesis of Bates now face a new kind of doubt, but likewise, suddenly the theory of evolution is no longer the sure "scientific truth" that Doonesbury assumes it is. Suddenly biologist Richard Dawkins' book The God Delusion, is no

73

longer so scientific. Maybe life on earth is the result of "intelligent design," not evolution. Maybe Christians should pay more attention to the biblical doctrine of angels; maybe God's angels have had work to do in creation, as well as in redemption.

Before he gets to UFOs, Bates asks in chapter 4, "Did Aliens Create Life on Earth?" (p. 119 ff.)

The answer is "No," as we might expect, but he refers to scientists like Francis Crick, who speculated concerning DNA and the "seeding" of life on planet earth. Later, Bates will deal with abduction researchers like Budd Hopkins and David Jacobs, who believe the aliens are conducting some type of breeding program. (p. 240 ff) All of these issues threaten the doctrine of biblical creation as Bates understands it.

In the early chapters of his book, Bates traces the idea of "aliens from outer space" in movies and in television. He places much of the blame for the development of the "UFO myth" on Donald Keyhoe, who through hearsay evidence wrote books claiming a government cover-up. (p. 165 ff) In regard to Roswell, Bates admits the government made a mistake, saying a weather balloon crashed, when in fact it was "a secret project known as Skyhook." (p. 167) The lie helped make the Keyhoe "myth" more believable. (Although Dolan and Zabel do not review the Bates book, they would be amazed at the ease with which Bates swallows the United States government position on UFOs.) It is really important to Bates to eliminate any suggestion that the governments of the world have crashed UFOs in their possession, and his desire is understandable. He wants to make the argument that UFOs are only demons, not space aliens. It seems a bit of a stretch to suppose demons would fly in UFOs that would crash. It is difficult enough to suppose space aliens would crash one or more of their craft.

Bates believes he has eliminated the scientific basis for most UFO reports. "First, it should be remembered that our investigation of UFOs (specifically unidentified flying objects) has revealed that there is no 'hard evidence' for ET craft, and that the majority of sightings could be accounted for as man-made or natural phenomena." (p. 226) But of those few cases that remain, researchers such as "J. Allen Hynek, Jacques Vallee, John Weldon, and John Keel, have noted that UFOs appeared to behave deceptively." (Ibid)

What remains to be explained are UFO abductions. Bates begins with the Betty and Barney Hill case, suggests how "science fiction" might have influenced their story. He then goes on to the Travis Walton story, then follows the work of folklorist Thomas Bullard who developed a typology of the typical abduction experience—capture, examination, conference, tour, otherworldly journey, theophany, return, and aftermath. (p. 235 ff)

BIBLICAL UFO REVELATIONS

How are we to understand what is going on? "Impartial research shows that most abductees have, in the past, dabbled in what is commonly known as the occult, even if it was on a relatively minor basis. For some, they may not have been aware of the potential of unlocking this doorway to the supernatural when they dabbled in New Age practices." (p. 255) And the occult leads to the demonic.

Bates refers to several of the New Testament encounters between Jesus and demons (Luke 11:24-26, Mark 5:1-15), and then remarks in regard to well known UFO author Whitley Strieber, his "increasing contacts with spirit beings masquerading as aliens leaves us no doubt about the progressive nature of the deception that enveloped him." "Because of his New Age beliefs, Strieber refused to believe that the beings were those as described in biblical terms," in other words, that Strieber's "visitors" were demons. (p. 282 ff.)

In the end, Bates joins Clifford Wilson, John Weldon and Timothy Dailey in seeing modern UFOs, and UFO abductions as demonic, rather than as space aliens. What about the views I have published that UFOs might carry the angels of God? This is apparently unthinkable to Bates, who describes me as a "former 'believer' [who has] been deceived and fallen away." (p. 326) He does not seem pleased that my book "is revered as a benchmark text among the more religious UFO believers, who hail him as a UFO 'master.'" (Ibid) Although he is aware that I have argued that a UFO parted the Red Sea, he not only does not discuss my biblical exegesis (See UFO REVELATION 4), he does not even quote a single sentence from my book. Nevertheless, it is no problem for Bates to condemn my work as failing to meet "the Scripture test." (p. 328)

THE DEMONIC THEORY: SOME OBSERVATIONS

There are major weaknesses with the demonic theory from a biblical point of view. None of the four authors (Wilson, Weldon, Dailey and Bates) give an overview of the biblical doctrine of demons.

Demons are mentioned first in connection with idols, and seem to refer to the evil spirits behind the idols made of wood or stone. (Deut. 32:17) This sense of connection between demons and idols continues in Paul (1 Cor. 10:20, 21), and in Revelation 9:20.

The major mention of demons is with the healing ministry of Jesus. We find that Jesus "healed many that were sick and cast out many demons; and he would not permit the demons to speak, because they knew him." (Mk. 1:34) Jesus never met a demon over which he was not the Lord, the victor.

One of the most famous exorcisms of Jesus was the healing of the demon possessed man in the country of the Gerasenes, where the demons in the man named themselves as "Legion." (Lk. 8:30) The demons asked permission to leave the man, and enter a herd of pigs that was nearby. Jesus gave them permission,

75

the pigs raced down a hill and drowned in a nearby lake.

A third dimension of demonology was the nature of Jesus himself. He was frequently accused of "having a demon," in a way we might say someone was crazy, or a little mad. (Like a UFO nut.) In fact, the only mention of demons in John's Gospel has to do with Jesus, and whether he was demon possessed. (Jn. 7:20; 8:48-52; 10:20,21) But there was a deeper question about Jesus, and that was, did he drive out demons by the Prince of Demons? (Mt. 12:27; Lk. 11:15)

One of the things that is clear in the Bible is none of the demons have a body of their own. They possess the body, or the mind, of a human. In the case of the Gerasene exorcism, the demons go into pigs, they do not suddenly appear with their own body. Wilson and Weldon say, "We shall see that demonic powers vary in their capacities. Some are extremely intelligent entities that are nonphysical in nature but have a capacity to assume a physical shape and to undertake certain physical activities." (p. 35) There is no biblical text in which demons take on a physical shape. That does not prove demons could not take on a physical shape, but they do not in the New Testament. Nor are there New Testament reports of demons "abducting humans," and then returning them to their bedroom.

A spiritual reality that does take on a physical shape in the New Testament is the resurrected body of Jesus. Jesus appears to his disciples in a room with "the doors being shut" (Jn. 20:19), in somewhat the same manner that beings came through the door of Betty Andreasson's house to abduct her.

A further difficulty with connecting demons and UFOs biblically is that demons are never connected with UFOs in the Bible. During the exorcisms of Jesus, UFOs are never reported. UFOs are reported in divine encounters, such as at the Transfiguration of Jesus (Mt. 17:1-9), or at the conversion of the Apostle Paul (Acts chapters 9, 22 and 26).

Bates is more careful than Wilson, Weldon and Dailey to make sure we do not believe UFOs are solid craft. Given the thousands of landing traces, radar sightings, and fighter jet encounters that those like Richard Dolan have documented, this point of view of Bates is very dubious. If the "Day of Disclosure" comes as Dolan and Zabel expect, and we find that one or more governments of the world have crashed UFOs in their possession, this will make the Bates point of view even more unbelievable than it already is. Nevertheless, if you are going to make the demonic argument, I think Bates is right to hope, if not believe, UFOs are nonphysical.

I have this fantasy that Wilson, Weldon, Dailey and Bates, the Four Prophets of the Demonic, are all riding in a car together to speak at a Christian UFO conference in Roswell, New Mexico. It is a dark night when suddenly a UFO hovers over their car, their car engine stops, and a bright light shines down on them. Then they all hear a voice saying, "Men, men, why do you persecute me?" In unison they all shout, "It must be demons." They may be right—or maybe not.

The other major theory of conservative Protestants in regard to UFOs is that they carry "fallen angels," the Nephilim, of Genesis 6:4. We will explore this theory, and the nature of the Satanic, in UFO REVELATION 10.

UFO REVELATION 10
UFOS AND CONSERVATIVE PROTESTANTISM: PART 2
THE FALLEN ANGEL THEORY

While the dominant theme of conservative Protestant UFO theology is that UFOs are demonic, a second view is that they are "fallen angels." At first glance, there might not appear to be much difference between the two theories: both are bad news, pick your poison. But if we carefully explore the "fallen angel theory," we will see that it opens no small Pandora's Box for the demonic theory, and perhaps for biblical theology as a whole. Furthermore, it would appear that the scientific evidence fits the "fallen angel" theory better than the "demonic" theory.

One of the main proponents of the fallen angel theory is Chuck Missler, who along with Mark Eastman, is author of the book Alien Encounters: The Secret Behind the UFO Phenomenon (1997). Missler gets high marks from Dolan and Zabel for his knowledge of the scientific evidence for the UFO mystery. [Patrick Heron, in books such as The Return of the Antichrist and the New World Order(2011), likewise believes Genesis 6 offers important end times clues in regard to fallen angels, and their connection to "the beast" of Revelation. There is at this time no firm agreement among conservative authors concerning how the "Nephilim" and fallen angels of Genesis 6 are to be understood, but there is considerable ongoing discussion.]

Dolan and Zabel say "Charles (Chuck) Missler is one of the world's leading Christian ufologists. He is a graduate of the United States Naval Academy, Air Force flight training, and holds a UCLA Masters Degree in Engineering. He also knows as much about UFOs as most non-Christian ufologists. He is well informed about their history, the cover-up, and specific cases. He knows about the testimony from astronauts, radar controllers, and jet pilots. He simply explains UFOs and aliens through the lens of Biblical interpretation as inter-dimensional beings that have a physical reality." (A.D., p. 255)

The main advantage of the fallen angel theory over the demonic theory is that it accepts the physical nature of the UFO phenomenon with ease, rather than trying to dismiss it, as Bates and the other demonic theory writers generally try to do.

The key text for Missler is Genesis 6 which Missler quotes at length: "And it came to pass, when men began to multiply on the face of the earth, and daughters were born unto them, that the sons of God saw the daughters of men that they were fair; and they took them wives of all which they chose......There were giants in the earth in those days; and also after that, when the sons of God came in unto the daughters of men, and they bare children to them, the same became mighty men which were of old, men of renown." (Genesis 6:1, 2, 4, Missler, p. 205)

Missler points out that most ancient translations called the sons of God angels, especially the Greek translation of the Old Testament, the Septuagint, which was the resource used by New Testament writers. These few verses from Genesis seem to be a sparse basis for a strong link between the Bible and modern UFOs. But there is further non-canonical evidence that Missler finds compelling.

"The Book of Enoch also clearly treats these strange events as involving angels. Although this book was not considered a part of the 'inspired' canon, the Book of Enoch was venerated by both rabbinical and early Christian authorities from about 200 B.C. through about A.D. 200 and is useful to authenticate the lexicological usage and confirm the accepted beliefs of the period. The Biblical passage refers to supernatural beings [Missler's italics] intruding upon the planet Earth. (There are alternative interpretations of this, which we will examine shortly.)" (Ibid)

Missler then goes on to make several connections in the Genesis text. He points out that the Hebrew word "Nephilim" translates "the fallen ones," and by mating with human women, the angels produced "unnatural offspring, the Nephilim, were monstrous and they have been memorialized in the legends" and myths of every ancient culture, including the "demigods" of ancient Greece.

Missler has a heading, "The Gene Pool Problem," based on Genesis 6:9, "These are the generations of Noah: Noah was a just man and perfect in his generations, and Noah walked with God." The perfection in generations, says Missler, is a genetic statement. "This term is used of physical blemishes, suggesting that Noah's genealogy was not tarnished by the intrusion of the fallen angels. It seems that this adulteration of the human gene pool was a major problem on the planet Earth, and apparently Noah was among the few left who were not thus contaminated." (p. 207)

Missler begins chapter 10, "The Return of the Nephilim," with this biblical reference from the words of Jesus, "And as it was in the days of Noah, so shall it be also in the days of the Son of man." (p. 203) The flow of divine history for Missler seems to be that the fallen angels created genetic and moral problems before the flood of Noah, and Jesus suggested that there would be another "Noah" time before his second coming. Since many modern UFO abductions seem to involve the taking of sperm samples, and removal of eggs from female abductees, we may have the fallen angels back, doing some kind of interbreeding again. That might mean the second coming of Christ is near.

Through the rest of his book, Missler draws on UFO writers like Jacques Vallee and John Keel, who focus on the deception and "trickster" dimension of the UFO phenomenon, and in this sense he is in unity with the "demonic" theory proponents like Wilson, Weldon, Dailey and Bates. There is concern about being under a "strong delusion," and being taken in by false Christs, and the antichrist.

But Missler is aware that his view is different from the demonic view. "Most students of the Bible tend to assume that the demons of the New Testament are equivalent to the fallen angels. Angels, however, seem to have the ability to materialize, etc. (that is, except those which are presently bound in Tartarus). In contrast, the demons seem desperate to seek embodiment. Angels and demons seem to be quite different creatures." (p. 213)

Gary Bates, well aware that the "fallen angel" theory does not fit well with the demonic theory, has a long discussion at the end of his book, in which he says, "even among Christians, the meaning of this passage is sometimes hotly debated. There are probably four major views regarding the expression 'sons of God' in Genesis 6, with some surprising connections to UFOlogy. " (Bates, p. 351) The views include the fallen angel view, the descendents of Seth, kings of the earth seen as gods, or humans possessed by demonic fallen angels. Bates does not openly dispute Missler, but by offering several alternatives, he weakens the fallen angel view.

Of course Bates is well aware that those like Erich von Daniken, and Zechariah Sitchin, have used the Genesis 6 text to argue that space aliens have been involved in a breeding program, directing the development of human life on earth. (p. 350)

THE FALLEN ANGEL THEORY: SOME OBSERVATIONS

The fallen angel theory has some advantages over the demonic theory, in that it explains the physical nature of UFOs better, and the suggestion of abduction UFO researchers like Budd Hopkins and David Jacobs that the aliens are involved in some type of genetic or cross breeding experimentation with humans seems somewhat consistent with the fallen angel theory.

The "disconnect" between the fallen angels and modern abductions with sexual content is that the fallen angels in Genesis saw that "the daughters of men were fair," and took them as wives for what seem to be normal human reasons— the joy of sexual union. In modern UFO cases, there are rarely reports of sexual unions, but rather instruments are used to extract sexual material from humans, and perhaps use this material in some type of incubation device. Sexual pleasure does not seem to be part of the story. (There are rare stories of sexual union with aliens, as in the case of Brazilian farmer Antonio Villas Boas who in October of 1957 reported being abducted from his tractor, taken aboard a UFO where he had sexual union with a beautiful, but not quite human, woman.)

Missler also describes these fallen angels as "supernatural," and as I have already said, I believe that eventually Protestants will see that the concept of the supernatural needs further study. Supernatural is not a biblical word, nor is there anything the "fallen angels" do in Genesis 6 to prove they are supernatural, whatever that word may mean to Missler. For contrast consider the angel that appeared to Gideon; the angel made consuming fire come from the tip of his staff, and then "the angel of the Lord vanished from his [Gideon's] sight." (Judg. 6:21). Or again in the case of the angel appearing to Manoah and his wife, after Manoah prepares an offering, "when the flame went up toward heaven from the altar, the angel of the Lord ascended in the flame of the altar while Manoah and his wife looked on; and they fell on their faces to the ground." (Judg. 13:20) The Genesis 6 "sons of God" show none of these signs. In addition, there is no UFO reported in the Genesis 6 passage, so connecting this passage to UFOs is very tenuous, to say the least. Furthermore, I do not think that the Missler argument that the flood of Noah served to get rid of a bad gene pool fits well with the Parable of Wheat and Tares of Jesus. Jesus seems to say, and modern DNA science would suggest, that the whole human race has a gene pool that is contaminated by a drive to dominate, which Jesus sees as a Satanic drive. In fact, it is the drive to dominate that leads Caiaphas and Pilate to crucify Jesus.

The Missler book was published in 1997, almost 30 years after mine, but like Dailey, there is no mention of my book, either to approve of my book, or refute it. Missler clearly knows his Bible well, and therefore even if he had not read my book, he would know that the "pillar of cloud and fire" seems very much like a UFO, but I find no comment on it in his book. In fact, Moses is mentioned only twice in his whole book, and the key to the Jewish faith is not Genesis 6:1-4, but rather the Exodus. That is where the core of Jewish revelation occurs. The fallen angel theory in Missler's hands seems very much to strain at gnats (Genesis 6:1-4), and then pretends there is no camel in the living room. (Exodus 13:21,22; sorry about the mixed metaphor.) I do not know why Missler did not simply argue for a dualism, that some UFOs may carry fallen angels, while other UFOs may be a sign of the presence of Christ and his angels, who for the present time, are willing to let the fallen angels torment planet earth, to lead us to repentance. Missler is well aware of the physical nature of the "good angels" in Genesis. (p. 211) But he does not even speculate on the possibility that some UFOs might carry the angels of God.

I suspect that the fallen angel theory makes some conservative Protestants like Gary Bates nervous on the grounds that people who are not Christian are more likely to see the von Daniken view of Genesis as correct, rather than the Missler view. We live in a scientific age, an age that doubts the supernatural. It would make more scientific sense to suppose that if "higher beings" from somewhere else were involved with human women, perhaps some type of cross breeding program was under way, not fallen angels "misbehavin."

It is not surprising that we find these words on the back cover of Missler's book. "Behind the hype, the hoaxes, and the government disinformation lies a reality so astonishing that the original publisher was too shocked to follow through with this book." The original publishers were probably not so much "shocked" as not wanting to tar their publishing reputation. In that sense, I very much see Chuck Missler as a brother.

THE SATANIC THEORY OF UFOS

So far as I know, there is no published book with the title "The Satanic Theory of UFOs." But as Chuck Missler pointed out, as some Christians confuse demons and fallen angels, I believe many conservative Christian writers confuse the Satanic with demons and fallen angels, although there is of course some overlap.

Satan or the devil makes a first brief appearance in 1 Chronicles 20:1, as a being who tempted David, but really only becomes a defined character in Job. The dating of Job is uncertain, perhaps around 750 B.C. Scholars are not sure when the book reached its current form, but we need to see that Satan as a testing angel of God came into Jewish thinking well after the Exodus, which may date before 1200 B.C. In the story of Job, God allows Satan to put Job into a kind of faith contest, which some religious skeptics see as a primitive game in which God and Satan make a bet or wager at Job's expense. Those of us who are trying to interpret the modern UFO mystery in light of Scripture seem to be very much in some kind of faith contest, not of our own creation.

Before Job, God was often understood to do his own testing. Thus it was the angel of God who through Moses confronted Pharaoh, and challenged Pharaoh to let Israel go. The angel of God brought all kinds of plagues on Egypt, and God tells Moses that "you may tell in the hearing of your son and of your son's son how I have made sport of the Egyptians and what signs I have done among them; that you may know that I am the Lord." (Ex. 10:2) Not only does God test the Egyptians, but Israel is tested in the wilderness. They find themselves without food and water after crossing the Red Sea, and they wish they were back in Egypt. Manna drops from the sky, Moses draws water from a rock. At Sinai, commandments are given, sometimes Israel disobeys, and is punished. But the whole purpose of God in the

Exodus is explained in these words from Moses to Israel: God "led you through the great and terrible wilderness, with its fiery serpents and scorpions and thirsty ground where there was no water, who brought you water out of the flinty rock, who fed you in the wilderness with manna which your fathers did not know, that he might humble you and test you, to do you good in the end." (Deut. 8:15, 16)

Thus the theme that God puts us through testing, to reward us in the end (with Promised Land), is not just a theme from Job, it is an Exodus theme. And the Apostle Paul confirms this as the theme of those who endure the cross with Christ. Paul says, "I consider that the sufferings of the present time are not worth comparing with the glory that is to be revealed to us." (Rom. 8:18) Our lot on earth is testing, suffering, but our destiny is a heavenly promised land.

Satan is the angel of God that tests us. We see this at the beginning of the ministry of Jesus, when we find that "Jesus was led up by the Spirit into the wilderness to be tempted by the devil." (Mt. 4:1) Jesus was led by the Spirit as Moses was led into the wilderness by the pillar of cloud and fire, the Exodus UFO. Jesus was led into testing, as the Jews were led into testing.

And Jesus taught us to pray, "Lead us not into temptation," because this is the world we live in, the Satanic is always here, within the biological drives of human flesh, programmed as it were by our DNA. We have a genetic drive to deceive and dominate those around us.

Where is the Satanic? It is in our desire to put the needs of the flesh ahead of the needs of the spirit, our bodily desires ahead of the will of God. We find Jesus is tempted to turn stones to bread, to meet his biological need for food. But he responds, "Man shall not live by bread alone." (Mt. 4:4) The third temptation was to bow down and worship the devil, and Jesus responded, "Begone, Satan, for it is written, 'You shall worship the Lord your God and him only shall you serve.'" (Mt. 4:10)

Notice that the first and third temptation seem very related to biological drives for food first, and then for power and control of territory, acting on the "territorial imperative" of the "beast" in all of us. The implication of this temptation is that with his divine power, Jesus would be the supreme warrior, who could conquer all the kingdoms of the earth. The temptation of leaping from the pinnacle of the temple seems to be the yearning of the ego for adoration, to be worshipped in God's place, which of course was exactly what made Satan the adversary of God, and is related to the original sin of Adam and Eve.

In light of the biblical understanding of God as not only our creator, but our tester, whether directly as in the Exodus, or through a "testing angel like Satan," how might we view some of our modern close encounter cases? One of my Christian friends is Rev. Michael J.S. Carter, author of the book Alien Scriptures: Extraterrestrials in the Holy Bible (2005). We have been friends for more than ten years, brought together by the challenge of understanding the UFO mystery in our time.

Carter experienced a series of bedroom visitations over a period of several months. The first meeting was with a being in a silver suit, and he had trouble sleeping out of fear the being would return, which it often did on the date of a full moon. On one occasion when he was in bed, "I felt a weight on my back as if someone or something was sitting on it. I could hardly breathe! I was paralyzed and could not open my eyes. I was terrified and I tried to calm myself by telling myself that it was just them visiting again. (Even today, I still have an initial feeling of fear when I get a visit). While paralyzed with this weight on my back, I was mentally shown a picture of a being that I can only describe as Spiderman-looking, except that this being was green and scaly with yellowish cat-like eyes. I heard a voice whisper in my ear saying, 'you're going to be rich and famous' (this has yet to happen by the way). I forced myself up by sheer will and forced open my eyes. To my astonishment, I watched this being simply walk through my window and outside of the building. I lived on the 15th floor at the time." (p. 27-8)

How are we to understand a report like this? If as I believe, all things are under the lordship of Christ, how do I make sense of this story? Carter and I, by the way, do not agree on how to interpret all the issues the UFO challenge gives us. But we agree that we need to face what is going on.

Certainly, there are aspects of his encounters that seem evil. We might suppose his fear is a sign that he is dealing with an evil force. But notice how the Bible describes one divine encounter: "As the sun was going down, a deep sleep fell on Abram; and lo, a dread and great darkness fell upon him." (Gen. 15:12) When the light from the angel of the Lord shone on the shepherds to announce the birth of Jesus, "they were filled with fear." (Lk. 2:9) Thus Carter's fear response seems natural, and similar to the human response to biblical divine encounters.

The physical nature of the beings might suggest they are "fallen angels." Or they might be "space beings" that have abilities we do not understand. But there is this issue. Those like Whitley Strieber, author of Communion, and others who go through multiple contacts—how are we to understand these modern "chosen people" who are contacted, for good or for evil, by another reality?

There is a biblical story of Jacob that may be helpful here. Jacob had cheated his brother Esau out of his father's blessing, had been separated from Esau for years, and was on his way home, seeking reconciliation with his brother. Jacob sent his wives on ahead one night, and was left to sleep alone. "And Jacob was left alone; and a man wrestled with him until the breaking of the day. When the man saw that he did not prevail against Jacob, he touched the hollow of his thigh; and Jacob's thigh was put out of joint as he wrestled with him. Then he said, 'Let me go, for the day is breaking.' But Jacob said, 'I will not let you go, unless you bless me.'And he said, "What is your name?'And he said, 'Jacob.' Then he said, 'Your name shall no more be called Jacob, but Israel, for you have striven with God and with men, and have prevailed." (Gen. 32:24-28) Jacob's own conclusion was he had seen God face to face. But the role of the stranger in the night seems very much like a Satanic role, for the being is clearly in an adversarial role with Jacob. The Jacob story appears before Satan became a figure in Jewish literature. But the theme of Jacob wrestling is the theme of Job: we go through bad trials, and are blessed in the end. It is the theme of the Exodus, wilderness journey, followed by Promised Land, and the story of Jesus, crucified, and raised from the dead.

I would not want to go through what Michael Carter has gone through in his close encounters. Yet it seems clear that these encounters have shaped who Michael now is, as Jacob's encounter reshaped not only his self understanding, with a new name, but it became the name of the whole people of God. The alien being promised Michael that he would be "rich and famous," which Michael is not. Is this Satan, the father of lies, speaking to Michael? Or might the alien promise refer to the Resurrection to come, when our true identity in Christ is revealed?

Missler better than those who argue for the demonic point of view understands the complexity we face. He says, "Because of Satan's sinister nature, many people naturally believe that his physical appearance is evil. However, because of Satan's supernatural ability to change his external form, he could take on a very pleasing, attractive, and even reassuring external form while remaining, in essence, the most evil entity in the universe! It is interesting that when Antonio Villas-Boas was abducted in 1957, he described the female alien entity he encountered as the 'most beautiful' creature he had ever seen!" (p. 245)

How then are we to read the Michael Carter experience, since one of his aliens had a "Spiderman" appearance? If the aliens are beautiful, does this mean they are Satanic, but if ugly, angelic? Should we link ugly aliens to Christ, who in the prophecy of Isaiah has "no form or comeliness that we should look on him, and no beauty that we should desire him. He was despised and rejected by men...as one from whom men hide their faces he was despised, and we esteemed him not." (Is. 53:2.3)

Or in the end of the day, do we have to look deeper than appearance to understand the "reality" behind the appearance? Carter goes on to say that he was eventually led to a form of healing called "Reiki," and that his asthma, an affliction since childhood, lessened. Even more, he was convinced that he had healing gifts, and enrolled in seminary in New York, and became a hospital chaplain.

I know much of Carter's story will seem "New Age" and "occult" in many of its dimensions to Christian conservatives. But I think we need to be careful to distinguish what may be an outpouring of the Holy Spirit in our time on one hand (Acts 2:15-18), and the occult on the other hand. One interesting aspect of Carter's experience is he is black, and he says, "I cannot tell you how many books and articles I have read which indict the so-called 'Grays' or 'Reptillians' as sinister or evil, while embracing the blond blue-eyed 'Swedes' or 'Pledians' as benevolent and loving. These portrayals may or may not be true. Intergalactic racism is a very real phenomenon in my humble opinion and needs to be called out when it is evident. After all, we humans can be pretty xenophobic when it comes to the so-called 'other.'" (p. 29)

Speaking of welcoming the other, the stranger, where has the voice of the church been? Jesus said, "I was a stranger, and you welcomed me." (Mt. 25:35) Neither the church, nor the world, has welcomed our UFO strangers. Might we be entertaining angels unawares? Or at the very least, God's testing angels?

AN ANGEL OF LIGHT—A CLEAR AND PRESENT DANGER

The point at which the danger of UFOs and the Satanic is clearly evident is in relation to what Dolan and Zabel call the "Breakaway Group." They say, "When Disclosure finally comes in the future, it will reveal the existence of a group that has pulled the strings on the UFO secret for years. It probably has a name, one that we are unaware of now, that will be exposed and become infamous. That name is probably not the Bilderbergers, the Council on Foreign Relations, the Free Masons, or even Majestic." (p. 94) Whatever the name of the group, it will probably be international in scope, in some sense beyond the reach of any of our elected officials, including the President of the United States. Dolan and Zabel say, "Let us hope that those people in the Breakaway Group who are dealing with the presence of the Others now and have been for so many years, are doing so in a way that is responsible to humanity as a whole. For at the present time, we have no way of knowing whether this is so, and no way of holding them accountable to the people." (p. 95)

If my imaginary alien Zorg does exist, in some real sense, and a secret human group is in verbal contact with the aliens, then the question is: What have the aliens offered to give us?

And what do they expect back in return, if anything? And what will we do with any "alien gifts?"

Richard Dolan is one of several UFO researchers who believe some aliens either look naturally human, or can make themselves look human. This means the aliens could infiltrate key positions in society and we would not even know it. (Dolan and others responded to the question, "The aliens that look just like us or make themselves to look just like us—how integrated do you think they are in our society?" "The Big Questions," MUFON UFO Journal, July 2011, p. 8.) The biblical view of angels is that they can seem very human, and can live in our society without being noticed. The three men who visited Abraham and Sarah were not known to be angels until after they left. (Gen. 18) The idea that we might entertain angels unawares assumes angels look human. (Heb. 13:2) When angels are distinguished from humans, it is often by their clothing. (Matt. 28:3; Acts 1:10) Thus we have a right to suppose that the angels of God may be living among us, but without our knowledge. Thus the conclusion of some UFO researchers that modern "aliens" are also living among us is shocking to Christians only because we have stopped believing the angels of God are still doing what they did in biblical times. But might we have a mixture of good and fallen angels living among us? If so, how would we tell the difference?

Those like Dr. Stephen Greer are sure that the aliens have given us the knowledge of anti-gravitational power, and with knowledge of this power, we can now run our technological society with pollution free energy. We no longer have to power modern culture with fossil fuels. Some researchers believe the "Breakaway Group" is holding back the secrets of this new power because they are so invested in profits from oil.

The second issue is that the "abduction phenomenon" indicates that the aliens have tremendous psychological power, they can take over the minds of abductees, they can make the abductees forget their experience. The aliens can control our psychological "reality," and turn it into fantasy.

What this means is, humans with alien technology, and alien paranormal powers, could control the world, and we would have no power to resist.

Here is the danger, it is the danger the Devil offered to Jesus to control all the kingdoms of the world "if you will fall down and worship me." (Mt. 4:9) As I have shown in UFO REVELATION 8, our animal drive to dominate is so much a given in human politics that I do not believe any secret "Breakaway Group" would be able to resist the temptation to use their power in an evil way. And any aliens/fallen angels who offered humans power to rule the whole world would very much be serving in the role of Satan.

The Apostle Paul understood that there are false apostles who disguise themselves as apostles of Christ, "And no wonder, for even Satan disguises himself as an angel of light." (2 Cor. 11:14) The original temptation of Eve in the garden was to "upgrade her power," to be more like God. The serpent said of the forbidden fruit, "For God knows that when you eat of it your eyes will be opened and you will be like God, knowing good and evil." (Gen. 3:5) If Zorg and his friends offer power to a secret group, which would enable that group to control the world, I cannot imagine any human group turning down the offer. Only if the Servant voice of Christ was in the Breakaway Group could the offer be resisted. And I suspect that whatever the name of the Breakaway Group, it follows the laws of the flesh, the spirit of antichrist, not the laws and spirit of Christ. But the bottom line for all Christians is not to have the right "theory" about the aliens, what we need to know is what is going on. We need our modern Pharaohs to confess the truth. If they do not willingly confess, then I hope God forces a confession from them. I believe it is in God's power to force such a confession. He forced a confession from Pharaoh in Egypt, and God can make sport of our modern Pharaohs. I hope all Christians long to see the glory of God as UFO REVELATION unfolds.

UFO REVELATION 11
ADVANCED PHYSICS, UFOS AND BIBLICAL INTERPRETATION

When I was a senior at Princeton Seminary, I told one of my theology professors I was going on to the University of Edinburgh to do further studies in the area of science and Christianity. He told me I was wasting my time, the two fields had become totally separate. I found his point of view difficult to understand. After all, physics is the study of energy, and whatever else the Holy Spirit is, it is one form of God's energy, what I sometimes call Holy Energy. (Col. 1:29) I believe the "Everywhere God" is the source of the energy that created our visible universe, not to mention the power that enabled the healing ministry of Jesus. The sense in which this power is "supernatural," whatever that means, needs to be raised in the modern church, and will be raised I believe in the future when the church begins to deal with the UFO mystery.

Whatever theologians may think, there are scientists who are raising the God question. One such scientist is Dr. Paul Davies, Professor of Theoretical Physics, University of Newcastle-upon-Tyne, England. He is author of several books, including God and the New Physics (1984). The jacket of the book summarizes the Davies view: "Demanding a radical reformulation of the most fundamental aspects of reality and a way of thinking that is in closer accord with mysticism than materialism, the new physics, says Davies, offers a surer path to God than religion."

Davies is well aware of the historical conflict between science and religion, but takes the position of scientific orthodoxy (Jung, Menzel, Sagan) that UFOs are a space age myth, not science. In regard to UFOs, "with the decline of organized religion, they [aerial phenomena] have re-surfaced again in technological guise, employing the language of spacecraft and pseudoscience, of mysterious force fields and mind over matter—a polyglot synthesis of primitive superstition and space-age physics." (p. 198)

In his book, Davies promotes the view that "science" is the trusted way to truth, and "revealed religion" frequently gets in the way of truth, promoting prejudice and warfare instead of truth. "Although individual scientists may cling tenaciously to some cherished idea, the scientific community as a group is always ready to adopt a new approach. There are no shooting wars over scientific principles." (p. 6) Thus from Davies' point of view, the enterprise of science as a whole is free from ideological divisions. (Science does, however, provide the weapons for shooting wars, which is no small issue, when searching for the government motive for a UFO cover-up.)

In contrast to the purity and ideological freedom of science, "religion is founded on revelation and received wisdom. Religious dogma that claims to contain an unalterable Truth can hardly be modified to fit changing ideas. The true believer must stand by his faith whatever the apparent evidence against it. This 'Truth' is said to be communicated directly to the believer, rather than through the filtering and refining process of collective investigation. The trouble about revealed 'Truth' is that it is liable to be wrong, and even if it is right other people require a good reason to share the recipients' belief." (Ibid)

It may be that some religious truth is said to be revealed "directly to the believer." In Roman Catholic Christianity, the doctrine of papal infallibility is based on the faith that the Holy Spirit will reveal the truth directly to the Pope, although Papal pronouncements will have been worked out carefully in light of Catholic theological tradition.

The Protestant Reformation, which is my tradition, came at the issue of truth from a different point of view. Protestants see the church as open to error, including the pronouncements of church councils.

While many Protestants see the Bible as a document of revealed truth that cannot be changed, nevertheless an important Reformation principle is that our interpretation of Scripture may be in error, and therefore the church must "always be reforming." My experience in exploring the issues regarding UFOs and biblical theology has been that Protestants who preach that the church must "always be reforming" do not seem very open to reform. (See my article "UFOs and Metanarrative Reformation," Strong Delusion archives.)

Nevertheless, scientists and Christians, need to understand this. Just as the universe is the object of study of scientists, physicists from Newton to the present may put forward new theories to explain the meaning of this reality. The theories may change, and have changed, nevertheless, the universe is the constant reality with which scientists work. In this sense, scientists have a kind of "revealed truth," the universe, which scientists may, or may not, understand correctly. In the same sense, the Bible is "the universe of the Christian theologian." And for Christians, the biblical testimony concerning who Jesus was, and why his life, death, and resurrection matter, is the core reality, the core universe, of the Christian theologian. The interpretations of this reality may change, but the reality stays the same. From my point of view, the biblical core reality is still there, but in light of UFOs, we need to reinterpret some of our beliefs about what the Bible means, especially the meaning of biblical angelology. I think this is a Protestant Christian thing to do.

Davies wants to make it clear that although he is suspicious of "revealed truth," that does not mean he is against religion. "It is a great mistake, however, to infer from the scientist's suspicion of revealed truth that he is necessarily a cold, hard, calculating soulless individual, interested only in facts and figures. Indeed, the rise of the new physics has been accompanied by a tremendous growth of interest concerning the deeper philosophical implications of science." (p. 7) What Davies sees happening is that many people now believe "that recent advances in fundamental science are more likely to reveal the deeper meaning of existence than appeal to traditional religion." (p. 8) My answer to Davies as a Christian is that there is no deeper meaning to existence than we find in Jesus Christ. But there are many spiritual powers in all of us that keep us from seeing the truth that is revealed in Jesus. (For instance, as explained in UFO REVELATION 8, our biological drive to dominate others is in conflict with the call of Jesus to servanthood. And there is more than a hint in the work of Davies that "science" ought to be in a "dominating" position in relation to "revealed" religion. Am I wrong to suspect that the arguments of Davies are as much about his power and status as they are about truth?)

Davies does raise issues concerning extraterrestrial life and Christianity, while not admitting belief in UFOs. "The existence of extra-terrestrial intelligences would have a profound impact on religion, shattering completely the traditional perspective of God's special relationship with man. The difficulties are particularly acute for Christianity, which postulates that Jesus Christ was God incarnate whose mission was to provide salvation for man on Earth. The prospect of a host of 'alien Christs' systematically visiting every inhabited planet in the physical form of the local creatures has a rather absurd aspect. Yet how otherwise are the aliens to be saved?

In this space-age era, when so many people apparently accept the reality of UFOs, remarkably little attention has been given to the 'alien dimension' by the world's principal religions." (p. 71)

Davies is right, the issue of extraterrestrial life does raise questions about "salvation" on other planets, although he does not explain the presumption that life on other planets would have to be "fallen" in order to need redemption. But Davies is quite right I think to say that "remarkably little attention" has been given to the issue of ET life and its implications for the Christian faith. What Davies, and scientists like him either do not understand, or do not want to admit, is that once you believe in, or have proof that UFOs are real, you then have the scientific possibility of religious revelation. By that I mean that if what Dolan and Zabel call the Day of Disclosure comes, religious revelation becomes a scientific possibility in a concrete sense. Revelation is already a "religious possibility" for those of us who are believers, of course. Scientists like Davies, Menzel and Sagan take the position, "I know of no scientific evidence of a 'revealing reality.'" Of course even if the government were to admit UFOs were real, that would not "prove" that UFOs are the source of biblical revelation. But then it would not be just a religious possibility, it would also be a scientific possibility. The fundamental position of the Bible is that there is a "revealing reality," an angelic reality, not of this world. Scientists like Davies simply write the whole idea of revelation off as "unscientific," and therefore beyond serious consideration.

The presence of UFOs raises the possibility that alien life is flying in our skies. What kind of alien life? How do they fly? And where are they flying from? Advanced physics can give us some clues to possible answers to these questions. We need to explore the concept of anti-gravity, and the concept of multiple universes, both areas where advanced physics raises questions that may give new direction to biblical interpretation.

ANTI-GRAVITATIONAL THEORY, UFOS AND BIBLICAL INTERPRETATION

The issue of UFO propulsion systems has many implications for the economy, the military, and civilian life. If some type of anti-gravitational system is part of the UFO story, then our oil based economy might be on the way out, which could be good for the environment, but bad for all the businesses that depend on oil.

As Dolan and Zabel remark, "For many years, leaks have occurred and claims have been made describing radical propulsion systems in alien flying saucers, as well as in the home grown variety. Certainly, anything that can move in perfect silence, hover indefinitely, and accelerate instantaneously is using something better than high-octane gasoline as its source of fuel, whether this be some form of the fabled zero-point energy field, a clean burning nuclear fusion, or something more exotic." (A.D., p. 195)

Nick Cook is an independent reporter who began to search within American industry for signs of anti-gravitational research. He published his results in his book, The Hunt for Zero Point (2001). Although he talked to some high level scientists in American industry, these scientists usually had a security person representing the interests of company secrets included in the interview. Consequently, there were limits to what Cook could learn. Nevertheless he points out the size of America's black budget, which "in 1988, the total was computed to be $30 billion for R&D and secret weapons programs— more than the entire annual defense budget of a major European NATO nation such as Britain, France or Germany." (p. 127) (See my review of Cook's book, MUFON UFO Journal, October 2002, p. 16-17) It seems reasonable to suppose that if we have been spending that kind of money since 1947, we now have air craft or space vehicle designs that are much more advanced than has been made public, and it is likely that something like anti-gravitational technology is part of that advance.

Do one or more of the governments of the world have in their possession crashed UFOs? Most researchers believe there may be a few, and these would be highly prized. By studying a crashed UFO, scientists might discover in a few years what otherwise might take decades of research. As Jenny Randles has said, "The prize of the secrets of alien technology would be enormous. I was told by a senior figure in Britain's Defence Ministry that finding out how UFOs do what they do is purpose number one behind any study of the data; as it was phrased, 'We have to learn to use this to build weapons before the other side do.' This same factor seems critical, from what little we know, to the thinking of security agencies, such as the CIA, and, probably, the NSA, which delve into UFO reports." (Jenny Randles, UFO Retrievals: The Recovery of Alien Spacecraft, 1995, p. 165)

Paul R. Hill has written the most comprehensive book thus far that explores the issues related to UFO propulsion technology. Hill, a former NASA scientist, experienced a personal UFO sighting, but as a member of NASA, he also heard of UFO reports that shaped his scientific thinking. Hill reports that UFOs have knocked persons down with some kind of force field, displaced tree branches when hovering over them, and rocked automobiles when flying above them, without direct contact.

What type of propulsion system would cause these effects? "In evaluating the force fields to determine which type is used, we shall examine the static-field types: the electric field, the magnetic field, and the repulsive force field. The first two are well known, but the third is not. As we have mentioned, the latter may be thought of as a negative gravity field, or a field with similar properties as yet undiscovered. Negative gravity is the field that theory indicates is associated with negative matter and possibly with some antiparticles. This field repels all matter." (Paul R. Hill, Unconventional Flying Objects: A Scientific Analysis, 1995, p. 109)

How does all this relate to the Bible? Many theologians refer to events in the Bible that are outside our normal experience as supernatural events. Events like the parting of the Red Sea, or the Resurrection of Jesus, are called examples of the supernatural. But "supernatural" is not a biblical word, and when strange events happen in the Bible they are often called "signs and wonders." (Mt. 24:24; Jn. 4:48; Acts

2:22 etc) My opinion is that "After Disclosure," theology will have to distinguish between "miracles" in the Bible that were caused by some type of advanced technology, while others will be seen as the direct work of the Holy Spirit. I believe the parting of the Red Sea is an example of the work of an advanced technology, while the Resurrection of Jesus is the work of the Holy Spirit, as were his healing miracles, and as was the giving of the Holy Spirit to the church at Pentecost. (Acts 2:4) If UFOs carry the angels of God, and operate by some type of anti-gravitational system, then these might be some of the signs of anti-gravitational power in the Bible: the parting of the Red Sea (Ex. 14:19-30), the earthquake effects at Mt. Sinai (Ex. 19:18), the stopping of the Jordan River (Josh 4:1924), and the falling of the walls of Jericho (Josh. 6:12-21), as well as the earthquake reported at the tomb of Jesus when an angel "descended from heaven." (Mt. 28:1-3)

What about the case of Jesus walking on water? Is this a case of anti-gravitational technology, or the work of the Holy Spirit? (Mt. 14:22-33) I don't know. There are reports among modern close encounter cases where humanoids are seen to "float" about a foot off the ground as they travel either from, or to, their space craft. Although Jesus spoke often about the Kingdom of Heaven, and its angelic occupants, we really have few details about the power that is basic to heavenly life. If angels are related to our modern UFO reports, then it seems likely that the Kingdom of Heaven operates on the basis of two different kinds of power, one that we might call impersonal and the source of heavenly technological power, and the other personal, what we usually call the power of the Holy Spirit, the third person of the Trinity.

PARALLEL UNIVERSES, UFOS AND BIBLICAL INTERPRETATION

When I published The Bible and Flying Saucers in 1968, I had one major concern about connecting UFOs to biblical angels. The biblical view of angels was they were eternal beings, they had eternal life. My understanding of the scientific world view at that time was that we live in a "running down universe," meaning that at some time in the future, the universe will run out of energy, and die. If this were true, then no one living in this universe could be eternal.

I began to explore the possibility that there might be more than one universe, that there might be a way to escape from the space-time continuum of our universe into a world that did not decay, did not run down. I thought Einstein's Theory of Relativity offered us the freedom to explore some possibilities within the framework of the as yet unfinished science of advanced physics. With that in mind, I began to look at the New Testament ideas of the angelic world looking for "some way out" of our universe, and looked for the possibility that UFOs did not come from our universe, but rather from another dimension. That was the basis for chapter 5 in my book, "Where Is Heaven?" I then expanded somewhat on these ideas in my two part article, "Wormholes, Heaven, and the God Hypothesis." (MUFON UFO Journal, November 2001, p. 10-12; December 2001, p. 11-14)

When my book was first published, the Christianity Today review of my book was predictably negative about chapter 5. "Space does not permit a complete account of the scientific distortions contained in the book. In the preface Downing states that he 'is not an authority on Einstein or on heaven...' This does not deter him, however, from devoting a chapter to the question, 'Where is heaven?' He admits that his discussion 'reads very much like science fiction' and 'is not necessarily true'; but it may, he says, 'help to set our minds free from the somewhat depressing agnosticism we now find ourselves in when we even being (sic) to entertain the idea that we might live eternally—as part of God's plan.' He then proceeds, with complete abandon, to do violence to both Einstein and heaven with over twenty pages of pure speculation." (Albert L. Hedrich, "Flying Saucers in the Bible?" Christianity Today, June 21, 1968.)

It should be clear to all who have read this series on UFO REVELATION my work has been rejected by both the liberal and conservative branches of Protestantism. Liberals do not want me to take stories like the parting of the Red Sea literally, they want it to be poetry, mythology.

They want to keep science out of the Bible. Religion is not about reality, it is about something we make up in our heads, much like music and poetry. Religion may have a beauty about it, it may represent human psychological longings, but it has nothing to do with the physical world.

The issue with conservative Christians is quite different. It has been more than 40 years since the publication of my book, and I still can't quite understand the conservative attack on my work. The conservative Christian mentality seems to be this: the church is a fort, the fort protects the basic treasure we have, which is the gospel, and the task of Christians is to attack all enemies who are trying to destroy the fort. They might be atheists (or other non-Christian religions, New Age mysticism, etc.,) or they might be false prophets, or as Gary Bates says of me, "former believers who have fallen away." Within this assumption, everyone has to be tested to see if he or she is a true believer, or an enemy.

From the point of view of Hedrich, I am the enemy, I proceeded "with complete abandon to do violence to both Einstein and heaven, with over twenty pages of pure speculation." For Hedrich, my speculation amounts to bombs dropped on the Christian fort. I am the enemy. Christians can "only hope that this book has a very limited circulation." Does Hedrich know where heaven is? If he does, he does not tell us in his review. Apparently he thinks it is sinful even to wonder about it. Since when is being full of wonder a sin? Since when is it a sin to believe that "with God all things are possible." (Mt. 19:26)

BIBLICAL UFO REVELATIONS

My view is not that the church is a fort, something we build to defend the gospel. God is our fort, "A Mighty Fortress Is Our God." And we are not called to live in a fort, we are called to live in the wilderness with God, on a journey, where we are moving toward the kingdom of God. If you hole up in a fort, you will not arrive at the kingdom of heaven. The incarnation of Christ means this journey through the wilderness is so important to God that God became human in Jesus, and lived, and died, on the journey with us. On this trip, we look for signs of buried treasure. (Mt. 13:44)

For more than 40 years I have been pointing at UFOs and saying, "This may be buried treasure hidden for us to find." UFOs are not buried in dirt, of course, but buried by the greed and lust for power of the military-industrial complex which decided years ago that UFO truth needed to be kept from us. Our modern Pharaohs are no different from the Pharaoh who challenged the God of Moses. I suspect that many world leaders did not want us to even think about the possibility that the angels of God are not only watching us, but are on occasion, shutting down our nuclear missile sites. And I suspect that for many conservative Christians, defending fortress America, and fortress Gospel, are so similar, that seeing UFOs as demons, rather than as angels, enemies of both America's military power, and enemies of the Gospel, was a very natural way to interpret the UFO mystery. This is my best understanding of why I am not only the enemy of liberal Protestants, but also conservative Protestants. By and large, it is Roman Catholics who have not demonized me.

One hundred years ago, physics and cosmology, the sister science of astronomy, were separate sciences. But with the advent of relativity theory, and particle physics, we now understand there is no way to explain the origin of the universe separate from advanced physics. The expanding universe, the way in which galaxies are formed, the cooling process of stars, and the action of the power of gravity on collapsing stars with the nuclear forces, all depend on advanced physics for interpretation.

Michio Kaku is professor of theoretical physics at City University of New York. He is an excellent interpreter of the current relation between physics and cosmology. He points out that there are four basic forces in the universe: gravity, electromagnetism, the weak nuclear force, and the strong nuclear force. (Parallel Worlds, 2006, p. 79-80) The search for a unified field theory uniting all four forces has thus far failed, but what is called the "Standard Model" is a formula that unites three of the four forces, leaving only gravity out of the equation. One might suppose that if a Unified Field Theory is achieved, this might help explain the apparent "gravity free" nature of UFO flight.

But the Standard Model, lacking the simplicity that physicists prefer, nevertheless has led to some strange cosmological conclusions. One theory about the "big bang" is that the original explosion at the creation of the universe was not exactly uniform, and the lack of uniformity might suggest that many universes might be created by the same process.

As Kaku suggests, "The multiverse idea is appealing, because all we have to do is assume that spontaneous breaking occurs randomly. No other assumptions have to be made. Each time a universe sprouts off another universe, the physical constants differ from the original, creating new laws of physics. If this is true, then an entirely new reality can emerge, within each universe." (p. 96)

From my Christian point of view, I find this interesting, because the suggestion that another universe might exist, parallel to ours, which operates by different laws of physics, leaves open the possibility that "death" might not be a natural part of that universe. In other words, a universe in another dimension might be eternal, unlike our own.

Kaku, as co-founder of string theory, presents the latest in dimensional theory in chapter 7, "M-Theory: The Mother of All Strings." Kaku points out that only a few years ago, scientists who "proposed the existence of unseen worlds were subject to ridicule."

"With the coming of M-theory, all that has changed. Higher dimensions are now in the center of a profound revolution in physics because physicists are forced to confront the greatest problem facing physics today: the chasm between general relativity and the quantum theory." "Of all the theories proposed in the past century, the only candidate that can potentially 'read the mind of God,' as Einstein put it, is M-theory."

With M-theory we can begin to ask fundamental questions: "What happened before the beginning? Can time be reversed? Can dimensional gateways take us across the universe?"(p. 185)

Einstein had shown that something like a "wormhole" exists at the heart of a black hole in space. "Mathematicians call them multiply connected spaces. Physicists call them wormholes because, like a worm drilling into the earth, they create an alternative short-cut between two points. They are sometimes called dimensional portals, or gateways. Whatever you call them, they may one day provide the ultimate means for interdimensional travel." (p. 118)

My purpose in presenting this material from Kaku is to demonstrate that the types of speculation that I presented in chapter 5, "Where Is Heaven?" in The Bible and Flying Saucers, is not far from the possibilities that are emerging even more clearly from modern physics and cosmology. I look at these possibilities with hope, and I do not think hope is a sin.

How does the issue of parallel universes relate to UFOs and biblical interpretation? There are two issues that I see clearly. There may be others. 1) Is there any connection between the idea of "portals" or gateways to other universes as we find in advanced physics theory, and UFOs, and the Bible? 2) And are there any indications that Jesus, or the angels, seem to go back and forth between earth and some kind of parallel universe?

Dolan and Zabel are aware that many of the strange aspects of the UFO mystery might be explained by the physics of multidimensionality. There are many cases of UFOs seeming to "wink in" and "wink out" of our reality, rather than flying away. Perhaps UFOs have a way of entering and exiting our reality.

They report the story of a young man and woman lying on their backs on a hill in Hawaii, when they see something strange. "Looking straight up, they noticed what looked like a huge, white door open up in the sky. It was either squarish or rectangular in shape, with four easily identifiable sides." (A.D., p. 144) The witnesses believed they saw a portal opening into another dimension of reality.

THE HEAVENS WERE OPENED

The concept of portals or doors is central to entering the Holy City of Jerusalem, and of course, in our human imagination, we suppose that after we die we meet St. Peter at the Pearly Gates to see if we will be admitted to heaven. (Rev. 21:21)

In the story of the baptism of Jesus, we find that after Jesus was baptized by John, "he went up immediately from the water, and behold, the heavens were opened and he saw the Spirit of God descending like a dove, and alighting on him; and lo, a voice from heaven, saying, 'This is my beloved Son, with whom I am well pleased.'" (Mt. 3:16, 17)

What does the phrase "the heavens were opened" mean? The biblical report suggests that something like a portal to another world is being described. What comes out of this portal? Something flies out of the portal, the "Spirit of God." Notice this is not God in his Godness exactly, but rather some kind of visible mediator of God. Apparently related to the Spirit of God, a voice from heaven identifies Jesus as "my beloved son."

What is this flying Spirit of God, which descends like a dove—white or silver, no wings moving, gliding, round, even saucer shaped in appearance? The "Spirit of God" flying connects back to Elijah. Elijah had been taken up into the sky in a chariot of fire, and Elisha had been anointed as his successor. The fifty prophets who supported Elijah asked Elisha's permission to go on a search for Elijah, for "it may be that the Spirit of the Lord has caught him up and cast him on some mountain or into some valley." (2 Ki. 2:16) Thus the "Spirit of God' was thought to provide a transportation system for chosen prophets.

If we look at the baptism passage in this light, then what may be suggested is that when Matthew says Jesus "went up immediately from the water," that Jesus "was levitated from the water," and that the Spirit of God, descending like a dove, "alighted" on Jesus, or perhaps more accurately, merged with Jesus.

After the merger of Jesus and the Spirit, "Jesus was led up by the Spirit into the wilderness to be tempted by the devil." (Mt. 4:1) The image of Jesus walking behind the Spirit, which flies ahead of him, fits the Exodus image of the pillar of cloud and fire, leading Moses and Israel into the wilderness for their time of testing. But the Greek words here for "led up" might also be translated that Jesus was "carried by the Spirit into the wilderness," which might be more in line with the Elijah tradition. In any case, in the baptism of Jesus we have a story of a possible heavenly portal, a UFO coming from the portal, and Jesus being lifted up and carried away by the UFO, or at least being led by it into the wilderness. (See my treatment of the Baptism issues in more detail in my book, The Bible and Flying Saucers, p. 134-148.)

Another example of the "the heavens being opened" is found in the speech of Stephen when he was about to be stoned to death. He gazed into heaven, saw the Glory of God, Jesus at the right hand of God, and said to the crowd, "Behold, I see the heavens opened, and the Son of man standing at the right hand of God." (Acts 7:56) Here we do not have a UFO flying out of the portal, but rather Stephen is somehow given a vision of a reality that is very near to him, but invisible to everyone else. The idea that the angels of God, the heavenly armies of God, can be present, but invisible to most humans, was also present in Old Testament history. On one occasion the king of Syria sought to kill Elisha, and surrounded the city where Elisha stayed with his army. Elisha's servant woke early in the morning, and saw the enemy army surrounding the city. In fear he went to Elisha, who prayed for the servant to see what Elisha saw. Elisha prayed, "So the Lord opened the eyes of the young man, and he saw; and behold, the mountain was full of horses and chariots of fire round about Elisha." (2 Ki. 6:21) There is also the strange story that an angel that was visible to Balaam's ass, but invisible to Balaam, until "the Lord opened the eyes of Balaam." (Num. 22:31)

What we see is that there is a biblical tradition that suggests we live in a universe of multiple dimensions, so that the heavenly reality can be in our space, but most of the time we do not see it. The kingdom of God can really be "in the midst of you" as Jesus said. (Lk. 17:21)

This brings us to the second issue: Are there examples of Jesus, and the angels, going back and forth between our universe and a parallel universe? A parallel universe theory seems to be one of the best ways to interpret the resurrection stories of Jesus that we find in the Gospel of John. We find these words in John: "On the evening of that day, the first day of the week, the doors being shut where the disciples were for fear of the Jews, Jesus came and stood among them and said to them, 'Peace be with you.'" (Jn. 20:19) It is made clear here that somehow Jesus entered the room even though the door was shut, probably locked, for fear that the powers that crucified Jesus would be coming for the disciples. How did Jesus "materialize" in the room? I do not know, but the resurrection stories suggest that the kingdom of heaven can be a place where beings have bodies, but maybe these bodies operate on the basis of different laws of physics. As Michio Kaku has suggested, the laws of physics might be different in a universe in another dimension. [We need to consider the possibility that what the Apostle Paul called a "spiritual body" (1 Cor. 15:44) represents both a different kind of physics and biology. (For further discussion see my book, The Bible and Flying Saucers, "Flying Saucers and the Resurrection of the Body," p. 203-212.)]

Eight days after he appeared to his disciples, Jesus appeared again, with the doors shut, to help doubting Thomas overcome his unbelief. (Jn. 20:26-29) Luke's Gospel also has a resurrection story that implies multidimensionality. Two disciples, one named Cleopas, were traveling the seven miles from Jerusalem to Emmaus, when they were joined by a stranger, who turned out to be Jesus. They spent the day walking with him, talking with him, but did not recognize him until he broke bread in front of them at their evening meal. "And their eyes were opened and they recognized him; and he vanished out of their sight." (Lk. 24:31) As Jesus vanished, so the angel that had met with Gideon also just vanished. (Judg. 6:21) As modern UFOs seem to "blink in" and "blink out," Jesus just vanished, only to appear somewhere else. Much later, as the disciples tried to understand these strange resurrection stories, "Jesus himself stood among them." (Lk. 24:36)

These kinds of reports bring to mind the experience of Betty Andreasson, who was abducted by beings who came through the door of her home without opening it, and left, taking her with them, without opening the door. Likewise in one of the bedroom encounters of Michael Carter, one of the beings left his room simply by walking through the window of his bedroom, which was on the 15th floor of his building.

The story of an angelic rescue of Peter reported in the book of Acts is also interesting in dealing with the issue of moving from one dimension of space to another. Herod had put Peter in prison, and was probably planning Peter's death. An angel appeared in the prison cell, struck Peter on the side to wake him (Peter was sleeping between two guards), and told Peter to get dressed. Peter's chains fell off of their own accord, and Peter was ordered to follow the angel. "When they had passed the first and second guard, they came to the iron gate leading into the city. It opened of its own accord, and they went out and passed on through one street; and immediately the angel left him." (Acts 12:10) While this is not proof that the angel "materialized" in the prison cell, it seems unlikely that the angel opened the iron gate on the way in, closed it, and then had to reopen it again on the way out. It seems more likely that as Jesus materialized in the upper room in his resurrection appearances reported in John, likewise the angel somehow came from another dimension into Peter's cell.

In the context of a discussion of proper head covering for men and women in prayer, the Apostle Paul said, "That is why a woman ought to have a veil on her head, because of the angels." (1 Cor. 11:10)

Scholars are not sure how to translate, or interpret, this verse. But the implication seems to be that angels are present when we worship, we cannot see them, but they can see us. It may be that the appearance of an angel to Zechariah as he served at the altar of incense is an example of an angel "materializing" during worship. (Lk. 1:5-23)

I believe modern physics opens doors of possibilities for interpretation of the UFO mystery in light of multidimensional space. Likewise, much of the biblical revelation seems to report some kind of UFO reality, which is connected to the angelic world, where Jesus is King of the Angels. I come to the UFO mystery with much more hope than fear. I do not believe we need, in the name of modern science, to stop believing in the angelic world, as some Christian liberals have done. Nor do I think it is helpful to come at the UFO mystery with a fortress mentality, as some conservative Christians have done. I believe we need to come to the UFO mystery with Christ's hope. I believe Christ understands that we now live in a basically godless culture. Scientists like Richard Dawkins mock our God openly in the name of science. The proper response is not to go into a fort, and shoot Bibles at those like Dawkins. The biblical witness, plus UFOs, plus the expanding field of advanced physics, have made it clear to me that God has the power to break us free from our modern form of Egyptian slavery—secular atheism, a culture with no godly hope. I believe the angels of God will some day expose the lies about UFOs spoken by our modern Pharaohs. Then we will have a new Exodus.

We will be able to journey with God in faith again, through another stretch of wilderness perhaps, but finally, Promised Land is up ahead. The resurrection of Christ is our ultimate promise that after wilderness comes Promised Land. But here in the wilderness, justification by faith should be our response to the current vision of the cloudy pillar which leads us to God's future.

UFO REVELATION 12
THE GOD HYPOTHESIS

If Dolan and Zabel are right in expecting the Day of Disclosure to arrive, when it arrives, suddenly all the world will know UFOs are real, and that governments of the world have been lying to us for decades. Things will change. Among the changes will be the religious response to, and assessment of, what UFOs mean for our religious beliefs. All this would happen whether the Christian religion existed, or not, whether Christian believers want this to happen, or not. And by and large, it appears most Christians do not want disclosure to happen.

Dolan and Zabel realize that Disclosure brings about a realignment of the old conflict between science and religion. With Disclosure we have to look at UFOs as a god-like force, we now have to deal with what Dolan and Zabel call "the God Hypothesis." (p. 282) "The God Hypothesis" is the title of an article I published in the MUFON UFO Journal (October 1988), as well as a book by Joe Lewels, for which I wrote the Introduction. (1997)

UFOs seem to have a spiritual dimension. "We are talking about existence of a spiritual realm, the existence of God, and all that goes with it. In other words, will Disclosure will (sic) offer us proof for this belief, or at least strong supporting evidence?"

"Within UFO research literature, there is no shortage of claims that the 'aliens' possess their own spiritual orientation. People who claim to recall abduction experiences have occasionally commented that the beings who took them pray to their concept of God. Indeed, it seems possible that these beings themselves exist in what we might loosely call the spiritual realm."

"What if these beings claim to be the 'divinities' worshiped by early human societies? Or to have created us?" "What if they have something provocative to say about Jesus Christ, Mohammed, or other important spiritual beings of human history. In other words, if Jesus or Mohammed or Buddha are seen as one of 'them?'" (A.D., p. 282)

The Day of Disclosure will present different problems for different Christian points of view, points we have examined in previous chapters. The Roman Catholic view at the present time seems to take the position that UFOs exist, and are probably highly evolved beings from our natural universe. They do not come from the supernatural world of demons and angels. (Msgr. Coraddo Balducci) But the Day of Disclosure could make it clear that it is not easy to distinguish between advanced technology and the supernatural, especially if our leaders are talking with Zorg, and Zorg and his alien companions are saying things like "we created you."

The Day of Disclosure creates a different problem for Christian liberals. Christian liberals like Bishop John Shelby Spong (Why Christianity Must Change or Die) do not believe there is a Higher Power that influenced the development of biblical Christianity. There is no Revelation, because no Revealer exists. Christians like Spong are not far from the atheism of biologist Richard Dawkins (The God Delusion), but might be inclined toward the scientific theism of Paul Davies (God and the New Physics) whose work we examined in the last chapter. But Davies, though a theist, is against religious "revelation." From the point of view of Spong, Dawkins, and Davies, the Day of Disclosure would mean the whole idea of religious revelation is alive and well again, and they will not like it. In fact, UFO Disclosure would undermine the whole intellectual basis of the "death of God" movement. Suddenly, maybe the "Ascension of Jesus" really did happen, maybe the angels do exist, maybe human life has a purpose that we only fully understand after death. Christian eschatology would become a live possibility again, Marxism would no longer look like a good alternative to the Christian belief in heaven. Liberals will not like this. None of the professors of "religious studies" in our public universities will like this. They have spent the past 50 years teaching that things like the parting of the Red Sea, and resurrection of Jesus, are mythology. With Disclosure, now what? Well, it depends on the type of Disclosure.

One might suppose that conservative Christians would be thrilled that Revelation is now a scientific possibility. The academic world that has mocked conservatives for so long as being backward and unscientific would now have to take the possibility of Revelation seriously.

But conservatives are not happy. From the conservative point of view, having Revelation is like having a wife. One wife is good, but having a thousand wives, like King Solomon, is not so good. Dolan and Zabel point to the issue that turns conservative Christians against the possibility of UFOs. Among many UFO contact reports we have mention of spiritual experiences, of alien beings that may pray to "their God." Or what if these beings claim to have created us? This is part of the Revelation of the Raelian cult, whose leader, Claude Vorilhon, learned special information about human history and the Bible through his contact with aliens.

BIBLICAL UFO REVELATIONS

Shirley MacLaine's "New Age" revelations about reincarnation, other lives, and channeling, drive conservatives to distraction. (MacLaine, Out on a Limb, 1983) Conservatives like Gary Bates have found it best to paint me as a New Age guru or 'Master.' (Bates, p. 327) To say the least, Disclosure of the UFO reality opens up a Revelation Pandora's Box. In the post Disclosure world, anybody can claim to have an alien contact, anyone can become a religious prophet. How do you tell the true prophets from the false ones? Thus for conservatives, it has seemed best to see UFO aliens either as demons (Wilson, Weldon, Dailey and Bates), or as fallen angels (Missler and Eastman, along with many others not examined here). As things now stand, for conservative Christians, there is only one Bible, and only the Bible has the story of God's true Revelation. Muslims believe the same thing about their Koran, of course. The problem for conservative Christians is after Disclosure it is not enough that we have a "great sign of power" in our skies. How do we know if modern signs are angelic, demonic, fallen angels, just a bunch of space guys, or the angels of Satan? Conservatives love to proclaim the absolute truth with certainty and conviction. When Disclosure comes, ambiguity, uncertainty comes with the package. Conservatives will not like the ambiguity at all. But from God's point of view, faith cannot exist without ambiguity, and as Hebrews chapter 11 teaches, Faith is the name of God's Game.

CHRISTIAN REVELATION: ENOUGH, BUT NOT TOO MUCH

UFOs present us with the scientific possibility that many of the strange things reported in the Bible happened. When the biblical people reported contact with beings from another world, it may have happened. The killing of the first-born in Egypt on Passover night may have happened, the parting of the Red Sea may have happened, giving of commandments at Sinai may have happened. The biblical religion may have been caused by beings from another world.

And these beings may have a special connection to or knowledge of God, the Everywhere God.

This is the scientific basis for "The God Hypothesis." Modern UFOs both in their flight characteristics, and in the psychological powers that the aliens exhibit in abduction cases, indicates that the alien reality has all the power necessary to have created the Christian religion, or any other world religion. It was and is my argument that "We need the God hypothesis because I don't think the governments of the world can keep the UFO lie going forever. It would be better for all of us if the God hypothesis could be discussed before world governments release their UFO information." ("The God Hypothesis," MUFON UFO Journal, October 1988, p. 13) I am thankful that the Dolan and Zabel book helps move the discussion in this direction.

Biblical revelation has a special character which needs to be understood, and this understanding may help interpret UFO behavior, and UFO goals, in our current situation. The Bible makes the case that the Jews were God's chosen people, they were chosen to be "a light to the Gentiles" (Is. 49:6, Acts 13:47). It was God's purpose to bring salvation to all the nations of the earth through the Jews.

Why were the Jews chosen to be the recipients of this special Revelation? Why from a Christian point of view, was the savior of the world, Jesus, a Jew? "For you are a people holy to the Lord your God; the Lord your God has chosen you to be a people for his own possession, out of all the people that are on the face of the earth. It was not because you were more in number than any other people that the Lord set his love upon you and chose you, for you were the fewest of all peoples; but it is because the Lord loves you, and is keeping the oath which he swore to your fathers, that the Lord has brought you out with a mighty hand, and redeemed you from the house of bondage, from the hand of Pharaoh, king of Egypt." (Deut. 7:6-8)

Notice that the biblical answer to the question: Why did God choose the Jews? is that they were anti-Egypt. In fact, they were the opposite of every other major world power. The Jews were "the fewest of all peoples." The Jews were chosen because from the world's point of view, they were nothing. This same theme shows itself again in the Christian story—Jesus was crucified, treated as if he were nothing. Jesus is "nothing" in terms of worldly power, but "everything" from God's point of view. This is the paradox of the biblical view of power. The biblical story, in both its Old and New Testament form, is an attack on biological enslavement, on our biological drive to dominate. (See UFO REVELATION 8) God's power works for freedom, freedom from the oppression of Pharaoh through Moses, and freedom from our enslavement to sin and death in the crucifixion and resurrection of Jesus. The powers of our political world control through killing, or threatening to kill. Jesus controls through love, through healing, feeding, raising the dead. Finally through his own death he buys us eternal life. Jesus is Lord because he gives and restores life, he is not a killing Lord. He becomes Alpha by being Omega, our Servant King.

FROM THE GOD WHO KILLS TO THE GOD WHO LOVES

But the God of Moses was a very good killer. How are we to make sense of this apparent contradiction? The biblical revelation began with human cultures that were very primitive in some respects. Yet, though we think of ourselves as "advanced," the basic rules of world politics still seem to apply. The way to deal with Osama bin Laden is to kill him. The nations with the best armies, and best weapons, win. During World War II, Germany had a very great army, and was defeated only with difficulty, and much loss of life on both sides. Law and order is maintained in our nation by police, who are armed to kill, if necessary. Thus, death is the ultimate authority in our biological world. The Darwinian laws of dominance are very much part of our modern world politics, even in a democracy. Ethics and laws do play a role in our society, and try to keep animal forces in us under control. Rapists, if caught, will go to jail. Thieves and murderers, if caught, will go to jail. There is a "social contract" that most of us follow, which means we treat each other with respect, that we "love our neighbor as we love ourselves," and therefore do not need government power to enforce civil behavior most of the time. But for those who prefer the laws of the flesh to the laws of the spirit, law enforcement agencies try to demand justice, or at least the human version of justice.

Into this world God seeks to introduce the idea of love over domination, even love of enemies, freedom over slavery, forgiveness over revenge, generosity over greed. How is God to do this in a world that is in "spiritual darkness," driven by a Darwinian code of survival of the fittest? If Moses had been sent to Pharaoh with the demand, "Let my people go," but with no power to back up the demand, what would have happened? There would have been no Exodus. The power of God in the Exodus is shown incrementally, a little at a time. A plague of frogs here, a plague of locusts there, but Pharaoh does not give in, not until Passover, not until the first-born males in Egypt are killed at midnight. The divine tactic used by God against Pharaoh is what I would call "Targeted Intervention." God does not land with an army of angels to take over Egypt, rather Moses announces a series of plagues, each more powerful, until Passover, when Pharaoh surrenders to God's demands. (See my article "UFOs, the Bible, and Targeted Intervention" at the Strong Delusion archives.)

People have to believe in a God who can out kill Pharaoh. The message in Deuteronomy was that God has rescued you from Egypt because "the Lord loves you." And the Jews are a sign to all nations that this same Lord loves all nations, a love that becomes more obvious in Jesus, and in his command to baptize all nations.

But how do we come to believe that the Killer God of Exodus is a God of love? This seems a bit of a stretch. God did not seem like love from the Egyptian point of view the morning after Passover. As we make our way through the Bible, we find that all is not happiness in the Promised Land. Israel finds it tempting to believe in the gods of their neighbors, gods that were mainly nature gods, sex and fertility gods. The prophets were sent to call Israel back to their God who could not be made in a graven image. To make the prophetic call to repent believable, the prophets turned to God's power to make their message stick.

King Ahab, and his wife Jezebel, represent typical corrupt political leadership in Israel, who had turned to the god Baal, a nature and sex god. The prophet Elijah speaks out against this corruption, and eventually arranges a contest at Mt.

Carmel between God and Baal. An offering is made, and the true God will answer by fire. (1 Ki. 18) The prophets of Baal call on their god, do their chants and dances, cut themselves with knives so that they bleed, but nothing happens. Elijah calls on the God of Israel, and fire comes from heaven, consuming the offering. Elijah ordered the prophets of Baal killed (a religious action which would not be viewed as politically correct today), but we find that Elijah's victory was not complete. Jezebel wanted Elijah's head, and he had to run for his life.

Finally in despair he hid in a cave, and we find this interesting passage in which God appears to Elijah in many forms of natural power, in a strong wind, in rocks broken apart, in an earthquake, and then fire. But God was in none of these, but after the fire came "a still small voice." (1 Ki. 19:12) What seems to be said here is that God's deepest inner nature is not raw power, but a quiet voice, a voice that might speak in love. What we meet in the Old Testament is a revelation that God can do the power thing, he can kill with the best of earth's kings, but it is not his first choice. And the problem is that we humans value power more than anything else, it is part of our biological nature. We have a spiritual nature that can appreciate love, but in a contest between power and love, power wins, love loses.

JESUS, THE POWER OF GOD AND THE LOVE OF GOD

When we come to the New Testament, we see how God deals with the ambivalence of power and love. The New Testament says that in Jesus we have God in human form, and God is love. (1 Jn. 4:7) In Jesus we have quite a different type of divine "Targeted Intervention." In his wilderness temptations, Jesus is challenged by the devil to use his divine power to meet his biological needs (Mt. 4:3), his desire for fame (Mt. 4:5), and his desire for political power (Mt. 4:9). We may suppose that if Jesus had the power that we see in the Exodus, that he could have easily become the ruler of the earth. Instead, when Jesus faces the cross, rather than being rescued by God's power, as were the Jews at the Red Sea, Jesus deliberately sacrifices his right to God's power. When Peter draws his sword to defend Jesus at the time of his capture, Jesus says, "Do you think that I cannot appeal to my Father, and he will at once send me more than twelve legions of angels?" (Mt. 26:53)

From the point of view of the Revelation of God in the Old Testament, it seems absurd to suppose that if Jesus really is the Son of God, that God would not have the power to protect Jesus from being crucified. What the Gospels say is that God did have the power to protect Jesus, but Jesus did not use it. On the cross, Jesus put love ahead of power. And in this act, the cruelty of the political powers (Pilate) and the religious powers (Caiaphas) were exposed. While the powers of this world played their biological game of Alpha, their game of domination, in Jesus we find God playing Omega, God's game of love. In Jesus we see the first being last, and the last being first. Jesus is God's first, but humans made Jesus last, a loser, on the cross. But God raised Jesus from the dead, the stone the builders rejected as unfit, is now the cornerstone, sitting at the right hand of God.

The way Jesus used his power in his ministry is interesting. He healed the blind, the lame, the sick, even raised the dead. And he fed thousands, but feeding thousands led to trouble. He gained followers who were just looking for a free meal. Jesus said to the crowd, "Truly, truly I say to you, you seek me, not because you saw signs, but because you ate your fill of the loaves." (Jn. 6:26) Jesus seems to face the kind of problem that a man who is a rich millionaire might face who goes into a local bar. He might receive a lot of female attention that is not all that interested in his personality. And if he said to the women in this bar scene, "I am here to speak on behalf of my heavenly Father, my Father and I are one," one can imagine that he might get more jeers than cheers.

Raw power can get in the way of love. Many women now earn their own money, and are less likely to marry a man for his money. At the same time, few women would want to marry a man who cannot even hold a job. God is in this kind of dilemma. God wants to be loved for himself, not for his money. But who would want a God who has no power? Who would want a God who says, "I did not create the heavens and the earth, because I do not have that kind of power." God seems to need to carry out a revelation process in which power gets our attention, but in which when we seek to encounter this power, we are driven away from power as the essence of God's character to a center where sacrificial love controls God's power. Targeted Intervention is the way God brings his power to bear in a way that does not overwhelm love.

We find this passage in the New Testament. "Then some of the scribes and Pharisees said to him, 'Teacher, we wish to see a sign from you.'" (Mt. 12:38) The religious leaders had heard of his healing miracles, but they wanted to see something with their own eyes. Jesus was not impressed with their request, for it really was a demand for a sign of "dominating power."

Jesus responded, "An evil and adulterous generation seeks for a sign; but no sign shall be given to it except the sign of the prophet Jonah. For as Jonah was three days and three nights in the belly of the whale, so will the Son of man be three days and three nights in the heart of the earth. The men of Nineveh will arise at the judgment with this generation and condemn it; for they repented at the preaching of Jonah, and behold, something greater than Jonah is here." (Mt. 12:39-41) What we see here is that there is a certain form of seeking after divine power that is corrupt. It is similar to the corruption that led a man to seek to buy the Holy Spirit from the disciples with money. (Acts 8:14-24)

The resurrection of Christ leads the disciples to understand that our calling is to do battle against the laws of the flesh in us, the laws that call us to dominate each other. They, after all, were the biological laws that led to the crucifixion of Jesus. Instead, if we live in love, if we forgive rather than seek revenge, we love freedom rather than domination. If we live in Christ's way, we will be called children of God. (Rom. 8:16) "Do not love the world or things in the world. If any one loves the world, love for the Father is not in him. For all that is in the world, the lust of the flesh and the lust of the eyes and the pride of life, is not of the Father but is of the world. And the world passes away, and the lust of it; but he who does the will of God abides for ever." (1 Jn. 2:15-17)

What God does is show enough of his power so that some people can believe in what I call "God's Game," that is, that we understand we are called to fight our own lusts of the flesh for success and dominance, whether it be in politics, religion, or sex. But most of the time we do not have "proof" this is God's Game. Sometimes God hits someone right between the eyes with proof, as with doubting Thomas (Jn. 20:24-29), or Saul who became Paul when he saw the blinding light on the Damascus Road (Acts 9:1-8). But for most of us, we have to decide to believe in the God of Jesus Christ on faith. Faith involves some evidence, it is not blind. But for many scientists, the Bible is not "proof" that God is real, that Jesus was raised from the dead, that after death we face judgment. In the Day of Judgment we will have to give answer to our faith response to the New Testament message. "Now faith is the assurance of things hoped for, the conviction of things not seen. For by it the men of old received divine approval." (Heb. 11:1,2) The biblical view is that the Revelation we find in the Bible, which covers a period of more than a thousand years, is enough "evidence" to bring us to belief, without proof.

Why not proof? Because if we are called to love God, then for it to be true love, we have to be free not to love God. True love is always given in freedom, not in compulsion. If we demand "signs" from God, it is a sign that we will only love God under protest, against our own will. But if God shows us a "sign," then we will believe out of necessity. The issue of belief and freedom provide an interesting division between liberals and conservatives at this point. Conservatives are glad to point to the miracles in the Bible as proof of God's power, and therefore as reason to believe. Liberals are glad to point out that we do not have "proof" of God's miracles, and that this leaves us "free" to love God, or reject God. But what we see is that all too often liberals, in their freedom not to believe in the biblical miracles, and the signs of God's power, end up not believing in God at all. That is why ours is a "death of God" generation.

For Jesus, faith is our proper path to God. If we have faith, we can move mountains. (Mt. 17:20) He condemned his disciples for being part of a "faithless and perverse generation."

(Mt. 17:17) Peter was able to walk on water with Jesus because of his faith, and then he sank when he lost his faith. Peter very strongly felt the "ambiguity" that goes with faith, and can turn it into doubt. (Mt. 14:22-33) We are justified by faith that Jesus is God's supreme gift to us, God's amazing grace through whom we are saved. (Rom. 3:21-26) Faith is that strange spiritual gift through which we become children of God, believing without seeing. (Jn. 20:29)

So what is God to do with our faithless scientific generation, our evil and adulterous generation, which does not even seek a sign? (Mt. 12:39; 16:4)

WHAT WILL BE GOD'S NEXT MOVE?

Christian liberals have given up on the doctrine of the Second Coming of Christ. Christian Protestant conservatives hold closely to this doctrine, but strangely, they do not expect angels to show up in our lives in any way other than at the Second Coming. Partly this is due to the conclusion of the Protestant Reformation that the Roman Catholic Church had too many miracles, almost on a daily basis, most of which were based on superstition, not on divine revelation. The New Testament view is that angels can show up any time, but we may not recognize them, so we have to be alert for strangers. "Do not neglect to show hospitality to strangers, for thereby some have entertained angels unawares." (Heb. 13:2)

If a Day of Disclosure comes, how might Christians interpret this disclosure in a way that suggested that the God of the Bible is still in business? One way might be for Jesus to land, if not on the White House Lawn, then perhaps in a poor village in Mexico, or Africa, or even Jerusalem, and declare that the Day of Judgment has come. But the Second Coming of Jesus would bring God's Faith Game to an end. What if God wanted the Faith Game to go on? What then might be God's next move? Is there some kind of "Targeted Intervention" strategy that the angels of God might use which would renew the faith of the Christian Church, without providing "scientific proof" that UFOs carry the angels of God?

If Dolan and Zabel are right, some kind of Disclosure might come any time, either from the governments of the world because they believe the time is right, or because the aliens take such decisive action that the governments cannot keep the lie going any more.

There are two main disclosure scenarios, which I suggested more than a decade ago, and which still seem to be possible:

"1) In one scenario, we have established direct contact with the aliens, and they have told us their purpose for being here. Maybe they have helped America achieve technological superiority, and maybe our government leaders have discussed religion with them. The main problem in this scenario would be whether or not the aliens can be trusted.

2) In the second scenario, our government does not know much more about

UFOs than the average MUFON member, except perhaps for better knowledge of their advanced technology. Even if we have examined dead alien bodies, we may have no idea why they are here, or what they are planning to do—and have done—with the human race." (Downing, "Religion, UFOs, secrecy and policy decisions," MUFON UFO Journal, December 1999, p. 8)

In the first scenario, my imaginary alien Zorg and his friends exist, and have been in contact with humans, perhaps the Americans in particular. They might say they are angels who work for and with Jesus. Or they might deny that they know anything about Jesus, or they might say that Jesus was some kind of fraud. The challenge for Christians in all of these situations would be: can we trust Zorg? Some conservative Christians would be quick to suppose Zorg is the Antichrist. But if Zorg claimed to be part of the biblical angels, how would we test this statement? It is shocking to think of the angels of Christ, who in the past seemed so against the corrupt powers of world politics, would work hand in hand with any world government. But at the same time, in the Old Testament we meet two Pharaohs, Good Pharaoh, and Bad Pharaoh. Good Pharaoh is the one who made Joseph in charge of his Egyptian grain program, after Joseph had been sold as a slave in Egypt by his own Jewish brothers. (Joseph is an early Christ figure, rejected by Jewish brothers and by Gentiles, but savior of both.) Then came Bad Pharaoh, "Now there arose a new king over Egypt, who did not know Joseph." (Ex. 1:8) This is the Pharaoh who opposed God and Moses, who enslaved the Jews in Egypt. So the God of the Bible worked with Pharaoh through Joseph, and against a later Pharaoh through Moses.

It is possible that the ecology of the earth is in such a bad condition that the angels of God are working directly with the governments of the world to try to save the earth from ecological collapse. Ecological collapse would be very much like the seven year famine that is central to the story of Joseph. (Genesis 41) And Richard Dolan in his UFOs and the National Security State series has recorded several instances of UFOs intervening with our nuclear weapons sites. We live in a time when direct angelic intervention with the governments of the world may have been necessary. If our aliens are the angels of God, would they admit that they belong to Christ and work under his authority? I do not know. And if they said they were the angels of Christ, would our government leaders believe them? Again, I don't know. In the case of direct contact between the angels and our government, or other governments, it is hard to see how this could extend God's Faith Game. People would demand to see the angels directly, and then they would demand to see Christ.

On the other hand, I believe it is no sure thing, despite rumors to the contrary, that our government leaders, or Dolan's Breakaway Civilization, have clear and easy access to Zorg, and his alien team. I suspect that there is much the governments of the world do not know about the aliens, even if we have received some kind of hi tech boost from them.

One way the Day of Disclosure might come about would be by the process of "Targeted Intervention," brought about by the aliens. This seems very much to be the mode of operation now in progress, very similar to the plagues in Egypt used against Bad Pharaoh. We have had 60 years of UFO sightings, UFO plagues, which is not scientific "proof," but almost everyone on planet earth suspects UFOs might exist. It would be in the power of the angels to expose the Big UFO Lie, not with a landing on the White House lawn, but through a series of more and more open appearances in our skies, easy to film for TV cameras, but without an open landing.

Then we would have proof of some kind of extraterrestrial power in our midst, but there would be a lot of questions for Christians: are these angels, demons, fallen angels, or Satanic powers? Non-Christians would perhaps see the aliens as just a bunch of space guys with no special religious significance for humans, except perhaps as fellow travelers in God's universe.

But with so many possibilities before us, the possibility of divine revelation would be back on the table for both scientific and theological discussion. Liberals would have to admit that the concept of revelation has theological validity, conservatives would have to admit that revelation creates both faith and ambiguity. Dealing with UFO questions might force conservatives and liberals a little more toward the center of the biblical witness, and therefore more toward the heart of Christ, which could be one of God's best gifts to Christians at this time. It would be clear that UFOs might have provided the power behind the parting of the Red Sea, or the resurrection of Jesus. But we would not have proof of this. We would be full of wonder, like "the throng wondered, when they saw the dumb speaking, the maimed whole, the lame walking, and the blind seeing, and they glorified the God of Israel." (Mt. 15:31) If UFOs carry the angels of God, and if it is not the purpose of God to have Christ return now, then I would think that the most likely divine tactic in our godless technological world would be for UFOs to show themselves in such a way that faith becomes real again, in a world of scientific doubt. But at the same time, the UFO REVELATION could remain so unclear in many ways, that doubt would still be a favorite choice for many. With a strong UFO Disclosure boost, God's Faith Game could go on for a while, because with God all things are possible. Is Jesus the Christ, or not, would still be the basic question. Jesus asked his disciples, "Who do men say that the Son of man is?" (Mt. 16:13) The disciples had heard a lot of speculation, Peter gave the right answer. In our age of UFOs, I expect this basic question to come before the human race with new power.

BIBLICAL UFO REVELATIONS

SPYING OUT UFO LAND

All of us who are Christians, and believe UFOs are some kind of new reality that Christians need to deal with, are a kind of vanguard for the church. Our situation reminds me of the time in the Old Testament when Israel had journeyed through the wilderness to the land of Canaan. Moses sent spies ahead to check out the land. Many of the spies came back with a very "evil report," even though the land "flowed with milk and honey."

"The land, through which we have gone, to spy it out, is a land that devours its inhabitants; and all the people that we saw in it are men of great stature. And there we saw the Nephilim (the sons of Anak, who came from the Nephilim), and we seemed to ourselves like grasshoppers, and so we seemed to them." (Num. 13:32, 33)

The fellow spies that I have mentioned in this series of UFO articles, Clifford Wilson, John Weldon, Timothy J. Dailey, Gary Bates, Chuck Missler and Mark Eastman, have all given an evil report in regard to UFOs, calling them demons or "fallen angels," related to the Nephilim of Genesis 6:4. Is history repeating itself? Are our modern "Christian spies" making the same mistake the Hebrew spies made when they saw the "giants" in Canaan?

My view of UFO land is like that of Caleb, "Let us go up at once, and occupy it; for we are well able to overcome it." (Num. 13:30) We are well able to overcome UFO land because we have Christ, and if God is for us, who can be against us? I understand the fear of those who believe UFOs are a threat to humanity, or that UFOs are an evil power out to deceive us. I do not deny that we may be being "tested" in a Satanic way. By and large the church is blind to the test, and would "rather go back to Egypt" than face the giants in UFO land. But what if UFOs are a sign of the presence of God's angels? I worry that if Sodom had been shown the signs given to our generation, that Sodom would have repented. (Mt. 11:23)

We need to remember our basics. John 3:16 is still true. "God so loved the world that he gave his only Son, that whoever believes in him should not perish, but have eternal life." Our scientific world view has cut millions off from faith, from faith in the God who walked on earth in Jesus. If there is a "Strong Delusion" in our Western culture, it is atheism. Richard Dawkins, Christopher Hitchens, and Sam Harris have all written best selling books promoting atheism. Our culture is more than ready to believe the preaching of these atheists. Dawkins sees himself as "an evangelist for atheism." The basic assumption of the "religious studies" programs in our universities is that all religions are "myth," that "God" is an idea humans invented out of some kind of Freudian need for a father figure. Political correctness demands that to be "fair," all religions must be treated as of "equal" value in Western politics. To suggest some religious beliefs are better than others is "prejudice." It is no wonder that the ethical teaching of Jesus, calling us to "deny ourselves," and the message of God's self denying love (the cross), have almost no impact on our government, our businesses, our education, our "entertainment," or our science. The world is busy playing "Alpha," its biologically driven dominance games: the flesh wins, and Holy Spirit loses. Christ's call to Servanthood, to be "Omega," goes unanswered.

I am not afraid of UFOs, I am afraid of the godless wilderness that Western culture has become, with all its technological power, and no moral integrity to control it. Random acts of violence are no surprise in our godless culture. The main question is choice of weapons.

I believe UFOs are God's way of saying to our godless culture: "I'm Back!" And if God is back, it is time to repent, and be glad that the world lives under the umbrella of God's love, with his angels watching over us. But does the church have the eyes to see, to open our church doors to welcome our UFO strangers, or will we continue to be "unaware?"

BIBLICAL UFO REVELATIONS

ADDED MATERIAL:
UFOS AND META-NARRATIVE REFORMATION
September 2010
Dr. Barry H. Downing
Published on line at Strong Delusion, September 2010
INTRODUCTION

A new and useful book has been recently published by former Boston Globe writer Leslie Kean. The title of her book is UFOs: Generals, Pilots, and Government Officials Go on the Record. It is very much a "nuts and bolts" book, words like "religion" and "UFO abductions" do not even appear in her very substantial index, in spite of the fact that in her acknowledgements she thanks abduction researcher and "friend Budd Hopkins for providing daily, steady support." (p. 293) Kean's goal is to break through the fact that UFOs are a taboo among America's elite, government and military leaders, scientists, and the mainstream media. It is a "taboo" for those in these power groups to take UFOs seriously. (See p. 269 ff.)

Thus Kean's book is based on a political strategy, to convince the American elite power makers to treat UFOs seriously. Part of that strategy is to have John Podesta, former White House Chief of Staff to President William J. Clinton, write the Foreword. But the core of her strategy is to present only UFO evidence from respected military, commercial airline and political authorities from around the world. By and large, the book is written so as not to "spook" unbelievers, and thus issues like abductions and the possible religious implications of UFOs are only hinted at by Kean.

But still this is a book that is worth reading by those who ponder at the Strong Delusion website. What Kean does is invite military leaders, military pilots, and high level political leaders (like former Arizona Governor Fyfe Symington), to write of their own UFO encounters. Kean does write connecting and introductory chapters, but by and large the power of her book is in providing "primary sources" for her story.

BIBLICAL UFO REVELATIONS

Her conclusion is not just that she "believes" UFOs are real, rather she "knows" UFOs are real. She says the evidence establishes UFOs as a scientific mystery, objects the origin of which we do not yet know. What is not yet proven is the extraterrestrial hypothesis. She says that "UFOs do exist. We have seen that there are solid, three-dimensional objects of unknown origin flying in our skies, stopping in midair and zooming toward outer space, which are apparently not natural or man-made. They've come very close and landed as well, leaving physical traces in soil while shriveling the leaves of nearby plants. They interact with aircraft and have physical effects upon them." (p. 291)

Although the extraterrestrial hypothesis is a possible, perhaps even likely explanation, Kean does not claim "anything beyond the reality of the physical phenomenon." (Ibid) That UFOs are extraterrestrial has not yet been proven.

The way in which Kean draws a sharp line between what UFOs look like, and act like, and the conclusion that UFOs are extraterrestrial, is her nod to what we have come to call the scientific method. I am not against the scientific method, but I also come from a religious tradition that speaks of justification by faith, not justification by the scientific method. To say UFOs are real, but we do not really know they come from another world, looks like straining at gnats, and swallowing camels to me. Kean supposes this little bow to the altar of science will result in American elite culture—scientists, politicians, military leaders, the main stream media—suddenly feeling okay about admitting that UFOs are real. (Good luck Leslie.)

UFOS AS A MODERN TABOO

One of key the chapters in her book is entitled "Militant Agnosticism and the UFO Taboo." It is written by political scientists Dr. Alexander Wendt and Dr. Raymond Duvall. Their argument is that UFOs are a kind of taboo among American elite culture. Government leaders, scientists, and main stream media have the power "that determines what 'reality' officially is." (p. 271) The problem with a taboo is that it prevents reasoned debate. One function of a taboo is to maintain the current power structure of the culture. The admission of the UFO reality might question the dominance of our science, our military, and our form of government.

Wendt and Duvall go on to say that a basic assumption of our society is that humanity more or less rules its own destiny, we answer to no one but ourselves. We have an anthropocentric world view. (Notice that God is assumed to be a non-issue in their view of our current cultural values.) Nature now and then gives us some trouble, with an earthquake or bad storm, but in general, we do not worship nature; natural things like disease, can be mostly controlled by human science, if not yet, then maybe in the future.

Then we find this interesting paragraph. "Significantly, it is on this anthropocentric basis that modern states are able to command exceptional loyalty and resources from their subjects. Because a possible explanation for the UFO phenomenon is extraterrestrial, taking UFOs seriously calls this deeply held assumption into question. It raises the possibility of something analogous to the materialization of God, as in the Christians' 'Second Coming.' To whom would people give their loyalty in such a situation?" (p. 276) Kean, Wendt and Duvall believe the UFO taboo can be overcome by "militant agnosticism," by which they mean they maintain UFOs are real, but do not claim to know what they are. We will see.

It is tempting to try the same strategy of militant agnosticism with Christians. I could say, "UFOs are real. I am not saying they are extraterrestrial, I am not saying they are angels, I am not saying they are demons. Of course they might be. But for now I am just saying UFOs are real." Does everyone feel safe now, has all anxiety gone away? Can we talk now? I doubt it. But I do commend Kean for the book she has created. I think it is another small step forward in the quest for UFO truth.

META-NARRATIVE REFORMATION

One value of the Kean book for me is that the "taboo" analysis helped push my understanding of the negative forces at work in my own attempt to understand the possible relation between UFOs and my biblical faith, and to get others to join in this attempt. I have attempted to publish articles in several main stream religious publications, but have faced almost universal rejection. If UFOs are "taboo" in American secular elite culture, I would say that my views in the eyes of religious leaders are seen as a "double taboo." I have been struggling for a long time to understand how to "name" my struggle. One possible name is: you are very stupid Barry to connect UFOs and the Bible. In fact, in the early review of my book in Christianity Today, the reviewer thought it very unwise to connect the Bible to something we do not have scientific proof even exists. I thought this a strange argument from a magazine whose existence is based on justification by faith.

But if by chance I am not as stupid, or out of line as my critics have claimed, then what? If by chance, or the grace of God, I have discovered a mystery that the church of Christ needs to face, to wonder about, and discuss, how am I to explain the resistance to my call to look at both the Bible, and the UFO evidence?

My conclusion is that the resistance to my work is related to the fact (whether my work is valuable or not) that the reality of UFOs, which Kean makes so clear, leads to what I am calling a "Meta-narrative Reformation."

I use the word Reformation in light of my own Protestant faith tradition. My Presbyterian heritage began in the 1500's with the work of John Calvin. Others like Martin Luther were part of this process. In this case, the Roman Catholic Church had gone in a direction which had undermined the central concept of grace, that we are justified by trusting the goodness of God toward us in Christ, not by our own efforts to be good or just-ified. (Roman Catholics by and large now agree that some of the concerns raised by Calvin and Luther needed to be dealt with.)

But one of the major tenants of the Protestant Reformation was that the church is not infallible, the church by its nature is limited in its understanding of God, its understanding of Scripture, and although this was not a major issue at the time, in our understanding of nature. The scientific revolution was just beginning, and names like Copernicus, Galileo, Newton, Darwin and Einstein would bring about a revolution, or a reformation, of our understanding of nature. In light of this, the church must always be ready to be Reformed. Well, this is the deal. UFOs mean the church of Christ has to be Reformed, again. This will probably be more fundamental, and more radical, than the Protestant Reformation of the 1500's. Of course, the church, being what it is, will not want to be Reformed. This reformation does not mean the church will be destroyed, as some skeptics have suggested. But it will be changed. What will this new Reformation look like? Only time will tell. I do not believe the Reformation depends on me. I feel like a kid watching a flood rise, and warning that the dam will break sometime. Perhaps not in my life time. But it will break, and the church will Reform in light of UFOs.

PROTESTANT'S LIBERAL/CONSERVATIVE SPLIT

Modern Protestantism, more than either Roman Catholicism or the Eastern Orthodox tradition, is divided between liberals and conservatives. Protestants do not have any human authoritative center like the Pope, and so this liberal/conservative split has no centering power.

Liberal Protestantism feels at home with secular religious scholarship, with what are usually called "Religious Studies" programs in our universities. In this mind set, religion is a human creation, all the world religions were "made up" by humans. Scholars do not say it exactly that way, they say that religion is a "cultural construct." Stories in the Bible like the parting of the Red Sea and the resurrection of Jesus are seen as "mythology," stories made up by a pre-scientific people. Likewise the sexual ethics in the Bible were "made up" by these people, but the priestly element in Judaism put the commandments in the form of a God who handed down ethical truth from Sinai. We moderns do not buy this any more. All ethical decisions are our own, liberals believe we make up our own ethics. It is all about our "choice." It is beyond the understanding of conservatives, who see the Bible as the infallible word of God, to see how liberals can call themselves Christians, and reject some of the biblical ethical teachings. But given the liberal view that all religion is created by the culture in which it exists, liberals feel free to "make up ethics" appropriate for our own age. They would say that things like birth control change the cultural context of our sexuality so much that some, if not most, of the biblical rules do not apply. Liberals look at the Bible the way modern artists might look at a Rembrandt painting: they would admire its beauty, but not feel duty bound to imitate Rembrandt's style. Liberals see beauty in the Scriptures, but they see flaws that they call "cultural constructs" from which we need to be "liberated."

When I published The Bible and Flying Saucers in 1968, I did not expect liberals to be too thrilled with my book. And they weren't. And aren't. By connecting UFOs and the Bible, and especially UFOs and the Exodus, I put forward the scientific possibility that the Ten Commandments were handed down from some heavenly power at Mt. Sinai. The whole liberal position, that the biblical religion was just something made up by the Jewish people—a cultural construct— would be put at severe intellectual risk if liberals were to believe UFOs were real. Now maybe there is a real God, maybe this real God has real ethical standards. Maybe God would approve of us "loosening the law," or maybe not.

In other words, UFOs challenge the basic liberal religious meta-narrative. Meta-narrative is a term sometimes used in theology to point to a fundamental world view of how things work. Where did the biblical religion come from? The liberal meta-narrative is that the biblical people made their religion up. But if in fact it was some kind of UFO inspired revelation, now what? So I was not surprised that liberals avoided getting involved in UFOs and biblical issues as if their whole religious view might go up in smoke, because it might. Likewise the agnostic liberal culture at large in our media, and our universities, would suddenly have to face a possible Meta-narrative Reformation. No wonder UFOs are taboo in America's dominant culture. How strange that two political scientists like Wendt and Duvall recognize that the UFO reality brings to mind the "Second Coming" of Christ, but that in the modern church, it would be "taboo" to utter such a thought.

THE SURPRISE OF CONSERVATIVE REJECTION

But I did make one major wrong assumption. I assumed that conservative Protestants in particular would see right away that UFOs are an issue that needs to be confronted out of our loyalty to Christ, our duty to interpret the signs of wonder in our skies. But I sure was wrong in that assumption.

Here is the biblical, conservative Protestant Meta-narrative. God created the universe, and humanity is made in the image of God, that is why we rule nature. But our biggest problem is ruling ourselves, we have powers in us that drive us to dominate others, steal from others, (adultery is a form of sexual stealing), use deception to have power over others. (We now recognize biologically based drives to dominate are part of all of the animal kingdom.) The call to love others, sacrifice our own gains for the sake of others, goes against our own "flesh" as the Apostle Paul would say. But in this struggle we are moving from slavery to sin to freedom in Christ-like love and salvation. That is God's plan. We need to live our struggle with hope, Christ crucified and raised from the dead is the cornerstone of that hope. He will return some day in victory and judgment.

That is the biblical Meta-narrative. That narrative has been undermined in the minds of many by the scientific revolution. Liberal Protestants did not conclude that the stories like the parting of the Red Sea and the Resurrection of Jesus are mythology for no reason. They believed that modern science made it impossible for educated people to believe these stories.

What has been going on for the past 500 years is that the Christian Meta-narrative has been challenged by, and to some extent, replaced by, our scientific Meta-narrative. That is, we do not know how the universe was made, but there is no sign of God. As far as life on earth is concerned, it just evolved in Darwinian fashion out of some cosmic goo. We live in an evolutionary universe, there is no need for God. Scientific atheists like Richard Dawkins of Oxford University have mocked Christian beliefs in his book The God Delusion.

Thus, for the past 500 years, we have had two Meta-narratives fighting it out in Western culture, the more or less Christian world view—God made the world, made humans, and because of Christ we have a promise of an eternal future after death—and the scientific world view, there is no sign of God, life just evolved on earth, there is no sign that we survive death. (But, Dawkins would say, life is good enough for him as it is.)

With the UFO reality here, now what? My thesis is that both the Christian world view (meta-narrative), and the scientific meta-narrative, are going to go through a "Meta-narrative Reformation." It was my thinking that conservative Protestants would understand that the UFO reality could restore the scientific credibility of the biblical understanding of angels, as well as the scientific plausibility of key biblical events like the Parting of the Red Sea, and the Resurrection of Jesus, not to mention the Second Coming of Jesus, as Wendt and Duvall point out.

But, alas, there were no shouts of joy in conservative land over linking UFOs and the Bible. It has taken me years to understand the resistance to doing what I believe will have to be done by Christian leaders, sooner or later.

Early resistance could be understood as based on the fact that the United States government said UFOs did not exist, and why shouldn't we believe our government? But as time has gone by, and as we have come to understand what Richard Dolan calls "UFOs and the National Security State," we no longer have a basis to trust American government statements about UFOs, unless we suppose our first duty is to Caesar, and not to Christ.

BIBLICAL UFO REVELATIONS

Yet, strong resistance continues, there is still no broad based Christian discussion of the meaning of the UFO reality for our faith. Why? Part of the answer can be seen in the book by Gary Bates: Alien Intrusion: UFOs and the Evolution Connection. Bates is concerned that if we admit the extraterrestrial hypothesis in regard to UFOs, scientists will use this as evidence that we live in an evolutionary universe, and that life has even evolved on other planets. Bates believes in a literal Genesis, he believes in an earth that is a few thousand years old. The best protection for his faith in a literal Genesis is to connect the UFOs to demons, not to extraterrestrial life. I suspect many conservatives understand, and support Bates because of these concerns.

A further concern, one embodied in the website title, "Strong Delusion," is rooted in the New Testament teaching that we Christians are in danger of being deceived by demonic and evil forces. How do we know if UFOs are angels, demons, or none of the above? Thus many would think I am naïve to hope UFOs carry the angels of God—that is just a little too easy. (And maybe it is.)

A further concern is the way in which Erich von Daniken, and those who created the History Channel series "Ancient Aliens," have developed a non-evolutionary, yet godless meta-narrative that takes the ancient aliens/UFO concept and creates a whole new meta-narrative, using a blend of the Bible and science. (Some have seen me as part of this point of view; I am not, although I do share some concepts with this group.)

The "Ancient Aliens" meta-narrative is this: aliens started life on earth, we are a designed species (in this sense they agree with "Intelligent Design" Christians), but they were not God inspired to do this, they just did it as perhaps a scientific experiment. Stories about angels in the Bible, such as the angels who destroyed Sodom, are not about angels, as such, but rather about ancient astronauts. Probably UFOs have always been part of our past, and they are directing our development, but at a safe distance, rather than ruling directly. (In this sense, my article in Strong Delusion, "UFOs, The Bible and Targeted Intervention," agrees with the "Ancient Aliens" group on alien/angelic strategy in directing life on earth.) Conservative Christians are concerned that if we take UFOs seriously, we end up with perhaps a creation story, and a salvation story, that does not involve God at all. When the biblical miracles are seen as the result of advanced technology, rather than the supernatural, God seems to be left out. Can the biblical doctrine of angels be reconciled with our modern UFO reality, and still maintain the Christian doctrine of God as Father, Son and Holy Spirit?

I do not see any way around these concerns. Sorry. I do not know how all this will work out, but I believe it is inevitable that the whole earth go through what I call a Meta-narrative Reformation. My faith is rooted in Scripture, I believe in the God of Scripture, I believe in Christ as Lord and Savior. I trust that in the end of our faith trial here on earth, Christ will be victorious. But I also believe the church will have to go through a powerful Meta-narrative Reformation because of UFOs, just as fundamental to our faith as the Exodus was to the Jews, as fundamental as the Resurrection of Jesus is to those who are Christians, as divisive as the Protestant Reformation was to the church in the 1500's.

Barry H. Downing
September 2010

BIBLICAL UFO REVELATIONS

UFO REVELATION BIBLIOGRAPHY

The Holy Bible, Revised Standard Version (Thomas Nelson, New York, 1959).

Ardrey, Robert, *The Social Contract* (Laurel Books, New York, 1970).

Barnstone, Willis, *The Other Bible: Jewish Pseudepigrapha, Christian Apocrypha, Gnostic Scriptures, Kabbalah, Dead Sea Scrolls* (Harper San Francisco, 1984).

Bates, Gary, *Alien Intrusion: UFOs and the Evolution Connection* (Master Books, 2004).

Behe, Michael J., *Darwin's Black Box: The Biochemical Challenge to Evolution* (Free Press, New York, 2006).

Berlitz, Charles, and Moore, William L., *The Roswell Incident* (Grosset and Dunlap, New York, 1980).

Blumrich, Josef F., *The Spaceships of Ezekiel* (Bantam, New York, 1974).

Bowen, Charles, ed., *Encounter Cases from Flying Saucer Review* (Signet, New York, 1977).

_____, *The Humanoids* (Neville Spearman, London, 1969).

Brasington, Virginia F., *Flying Saucers in the Bible* (Saucerian Books, Clarksburg, W.Va., 1963).

Brueggemann, Walter, *Mandate to Difference: An Invitation to the Contemporary Church* (Westminster John Knox, Louisville, 2007).

Campbell, Joseph, *The Inner Reaches of Outer Space: Metaphor as Myth and as*

Religion (Harper and Row, New York, 1988).

_____, with Bill Moyers, *The Power of Myth* (Doubleday, New York, 1988).

Carter, Michael J.S., *Alien Scriptures: Extraterrestrial in the Holy Bible* (Blue Star Productions, Sun Lakes, AZ, 2005).

Clark, Jerome, and Coleman, Loren, *The Unidentified: Notes Toward Solving the UFO Mystery* (Warner, New York, 1975).

Condon, Edward U., *Scientific Study of Unidentified Flying Objects* (Bantam, New York, 1969).

Cooke, Patrick, *The Greatest Deception: The Bible UFO Connection* (Oracle Research, Berkeley, CA, 2002).

Corso, Col. Philip J., *The Day After Roswell* (Pocket Books, New York, 1997).

Davies, Paul, *God and the New Physics* (Touchstone Books, New York, 1983).

Dailey, Timothy J., *The Millennial Deception: Angels, Aliens & the Antichrist* (Chosen Books, Grand Rapids, MI, 1995).

Dawkins, Richard, *The God Delusion* (Houghton Mifflin, Boston and New York, 2006).

Dembski, William A., *The Design Inference: Eliminating Chance Through Small Probabilities* (Cambridge University Press, New York, 1996).

Denzler, Brenda, *The Lure of the Edge* (University of California Press, Berkeley, 2001).

Dione, R.L., *God Drives a Flying Saucer* (Bantam, New York, 1973).

_____, *Is God Supernatural? The 4,000-Year Misunderstanding* (Bantam, New York, 1976).

Dolan, Richard, and Zabel, Bryce, *A.D.: After Disclosure; The People's Guide to Life After Contact* (Keyhole Publishing, Rochester, NY, 2010).

Dolan, Richard, *UFOs and the National Security State: 1941-1973* (Keyhole Publishing, Rochester, NY, 2000)

_____, *UFOs and the National Security State: 1973-1991*(Keyhole Publishing, Rochester, NY, 2009).

Downing, Barry H., *The Bible and Flying Saucers* (J.B. Lippincott, Philadelphia, 1968; Avon, New York, 1970; Sphere Books, London, 1973; Berkley, New York, 1989; Marlowe & Co, New York, 1997).

Edwards, Frank, *Flying Saucers—Serious Business* (Lyle Stuart, New York, 1966).

Emenegger, Robert, *UFO's: Past, Present and Future* (Ballantine, New York, 1974).

Fawcett, Lawrence, and Greenwood, Barry J., *Clear Intent: The Government Coverup of the UFO Experience* (Prentice-Hall, Englewood Cliffs, N.J., 1982).

Fowler, Raymond E., *The Andreasson Affair* (Bantam, New York, 1980).

_____, *The Watchers: The Secret Design Behind UFO Abduction* (Bantam, New York, 1990).

Fuller, John G., *Aliens in the Skies* (G.P. Putnam's, New York, 1969).

_____, *The Interrupted Journey* (Berkley, New York, 1974).

Friedman, Stanton T., and Berliner, Don, *Crash at Corona: The U.S. Military Retrieval and Cover-up of a UFO* (Paragon House, New York, 1994).

_____, *Flying Saucers and Science* (New Page Books, Franklin Lakes, NJ, 2008).

Good, Timothy, *Above Top Secret: The Worldwide UFO Cover-up* (William Morrow, New York, 1988).

_____, *Alien Contact: Top-Secret UFO Files Revealed* (William Morrow, New York, 1993).

Graham, Billy, *Angels: God's Secret Agents* (Guideposts Associates, Carmel,

New York, 1975).

Harris, Sam, *The End of Faith* (Norton, New York, 2004).

Hansen, George P., *The Trickster and the Paranormal* (Xlibris, 2001).

Hansen, Terry, *The Missing Times: News Media Complicity in the UFO Cover-up* (Xlibris, 2000).

Hitchens, Christopher, God *is not Great: how Religion Poisons Everything* (Twelve, New York, 2007).

Hopkins, Budd, *Intruders: The Incredible Visitations at Copley Woods* (Random House, New York, 1987).

_____, *Missing Time* (Ballantine, New York, 1988).

_____, *Witnessed: The True Story of the Brooklyn Bridge UFO Abductions* (Pocket Books, New York, 1996).

Hill, Paul R., *Unconventional Flying Objects: A Scientific Analysis* (Hampton Roads, Charlottesville, VA, 1995).

Howe, Linda Moulton, *An Alien Harvest* (Linda Moulton Howe Productions, Littleton, CO, 1989).

Hunter, James Davison, *To Change the World* (Oxford University Press, 2010).

Hynek, J. Allen, *The UFO Experience: A Scientific Inquiry* (Henry Regnery, Chicago, 1972).

_____, and Imbrogno, Philip J. with Bob Pratt, *Night Siege: The Hudson Valley UFO Sightings* (Ballantine, New York, 1987).

Jacobs, David Michael, *Secret Life: Firsthand Accounts of UFO Abductions* (Simon and Schuster, New York, 1992).

_____, *The UFO Controversy in America* (Signet, New York, 1976).

_____, ed., *UFOs and Abductions: Challenging the Borders of Knowledge*

(University Press of Kansas, Lawrence, Kansas, 2000).

Jessup, M.K., *UFO and the Bible* (Citadel Press, New York, 1956).

Johnson, Phillip E., *Darwin on Trial* (Intervarsity Press, Downers Grove, IL, 1993).

Jung, C.G., *Flying Saucers: A Modern Myth of Things Seen in the Skies*, trans. R.F.C. Hull (MJF
Books, New York, 1978).

Kaku, Michio, *Parallel Worlds: A Journey through Creation, Higher Dimensions, and the Future of the Cosmos* (Anchor Books, New York, 2005).

Kean, Leslie, *UFOs: Generals, Pilots and Government Officials Go on the Record* (Harmony Books, New York, 2010).

Keel, John A., *The Mothman Prophecies* (Signet, New York, 1976).

Kelleher, Colom A., and Knapp, George, *Hunt for the Skinwalker* (Paraview Pocket, New York, 2005).

Keyhoe, Donald E., *Aliens from Space* (Signet, New York, 1974).

_____, *The Flying Saucer Conspiracy* (Holt, New York, 1955).

Kitel, Lynne D., *The Phoenix Lights* (Hampton Roads, Charlottesville, VA, 2000).

Lewels, Joe, *The God Hypothesis: Extraterrestrial Life and Its Implications for Science and Religion* (Wild Flower, Mill Sprint, NC, 1967).

Lorenzen, Coral and Jim, *Flying Saucer Occupants* (Signet, New York, 1967).

Mack, John E., *Abduction: Human Encounters with Aliens* (Charles Scribners, New York, 1984).

_____, *Passport to the Cosmos* (Crown Publishers, New York, 1999).

MacLaine, Shirley, *Out on a Limb* (Bantam, New York, 1983).

BIBLICAL UFO REVELATIONS

Maruyama, Margoroh, and Harkins, Arthur, *Cultures Beyond the Earth* (Vintage, New York, 1975).

McCampbell, James M., Ufology: New Insights from Science and Common Sense (Jaymac Company, Belmont, CA., 1973).

Michel, Aime, *The Truth About Flying Saucers* (Pyramid, New York, 1967).

Missler, Chuck, and Eastman, Mark, *Alien Encounters: The Secret Behind the UFO Phenomenon*
(Koinonia House, Idaho, 1997)

Moody, Raymond A., *Life after Life* (Bantam, New York, 1976).

Moyer, Ernest P., *The Day of Celestial Visitation* (Exposition Press, Hicksville, New York, 1970).

Murchland, Bernard, ed., *The Meaning of the Death of God* (Random House, New York, 1967).
Peters, Ted, *UFOs: God's Chariots?* (John Knox, Atlanta, 1977).

Rael, Claude Vorilhon, *The Message Given to me By the Extraterrestrials* (AOM Corporation, Tokyo, 1986).

Randles, Jenny, *The UFO Conspiracy: The First Forty Years* (Javelin, London and New York, 1987).

_____, *UFO Retrievals: The Recovery of Alien Spacecraft* (Blandford, London, 1995).

Ring, Kenneth, *The Omega Project: Near Death Experiences, UFO Encounters and Mind at Large* (William Morrow, New York, 1992).

Rogo, D. Scott, ed., *Alien Abductions: True Cases of UFO Kidnappings* (Signet, New York, 1980).

Ruppelt, Edward J., *The Report on Unidentified Flying Objects* (Ace, New York, 1956).

Sagan, Carl, *The Demon-Haunted World* (Ballantine, New York, 1996).

_____, and Page, Thornton, ed., *UFO's: A Scientific Debate* (Cornell University Press, Ithaca, NY, 1972).

Saunders, David R., and Harkins, R. Roger, *UFOs? Yes!: Where the Condon Committee Went Wrong* (Signet, New York, 1968).

Spong, John Shelby, *Why Christianity Must Change or Die* (HarperSanFrancisco, 1998).

Steiger, Brad, *Project Blue Book* (Ballantine, New York, 1976).

_____, *Revelation: The Divine Fire* (Prentice-Hall, Englewood Cliffs, NJ, 1973).

_____, and White, John, ed., *Other Worlds, Other Universes* (Double Day, New York, 1975).

Steinhauser, Gerhard R., *Jesus Christ: Heir to the Astronauts* (Pocket Books, New York, 1976).

Story, Ronald D., ed., *The Encyclopedia of UFOs* (Doubleday, New York, 1980).

_____, ed., *The Encyclopedia of Extraterrestrial Encounters* (New American Library, New York, 2001).

Strieber, Whitley, *Communion: A True Story* ((Beech Tree Books, New York, 1987)

_____, *Transformation: The Breakthrough* (Beech Tree Books, New York, 1988).

Thompson, Richard L., *Alien Identifies: Ancient Insights into Modern UFO Phenomena* (Govardhan Hill, Badger, CA, 1993).

Trench, Brinsley Le Poer, *Mysterious Visitors: The UFO Story* (Stein and Day, New York, 1971).

_____, *The Sky People* (Award Books, New York, 1970).

Vahanian, Gabriel, *The Death of God: The Culture of Our Post-Christian Era*

(George Braziller, New York, 1961).

Vallee, Jacques, *Anatomy of a Phenomenon: Unidentified Objects in Space—A Scientific Appraisal* (Henry Regnery, Chicago, 1965).

_____, *Passport to Magonia: From Folklore to Flying Saucers* (Henry Regnery, Chicago, 1969).

_____, *Dimensions: A Casebook of Alien Contact* (Contemporary Books, New York and Chicago, 1988).

_____, *The Invisible College* (E.P. Dutton, New York, 1975).

Velikovsky, Immanuel, *Worlds in Collision* (Laurel, New York, 1967).

Von Daniken, Erich, *Chariots of the Gods?* Trans. Michael Heron (Bantam, New York, 1971).

_____, *Gods from Outer Space*, Trans. Michael Heron (Bantam, New York, 1972).

Walton, Travis, *The Walton Experience* (Berkley, New York, 1978).

Warren, Larry and Robbins, Peter, *Left at East Gate* (Marlowe, New York, 1997).

Weldon, John with Levitt, Zola, *UFOs: What on Earth is Happening?* (Bantam, New York, 1976).

Wilson, Clifford, *Crash Go the Chariots* (Lancer, New York, 1972).

_____, and Weldon, John, *Close Encounters: A Better Explanation* (Master Books, San Diego, CA, 1978).

_____, *The Alien Agenda* (Signet, New York, 1988).

Wolf, Fred Alan, *Parallel Universes: The Search for Other Worlds* (Touchstone, New York, 1988).

BIBLICAL UFO REVELATIONS

THE GOD HYPOTHESIS REVISITED
MUFON UFO Journal
October 1988, p. 10-13
Dr. Barry H. Downing
(Published on line at Strong Delusion)

At the end of my article, "UFOs and Religion: The French Connection," in the June issue of the *Journal*, I asked the question: "Could UFOs be a manifestation of the God of the Universe? At this point it would only be a hypothesis, of course." In this article I will explore why we need the God hypothesis in our current UFO context.

As a Presbyterian Pastor I get asked to perform many wedding ceremonies. I occasionally get a call from a couple who obviously has never darkened the door of a church in their lives—but they want to get married in a church.

They really don't care what kind of God I believe in, or what my theology is, as long as I "do the job."

After the wedding ceremony is over, they will never darken the door of a church again (at least while alive.)

For over fifteen years I have been a theological and religious consultant to MUFON, and it has been a task I have enjoyed. My task has been seen by most as of marginal importance. After all, MUFON is an independent organization devoted to the scientific study of UFOs, it is not a religious organization. The UFO subject has been seen by most MUFON members to be an essentially scientific animal with a few religious warts.

My job has been to explain the religious warts, if I could. If I couldn't it wouldn't matter much, because the apparently religious warts would probably turn out to be scientific in the end anyway.

In recent times, the religious wart has grown. A few MUFON readers may begin to wonder more carefully what kind of a theological consultant the *MUFON UFO Journal* has. Is one enough? Do we need more than one brand? Do we really want this guy in charge of the UFO-religion marriage? I leave it to the MUFON board of directors to ponder these questions, while I try to the best of my ability to describe how the religious UFO wart looks to me.

In his introduction to the June 1988 issue of the *Journal*, editor Dennis Stacy says, "Science and technology, religion and magic, would seem to be separate pigeonholes and never the twain shall meet." But in the June issue they do meet. Stacy says, "We're not aiming to make converts here to any particular cause, but rather to referee what otherwise might be considered an unwieldy contest between opponents who don't usually square off in the same ring."

Stacy's disclaimer of "not aiming to make converts" is one hint of how religion makes the study of UFOs even more uncomfortable than it already is. Few readers of the *Journal* would want it to become an advocate for a Roman Catholic, or Methodist, or Presbyterian, or Hindu, or Jewish, or Islamic view of UFOs, whatever that might be.

I would say that the *Journal* would do well to imitate the United States Constitution in its policy on religion: make no laws regarding the establishment of religion, nor prohibiting the free exercise thereof.

That is to say, no one religious view should be the dominant or "established" view of the *Journal*, but at the same time I would not want to see the *Journal* exclude discussion of the religious issues in regard to UFOs from its pages.

STRANGE BEDFELLOWS

The fact that UFOs are now more openly admitted to have a religious dimension is due in a sense to the growing confidence among MUFON members that UFOs are a legitimate scientific problem. This may seem like a strange observation.

But in the early years of UFO studies, those who took the UFO phenomenon seriously had to contend with the view of scientists like Cornell's Dr. Carl Sagan and the late Harvard astronomer Dr. Donald Menzel, who argued that UFOs were not really a scientific problem, they were some form of modern religious myth.

These arguments advanced by scientists, together with the "lunatic fringe" of ufology, the contactees who went around giving us messages from the "space brothers," made those who took UFOs seriously from a scientific point of view want to keep religion as far from the UFO debate as possible.

But with the developing data base of UFO reports, the excellent scientific work of Dr. J. Allen Hynek, and Dr. Jacques Vallee among others, together with mounting evidence of a world-wide lie by governments to deny the existence of UFOs (see Fawcett and Greenwood, *Clear Intent*, Randles, *The UFO Conspiracy*, Good, *Above Top Secret*), UFO researchers now have the confidence to believe that UFOs are a real scientific animal, and perhaps we ought to look more closely at the religious warts on this animal—they may be an important clue in solving the scientific puzzle.

From my point of view, this is both good news and bad news. The good news is that my warts are now going to get more serious attention. The bad news is, the wart is bigger than I wish it were.

UFOs, of course, are still not seen as a "religious problem" by most UFO writers, though there are those who already worry about the possibility. Thus Jerome Clark, in his article "Ufologists and the Extraterrestrial Hypothesis," is critical of Jenny Randles for admitting that she is interested in UFOs in part because she hopes UFOs "will change the world and maybe help us get out of the mess we are in."

Clark says, "To the overwhelming majority of ufologists, the investigation of the UFO phenomenon is not anything remotely like a religious pursuit."

I would not want to argue with Clark about what may be the motives of those studying UFOs. What I would want to say to Clark, however, is that UFOs have a huge religious dimension, and it is important that we be allowed to take this dimension out of the closet. I would also say that if Jenny Randles want to admit in public that she has a kind of messianic hope in regard to UFOs, she ought to be able to admit this without ridicule.

Clark's closing paragraph is interesting. He argues that many people are afraid of dealing with "CE3s, abductions and the ETH" because they are seeking "a comfortable, non-threatening alternative which reassures them that humans beings and their gods are still the lords of this earth."

RELIGIOUS DIMENSIONS

I hope Mr. Clark recognizes the religious dimensions of this closing statement. Our emerging UFO scenario, including the abduction phenomenon, is that the UFO reality seems to be acting in a god-like way toward humans. That is, UFO beings can abduct humans, can control our minds, may take sperm samples from us, impregnate women, and apparently carry out breeding experiments with us. In other words, as Jacques Valle has argued in *Dimensions*, UFOs are a control system. They carry on many of the functions the Judeo-Christian tradition used to ascribe to God.

Our culture as a whole has little idea that many in the UFO field now believe UFOs are acting in a god-like way in regard to planet earth. The government lie about UFOs has kept the media, and therefore our religious institutions, from carrying on the religious debate that the UFO concept demands.

Let us make no mistake about how revolutionary an idea this will be to our religious institutions (and by our, I mean the Judeo-Christian tradition, the main religion of Western culture and of America).

BIBLICAL UFO REVELATIONS

When Copernicus and Galileo suggested that the sun, not the earth, was the center of our solar system, the idea was seen as a huge threat to the Roman Catholic faith. Yet, when we think about the basis of the Biblical religion, the location of the sun in the sky is really a minor issue.

Likewise, Fundamentalist Protestantism is still battling Darwin's theory of evolution. Darwin does not fit well with a literal reading of Genesis. Roman Catholics and liberal Protestants have been willing to read Genesis in a more metaphorical way, and so Darwin did not cause a great crisis for these "brands" of western religion.

But the emerging concept of UFOs as the controlling force directing life on earth, as Vallee argues in *Dimensions*, a force developing our religious belief systems, is a concept which cuts right to the core of Western religious faith. If Copernicus and Darwin could register a seven on the religious Richter Scale, I cannot imagine what numbers we need to read the scale of religious revolution that will take place when the rest of the world catches up with current UFO studies.

On behalf of the Fund for UFO Research, Dr. Thomas Bullard compiled a study of over 400 pages entitled, *Comparative Analysis of UFO Abduction Reports.* Bullard argues that the typical abduction victim goes through a sequence of eight stages: 1) Capture, 2) Examination, 3) Conference, 4) Tour, 5) Otherworldly Journey , 6) Theophany, 7) Return, 8) Aftermath.

He defines number 6, Theophany, as follows: "The witness has a religious experience or receives a message from a divine being."

One of the most famous theophanies in UFO literature is the story of Betty Andreasson, reported by Raymond Fowler in *The Andreasson Affair,* and *The Andreasson Affair: Phase II.* In this abduction report Betty Andreasson confronts a being who seems to speak with the authority of God.

How are we to interpret this aspect of the UFO phenomenon? Here are some possibilities: 1) We can put forth the hypothesis that all UFO abduction reports are mysterious psychological experiences, and the theophany in these reports is simply one aspect of the whole psychological process. 2) We can suppose that much of the UFO abduction report is real, but the theophany aspect of the reports is a kind of natural human response elicited by being in the presence of this frightful being (see Whitley Strieber's reaction in *Communion*). 3) We can suppose that all of the abduction experience is real, and that the theophany is caused deliberately by the UFO beings, whoever they are, but their motive in presenting us with this theophany is deceptive: They want to give us the appearance of being God, but they are not God. This is essentially R.L. Dione's argument in *God Drives a Flying Saucer.* More serious UFO researchers, like John Keel and Jacques Vallee, are fearful that UFOs are influencing our religious beliefs for motives we would not like if we understood them. 4) We can suppose that UFOs are, or represent, the ultimate force behind the universe. UFOs are God, or are of God. This is the God hypothesis. This says the reason that theophanies occur in UFO abduction cases is because God is behind the abductions.

This may be an unpleasant hypothesis. There may be insufficient evidence in favor of this hypothesis at present time for it to be given much weight. But for the time being, that is beside the point.

My main argument for now is that the God hypothesis ought to be seen as a legitimate scientific hypothesis. We have reached the point in UFO research where it should be considered along with the ETI theory, and the psychological theory, which are the main theories now under consideration.

There is no logical reason why God might not be the ultimate cause of UFO events. I realize that this is an unpleasant thought to scientists with good memories. Not long ago, the idea of God was used to explain why the sun moved across the sky and why rain fell. Do we not have a right to suppose that when the real truth about UFOs is known, that once again we will find "God" is an unnecessary part of the explanation? We may suppose this, but we do not know if it is true at this point.

GOD CONCEPTS

There are many difficulties with the God hypothesis, of course. The first problem is that when we use the term God, we are thinking in Western culture of the God of Judeo-Christian tradition. Islam is also an off-shoot of this tradition.

Hinduism does not have a comparable concept of God, nor does Buddhism, which grew out of Hinduism. Foster Morrison, in his article, "UFOs—Science and Technology in the Service of Magic," in the June issue of the *Journal*, says that "The universe of UFOs is animistic. Exotic celestial beings travel from world to world. Life is everywhere and more diverse than the Hindu pantheon."

Morrison further argues that "The Gods of the messianic faiths are similarly removed from human understanding" in our scientific culture, in which science is our real religion, religion having the function of justifying "the prevailing political and social system."

Thus from Morrison's point of view, Western religion, which is messianic, is of little use either in our current scientific culture, or in understanding UFOs.

Morrison has arrived at this conclusion in part because he has not traced the God of Western culture back to its two roots. Our idea of God is partly formed by the Greek philosophy of Plato and Aristotle, who saw God not so much as a person as prime mover, or as being itself.

This idea of God was blended by theologians like Aquinas with biblical theology, the theology of a God who made man in his own image, a biblical tradition in which angels flew down from the sky, met with humans, intervened with "chosen people" like Moses and Jesus, Messiahs who save us from Egypt or death.

Thus Western religion, messianic religion, is by no means by-passed by our emerging UFO stories. Part of Jerome Clark's fear is that some kind of new messianic faith will emerge from UFO studies. Jenny Randles hoping that UFOs will "help us get out of the mess we are in" may be only the tip of the iceberg.

Whitley Strieber is clearly fearful of the messianic dimensions of the UFO story. In his Forword to Vallee's *Dimensions*, Strieber says, "The only thing now needed to make the UFO myth a new religion of remarkable scope and force is a single undeniable sighting. Such a sighting need last only a few minutes—just long enough to be thoroughly documented. It will at once invest the extraterrestrials channels, the 'space brothers' believers, and the UFO cultists with the appearance of revealed truth." Vallee shares Strieber's fear that we humans will be too quick to believe.

I would not deny that there is huge potential for fanaticism in the UFO concept. Furthermore, if Strieber's "one undeniable sighting" were to occur, Christian fundamentalists would undoubtedly assume that the Second Coming of Christ is here. John Weldon and Zola Levitt's *UFOs: What on Earth is Happening?* Has already led the way in that direction.

Let us suppose that the governments of the world are not as dumb as we in the UFO field have been inclined to think. Jerome Clark, Jacques Vallee and Whitley Strieber all see tremendous danger in linking UFOs and religion. They see a frightening potential for social disaster.

That is undoubtedly one of the main reasons our government has lied to us about UFOs. Like Clark, Vallee and Strieber, they fear social and religious disaster if UFO information is released.

At the same time, Foster Morrison has argued rightly, "The only identifiable thing the UFO phenomenon is doing is discrediting the scientific and political establishments."

I have argued that the UFO phenomenon, through the "pillar of cloud and fire" during the Exodus, in the same way discredited the scientific and political establishment of Pharaoh's Egypt, and likewise the resurrection of Jesus discredited the Roman political and Jewish religious establishment of his time.

I believe that the humbling of the established powers that UFOs are now bringing about has occurred before. And although Jenny Randles may not have a lot of evidence to support her hope that UFOs may "help us get out of the mess we are in," at the same time what are we to make of stories like those reported by Fawcett and Greenwood in *Clear Intent*, in which UFOs hover over our nuclear silos, and reprogram the computers in the warheads? Is it not possible that UFOs have used their power to cause the political and scientific powers of the world to rethink their nuclear strategy? If so, is this messianic activity God-like activity?

I think we need the God hypothesis. At the very least, many reports indicate that UFOs are behaving in a God-like way toward life on planet earth.

Speaking as a Christian, I have to say that UFOs create a huge problem for my theology if they are not God-directed. UFOs are reported in the Bible that are very similar to modern UFOs. Furthermore, modern UFOs, and their occupants, are reported to control human minds, and human speech (in the manner of Pentecost, Acts, chapter 2), they can control human reproduction, and therefore all biological development; reports indicate that they can distort time as well as space. They have the power to heal human diseases, to overpower human technology, and to confound the political and scientific powers of the world. Jacques Vallee has argued in *Dimensions* that the main purpose of UFOs is to control our religious belief systems. The God of the Bible is known by his ability to do all these things. I know nothing in my theological training that gives me the ability to distinguish between the world of God, and the world of the UFO reality. If UFOs are not of God, where is my God, and how am I to know Him?

We need the God hypothesis because I don't think the governments of the world can keep the UFO lie going forever. It would be better for all of us if the God hypothesis could be discussed *before* world governments release their UFO information. This way the discussion could occur in a more rational atmosphere, rather than in the face of the fear that those like Whitley Strieber obviously felt so deeply.

At this point we need to raise the God hypothesis in a scientific way. I say in a scientific way because the religious community is too fearful to explore this concept in even a preliminary fashion at this point. But the UFO community, as a scientific brotherhood, can ask the theoretical question: If there is a God in the universe, and if this God were to be the cause of the UFO phenomenon, how would we know it? This question is only a slight extension of the basic question we are all asking: Who are these guys, and what do they want?

Barry H. Downing

October 1988

BIBLICAL UFO REVELATIONS

UFOS, THE BIBLE AND TARGETED INTERVENTION
January 2010
Dr. Barry H. Downing
Published on line at Strong Delusion

INTRODUCTION

In October 2009 I published an article on the Strong Delusion web site entitled "Hermeneutical Rape." I wrote the article as an answer to some of my critics such as Michael Heiser, Gary Bates and Guy Malone. The title of the article was taken from a criticism of my work made by Heiser, who suggested my UFO theology involves hermeneutical rape of the biblical text. My basic question, asked more than 40 years ago in my book, *The Bible and Flying Saucers*, is this: is it possible that what we now call UFOs carry the angels of God? In this context, the biblical question would be: was the pillar of cloud and fire, the UFO of the Exodus, a form of space transportation for the angels?

Heiser began blogging a response to my article in October, and finally finished sometime in December of 2009. I have waited until he finished to make a response to his blogs, five in number that contained critical content. When I quote Heiser in this response, I will refer to Blog 1, 2, 3, 4, or 5 as a way to make reference.

I have framed my response under three major headings: I. Exodus and Biblical Angelology. Heiser has been critical of my treatment of the Exodus material, and I will try to clarify my interpretation of that material in light of the larger biblical concept of angelology. II. Faith, Science and Epistemology. Heiser and I are closer in our method of biblical interpretation than might at first glance be obvious, but there are areas of difference that need to be explored. These issues relate to the tension between faith and what Heiser calls "hard science, " the general area of epistemology. He sees my arguments as "nonsense," or lacking "coherence." (Blog 1)The issue here is: is the nonsense my fault, or Heiser's? Many Newtonian scientists thought Einstein's theory of relativity was "nonsense" when they first heard of it. Nonsense maybe, but it turned out to be true. III. Targeted Intervention as a Ruling Strategy. Heiser is right in wondering if there is any larger pattern, any coherence, that would make sense of the biblical stories in our faith tradition, and modern political and religious powers as they relate to the UFO issue. I will present the concept of "targeted intervention" as a paradigm for interpreting the current UFO situation in light of the Bible.

1. EXODUS AND BIBLICAL ANGELOLOGY

In my article I had suggested that the pillar of cloud, the Exodus UFO, met Moses at the burning bush, and orchestrated the plagues in Egypt, including Passover.

Michael Heiser says, "Uh, check the text, Barry—there is no reference to a pillar of cloud at the burning bush (Exodus 3 for all you who want to read it.) THIS is precisely why your hermeneutic and eisegesis cannot be trusted. You simply insert details into the text that favor what you're saying, assuming people won't look (And you've been right there to a large extent). Ridiculous." "Guess what? No pillar of cloud ever mentioned with the plagues or Passover either! Who'da thunk that?!" (Blog 5)

I realize the pillar of cloud and fire is not mentioned at the burning bush, nor in connection with the plagues. But this is why we do hermeneutics. Hermeneutics is not just reading a chapter in the Bible, it is looking at the chapter in light of the Bible as a whole. I did not go through detailed analysis in my article, "Hermeneutical Rape," because I hoped that those who criticized my work would read the details of this analysis in my book, Chapter 3. But for those who have not read my book, I will do a review here.

The pillar of cloud and of fire is central to the Exodus, it is understood to be the power of God that takes over before the parting of the Red Sea, and continues on, dropping the manna to feed Israel daily, landing on Mt. Sinai to deliver the commandments to Moses, and leading the way to the Promised Land. Here is a most basic question: what was the pillar of cloud and fire? To the biblical writers, it was a sign of the presence of God. In fact, sometimes, it was referred to as "My presence." (Ex 33:14; all biblical references will be to the Revised Standard Version, RSV, unless otherwise noted.) It was also called "the Lord," and "the angel of God," and is sometimes referred to as "the Lord in the pillar of cloud and of fire." (Ex. 14:19-30) Did some of the Jewish leaders at that time believe either that the pillar of cloud and fire was God, or that God was contained in it? It seems clear they did. In the burning bush sequence, the text says "Moses hid his face because he was afraid to look at God." (Ex. 3:6) [Israel was conditioned to the idolatry of Egypt, and soon created a molten calf at Sinai, a god they could see. (Ex. 32:1-6)] When Israel gets to Mt. Sinai, we find the text saying, "And Moses went up to God." (Ex. 19:3) The book of Deuteronomy finishes its praise of Moses by saying "And there has not arisen a prophet since in Israel like Moses, whom the Lord knew face to face." (Deut. 34:10) Are we to believe that God is some kind of physical reality that only special humans like Moses can see? Was the pillar of cloud and fire in some sense God? Was the burning bush God?

Heiser says, "Christianity and Judaism never claim that God is part of the created world. His existence is therefore not in the realm of scientific inquiry." (Blog 1) I agree with this statement by Heiser, but I do not think the invisibility and non-physicality of God is a clear doctrine in the book of Exodus; a distinction between God and God's angels would develop later. The concept of the invisibility of God is a doctrine that evolved over a period of time. (The word angel appears only 6 times in the book of Exodus, but over 50 times in the book of Revelation.)The pillar of cloud and fire is portrayed as something everyone saw, something apparently as physical and scientific as our created world. But the pillar of cloud had divine authority.

It is clear that Heiser believes that by claiming the pillar of cloud is a UFO, that I follow R.L. Dione who wrote the book *God Drives a Flying Saucer*. I do not believe God drives a flying saucer, but I believe his angels may. Heiser says that "your reading of this passage [the pillar of cloud at the Red Sea] has the God of Israel in a space craft, meaning that he needs technology to travel. What happened to omnipresence? Omnipotence? The idea that Jesus expressed with complete clarity, that God 'is a spirit' (John 4:24). You've just made God subject to the laws of nature, which means he's a created being, which means he isn't God by ANY biblical definition. In short, you don't have much of a theology." (Blog 5) Like most Protestant Christians, Heiser does not have a functioning angelology. He may say he believes in angels, but he does not give them anything to do. Instead, many Protestants hold an almost unconscious view of God as a kind of supernatural magic bullet who can do anything any place. But then who needs angels? But God does use angels, perhaps because it pleases him, and uses humans for the same reason. Heiser claims that God is not physical, and I agree, but Heiser fails to notice that often the angels are very physical, they even eat with Abraham, as the resurrected Jesus ate with his disciples.

How do we claim the Exodus UFO had divine authority, but was not God? By claiming that the pillar of cloud either was, or carried, the angels of God, but was not God in God's essence, but rather God in mediated form. Of course the text itself does refer to the Exodus UFO as an angel, but there is not a fully developed angelology in Exodus. The development of biblical angelology was a gradual process. The angelology of Zechariah, the next to last book in my Old Testament, has some of the flavor of the angelology of the book of Revelation. Angelology expanded during the intertestamental period, sometimes in ways the church could not affirm. In the Apocryphal book of Tobit, the angel Raphael seems to be a blend of a traveling companion and a match maker straight out of "Fiddler on the Roof." (Enoch is seen as a Merkabah text, influenced by the "throne-chariot" tradition of Ezekiel.) By the time we get to the New Testament, this is understood: "No one has ever seen God; the only Son, who is in the bosom of the Father, he has made him known." (Jn. 1:18) Jesus is the ultimate mediator, the Word made flesh, "the image of the invisible God." (Col 1:15) But if it is true that no one has ever seen God, then what of all those passages in Exodus where God seems to be visible, and in charge? By the New Testament era, it was understood that all of the Exodus was brought about by the angels of God. This is clearly illustrated in Stephen's speech in Acts chapter 7. Stephen gives what is certainly understood by the high priest and all who heard it to be "orthodox Jewish belief" at that time, or at least orthodox Pharisee theology. Stephen says that an angel of God contacted Moses at the burning bush (7:30), and goes on to say "This Moses whom they refused, saying, 'Who made you a ruler and judge?' God sent as both ruler and deliverer by the hand of the angel that appeared to him in the bush. He led them out, having performed wonders and signs in Egypt, and at the Red Sea, and in the wilderness for forty years. This is the Moses who said to the Israelites, 'God will raise up for you a prophet from your brethren as he raised me up.' This is he who was in the congregation in the wilderness with the angel who spoke to him at Mount Sinai, and with our fathers; and he received living oracles to give to us." (7:35-38) At the end, Stephen condemns his listeners for killing the "Righteous One," "you who received the law as delivered by angels and did not keep it." (7:53)

We should note that there were no complaints about Stephen's review of Jewish history. The rage came when he proclaimed that they had killed Jesus, the "Righteous One." I take this to mean that at least one segment of Judaism at this time had a strong angelology, and it was by this means that the "otherness" of God was maintained, while at the same time saying that the Jews were indeed chosen people, singled out for a special revelation through the angels of God. And since the book of Acts is included in the New Testament canon, I take it as Christian orthodox truth that the whole of the Exodus was carried out "by the hand of the angel," meaning the power of God was exercised through angelic beings, just as the power of God is exercised through humans when we preach the gospel (Mt. 28:19-20). If we read the book of Exodus in isolation from the New Testament, as Heiser does, then it appears that the essence of God was present at or in the burning bush, at or in the pillar of cloud and fire. But by New Testament times, angelology separated visible angelic signs of God from the essence of God's uncreated invisibility. As New Testament scholar G.H.C. Macgregor says, "The angel as a mediator is a later tradition added to the original account, in which Yahweh himself gives the laws to Moses." (*Interpreter's Bible*, Vol. 9, p. 100)

Biblical writers knew from Genesis that the angels of God appeared to Abraham and Lot in human form. This led to the warning "Do not neglect to show hospitality to strangers, for thereby some have entertained angels unawares." (Heb. 13:2) Do angels have wings? Not the ones that are going to knock on our doors and catch us "unaware." The angel that rolled back the stone in front of the tomb of Jesus and sat on it "descended from heaven." (Mt. 28:2) Angels come from the sky, and generally do not have wings. But Christian artists added wings to angels to explain how they got from earth to heaven. Whatever the pillar of cloud and fire is, or was, it relates to the angelic order, and in some sense, the pillar of cloud relates to all of the Exodus—burning bush, plagues, Passover, parting of the Red Sea, manna, Sinai Revelation, and finally Promised Land. Stephen says that the same power that met Moses at the bush, this same angel, performed wonders and signs in Egypt, as well as at the Red Sea, and in the wilderness journey.

The Apostle Paul briefly noted this view of the work of the angels at Mt. Sinai when he says, "Why then the law? It was added because of transgressions, till the offspring should come to whom the promise had been made; and it was ordained by angels through an intermediary. Now an intermediary implies more than one; but God is one." (Gal. 3:19,20) Authors of scripture understood that there was a danger that we might worship angels, and John Calvin was concerned not to give power to the angels that only rightly belonged to God and Christ, but Calvin affirmed "For we must so understand, however much it may be twisted, what Stephen and Paul say, that the law was given by the hand of the angels." (*Institutes of the Christian Religion*, translated by Ford Lewis Battles, Book I, XIV, 9.)

How did the biblical doctrine of angels develop? Even in the Hebrew testament there was anxiety about saying that Moses saw God. There is a very interesting passage in Exodus where Moses asks to see the face of God, and God denies the request, hiding Moses in a rock, while allowing Moses to see God's back side. (Ex 33:17-23) New Testament angelology represents a thousand years of interpretation since the time of Moses. During the time of Jesus, the Pharisees believed in angels, the Sadducees did not. (Acts 23:6-8) Paul was a Pharisee, and thus believed in angels, and was in fact a witness to the speech of Stephen before Saul/Paul was converted (Acts 7:58; 8:1) Also Paul reported that he was carried off to the "third heaven," (2 Cor. 12:1-4), thus giving Paul a special view of the angelic world. In his teaching Jesus had connected the world of the angels and the world of the resurrection. Consequently, when Jesus preached about the kingdom of heaven, this angelic world was understood to have been directly involved in the events of "special revelation" that are part of the Jewish and Christian tradition.

The angels brought about all of the Exodus under God's command. Thus we have the right to suppose that the pillar of cloud and fire is in some sense connected to all of the Exodus as part of the angelic reality. Consequently we have a right to raise this question: Does the pillar of cloud and fire provide extra-terrestrial transportation for the angels? The Second Coming of Christ is expected to be brought about by the angels coming on the clouds of heaven, as if the "clouds" are part of their transportation system. (Mt. 24:30) And if the "clouds" are some kind of transportation system for the angels, is this system technological? How would we know if the angels use a technological system of transportation? The biblical people had no understanding of technology as we know it. [Heiser would I think agree. He says "The Bible never claims to be a science book." (Blog 3)] And that leaves us with our current mystery: if modern UFOs are an advanced technology, how do we know they are **not** the angels of God? Putting it in a more positive form: on the basis of my study of modern UFOs, they seem to have more than enough power to do all the things reported in the Exodus. Heiser would say this is not yet "proven by hard science." (Blog 4) We will return to the issue of "hard science" in Part II of my article.

Interpreting the Burning Bush in Light of the Pillar of Cloud and Fire

Having established that the orthodox New Testament view of the Exodus is that it was the work of the angels of God, from beginning to end, let us look at the burning bush text in Exodus chapter 3.

Moses is caring for his sheep in the wilderness when we read the following. "And the angel of the Lord appeared to him in a flame of fire out of the midst of a bush; and he looked, and lo, the bush was burning, yet it was not consumed. And Moses said, 'I will turn aside and see this great sight, why the bush is not burnt.' When the Lord saw that he turned aside to see, God called to him out of the bush, 'Moses, Moses!'" (Ex. 3:2-4)

If we approach the Exodus story as a unified angelic event, then we have a right to wonder about the connection between the pillar of cloud, called the angel of God, at the Red Sea, and the angel of God at the burning bush. Might this not be the same angel? Notice that at the Red Sea, the angel of God is in voice communication with Moses (Ex. 14:26 etc). This voice in some sense comes "from above."

But at the burning bush, the voice comes from ground level. Are we to suppose that the pillar of cloud, which seems able to fly anywhere, could not land on the ground? And what if it were to land in a thicket, or a clump of bushes? (This is one possible translation of the Hebrew word for bush. And this would seem to explain the need to use the words "out of the midst of." Some bright light or fire might have been glowing in the middle of a thicket.) The pillar of cloud was also a glowing object. If it were to land in a thicket, would it light up the leaves and branches of the bushes? When modern UFOs land in a woods, they often light up the trees around them, sometimes leaving an "after glow." Exodus chapter three does not say the pillar of cloud and fire was present, this is true. But hermeneutics is the process of looking at the larger biblical context. I do not believe we can say with full assurance, "the pillar of cloud and fire was not on the ground, in a thicket, causing the thicket to appear to be on fire to Moses, but not really on fire, which is why the bush did not burn up." If the pillar of cloud and fire were to land in a clump of bushes, its basic shape would be disguised by the bushes, but its glow would cause the bushes to light up, but not burn up. I do not believe this is absurd, or irresponsible, biblical exegesis. And I believe New Testament angelology favors moving in this direction.

What is somewhat unusual about the burning bush story is that the voice of the angel comes from ground level, rather than from some light in the sky. When Isaiah hears his call from God, the Lord was "sitting on a throne high and lifted up." (Is. 6:1) The voice of angels to the shepherds at the birth of Jesus come from above, from a glowing light. (Luke 2:9) At the baptism of Jesus, the "Spirit" flew down from the sky, and the divine voice was heard coming from above, from heaven. (Mt. 3:17) [I have dealt with the baptism sequence in detail in chapter 4 of my book, *The Bible and Flying Saucers*.] Likewise a divine voice came from the "bright cloud" at the Transfiguration of Jesus. (Mt. 17:5) The voice of Jesus came to Saul/Paul on the Damascus Road from a bright light in the sky . (Acts 9:4-6; 22:7,8; 26:14-18) There are exceptions about voice contact coming from the sky. When the young boy Samuel hears the voice of God, it seems to be disembodied, and comes from something like ground level. (1 Sam. 3:1-14) But it would seem to be consistent with much of biblical "voice revelation" to suggest an extraterrestrial vehicle helped provide the source of the voice at the burning bush, a source that could fly, like the pillar of cloud, or land on the ground in "the midst of a thicket." I believe this argument is consistent with New Testament angelology; modern UFOs raise technological questions that might relate to the burning bush story, questions that the biblical culture with its lack of scientific knowledge could not address.

The Pillar of Cloud and the Parting of the Red Sea

The story of the parting of the Red Sea begins by saying it did not have to happen. God could have avoided the Red Sea, but decided to lead the way to the Red Sea deliberately. (Ex. 13:17-18) Then the "pillar of cloud and fire" is introduced and described, saying that it "did not depart from before the people." (Ex. 13:22) The Exodus UFO was a constant presence, which we still sing about in hymns such as "Guide Me O Thou Great Jehovah." When Israel arrived at the Red Sea (biblical scholars do not really know for sure what body of water), we find the following narrative, which I have no desire to hide from anyone.

"Then the angel of God who went before the host of Israel moved and went behind them; and the pillar of cloud moved from before them, and stood behind them, coming between the host of Egypt and the host of Israel. And there was the cloud and the darkness; and the night passed without one coming near the other all night.

Then Moses stretched out his hand over the sea; and the Lord drove the sea back by a strong east wind all night, and made the sea dry land, and the waters were divided. And the people of Israel went into the midst of the sea on dry ground, the waters being a wall to them on their right hand and on their left. The Egyptians pursued, and went in after them into the midst of the sea, all Pharaoh's horses, his chariots, and his horsemen. And in the morning watch the Lord in the pillar of fire and of cloud looked down upon the host of the Egyptians, and discomfited the host of the Egyptians, [clogging] their chariot wheels so that they drove heavily; and the Egyptians said, 'Let us flee from before Israel; for the Lord fights for them against the Egyptians.'

Then the Lord said to Moses, 'Stretch out your hand over the sea, that the water may come back upon the Egyptians, upon their horsemen.' So Moses stretched forth his hand over the sea, and the sea returned to its wonted flow when the morning appeared; and the Egyptians fled into it, and the Lord routed the Egyptians in the midst of the sea. The waters returned and covered the chariots and the horsemen and all the host of Pharaoh that had followed them into the sea; not so much as one of them remained. But the people of Israel walked on dry ground through the sea, the waters being a wall to them on their right hand and on their left." (Ex. 14:19-29)

There has never been a known explanation for the pillar of cloud and fire. Some have given natural explanations, such as that it might have been the shared memory of a volcano. It is sometimes called a "theophany," which only means it was a sign of God's presence. More commonly I suspect it is thought by conservative Christians to be something supernatural, but visible. Likewise the parting of the Red Sea is assumed to be supernatural, although no one can say what supernatural is, since it is beyond nature. But suppose that the angels of God use not the supernatural, but super technology, as one source of their power. And suppose the pillar of cloud and fire is some kind of space vehicle used by the angels. When we read the story this way, these are the possibilities.

BIBLICAL UFO REVELATIONS

The Exodus UFO leads Israel up to the Red Sea, and then moves behind Israel, keeping the Egyptian army away from Israel until it is dark. The fact that it was dark suggests on this night, whatever caused the UFO to glow in the dark was turned off.

During the night, "the Lord drove the sea back by a strong east wind all night, and made the sea dry land." Those who have supposed there was a "natural" explanation for the parting of the Red Sea try to imagine a powerful wind coming up at just the right time. Or if we approach this story with standard Christian thinking, we imagine the "Lord" as an invisible supernatural force who can do anything any time. Part the Red Sea, no problem! God can do anything.

But the text makes it clear that the Lord is present in the pillar of cloud. Therefore, the writers of the story understood that the "strong east wind" was somehow created by the pillar of cloud. The text does not tell us when the pillar of cloud moved from between the army of Israel and Egypt to a position right over the sea channel, but when we next find the Exodus UFO reported, it is above the sea channel, according to verse 24, "in the morning watch."

I believe the Exodus UFO moved to a position above the sea, and then used its propulsion system, some kind of power beam, to part the sea. I do not know what kind of power this is, UFO researchers do not know what kind of power makes modern UFOs fly. By and large, modern UFO propulsion systems seem almost silent. Whatever the system is, that is what I believe caused the "walls of water," one on the right, one on the left, an idea that seems impossible to our scientific minds. But it may not be impossible to those flying our modern UFOs.

One of the side effects of this propulsion beam would be that wind would blow out each open end of the channel. The Jews were going from West to East, they reported an East wind blowing "caused by the Lord" in the UFO. If the Jews had been on the Eastern shore, heading West, I suspect they would have reported that the Lord caused a strong West wind to blow all night. One further effect of this beam technology would be to dry out the sea bed. There has been speculation among UFO researchers that UFO propulsion systems have a microwave effect on the ground, often drying it out for a long period after a UFO has landed. What should be noted is that there was no wind reported during the crossing. What held the walls of water in place during the crossing? Or, if a strong wind were blowing in their face, why didn't this make crossing difficult, or impossible?

A similar question can be asked concerning beam technology. If some kind of power beam moved the water back, and dried out the sea bed, why didn't this power beam crush, or fry, the Jews when they crossed? A possible answer would be that the power beam could be phased out in the center, leaving two walls of power on each side to keep the water in place, while leaving the center of the channel power free for the Jewish crossover.

The textual evidence for this possibility comes next. The Egyptians pursued Israel into the open sea channel. "And in the morning watch the Lord in the pillar of fire and of cloud looked down upon the host of the Egyptians, and discomfited the host of the Egyptians, [clogging] their chariot wheels so that they drove heavily;" (Ex. 14:24-25a)

Most of us forget these verses in the text. Our minds go naturally to the next step, Moses raises his hands, and the walls of water fall in on the Egyptians. But we have this text to deal with first. The Jews have crossed safely, they think they are safe, except here come the Egyptian chariots. Has God saved them by this miracle of the parting of the Sea, only to let the Egyptians kill them anyway?

Something strange happens. The pillar of cloud is the focus of what happens next. The Lord in the pillar of cloud and fire "looked down upon the host of the Egyptians."

This is a strange image. When I look at someone, in a way, nothing has really happened. But the text says that the Lord, by this "look down," did damage to the Egyptians. The text does not say, "The Lord turned on the beam technology, and crushed the Egyptians." These were not technological people, they would not say that. But they knew that something—an invisible force, like a stunning glance—came down from above. What happened?

The phrase says the Lord's look down "discomfited the host of the Egyptians, [clogging] their chariot wheels so that they drove heavily." The "look down" defeated the Egyptians, stopped them in their tracks, by doing something to the chariot wheels, so that the chariots drove heavily. The horses could only move the chariots with great effort. The reader will notice that I have placed the word "clogging" in brackets. That is because the proper translation here is in dispute: there are three possible translations of what happened to the chariot wheels according to the RSV: clogging, binding, or removing (breaking).

Here is Michael Heiser's response to my analysis of the parting of the Red Sea. " These details are not in the text. I challenge you, Barry, to give us all the text—chapter and verses—where Egyptians were knocked flat off their horses by 'an invisible force" (it was by the water, and water isn't invisible), chariot wheels broken, horses paralyzed. Give it to us. Again you are deliberately duping readers here. NONE of this is in the exodus account of the account of the crossing. ZERO. This is inexcusable on your part. " And then later he says, "show me the RSV note (give me an edition, a copyright year, something) that says the wheels were affected by the cloud. I don't believe it exists." (Blog 5)

Here is as direct an answer as I can give. I have several editions of the RSV. The one I have used lists the Old Testament as having a copyright date of 1952,

BIBLICAL UFO REVELATIONS

New Testament 1946, and references 1959, published by Nelson. But all editions have the same footnote. The word in the text itself is "clogging," but there is a "q" after clogging, and the footnote reads as follows: "Or binding. Sam Gk Syr: Heb removing." At this point we have three possible words: clogging, binding, or removing (which I take to be breaking off the wheels.)

Heiser himself says further, ""My reason is that the Hebrew word behind the RSV English is a very common verb (swr—'to turn aside'; note that the LXX may have something different—it is where the "clogging" translation actually comes from). Doesn't seem too complicated to me. " Heiser then makes the case for mud being in the sea bed even though the text says several times that the sea bed was dry. "It doesn't mean there's no water in it like it's a desert. Humans can walk on ground that heavier object (sic)(like horses and chariots) cannot. Anyone who's had a bike or car stuck knows the wheels 'turn aside' in ways you don't want them, making for inoperative conditions. Pretty simple. A common word." (Blog 5)

Now we have four choices for translation of the key word: Heiser's—to turn aside, and three from the RSV—clogging, binding and removing. Heiser supposes that the RSV choice of clogging is based on the Septuagint (LXX) version. But my understanding of the RSV footnote is that the LXX version, along with the Samaritan Hebrew text, and the Syriac Version of the Old Testament, read "removing." I believe the word "clogging" is just something the RSV translators made up, because they could understand how the Lord's "look down" could either bind or remove the chariot wheels, and therefore joined Heiser in inventing mud for the wheels to get stuck in, or slide around in, if you prefer Heiser's "to turn aside" explanation. [Heiser complains that in suggesting the pillar of cloud and fire was a space craft, I make "the Israelites sound like idiots. Give them some credit." (Blog 5) But when Heiser is doing his exegesis, he says the Israelites do not know the difference between dry ground and mud. I say, give the Israelites some credit.]

[Nelson's *Complete Concordance* to the RSV indicates that Ex. 14:25 is the only place in the RSV where the word "clogging" is used. The New Revised Standard Version follows the RSV in using "clogging," but omits "binding" while retaining "removing" in the footnote. The King James version reads, "And took off their chariot wheels;" the Revised English Bible reads "He clogged their chariot wheels;" the footnote reads "clogged: so Samar; Heb. removed." One Jewish translation of the *Torah*, published in 1962, reads, "he locked the wheels of their chariots so they moved forward with difficulty." The possibility of "locked" is very instructive.]

My interpretation is this: the Lord's "look down" was some kind of power beam, which either broke the wheels off from the chariots, or else heated up the

148

metal in the axles so much that the metallic expansion caused the wheel hubs to lock, freeze up or bind on the axles. Iron and bronze would be used in making the axles, as well as the hubs, of the wheels. If some type of "beam technology" caused the metal in the axles, or hubs, to heat up, they would expand, and the wheels would fail to turn. They would bind or lock. If the Jews, witnessing the difficulty of the horses trying to pull chariots, saw that the wheels were to bind, or lock up, then they would indeed "drive heavily." On the other hand, if some type of beam technology "removed" the wheels, or broke them off, likewise the chariots would "drive heavily." If the wheels where broken off, then "removing" would be the correct translation. If the wheels locked up on the axle, then "binding" would be the correct translation. In any case, if the wheels either "bound" or were "removed," we do not need mud to explain the difficulty the chariots faced and that the Jews witnessed. The Bible says the sea bed was dry ground.

One of the best UFO books published in 2009 was *UFOs and the National Security State: The Cover-up Exposed. 1973-1991*, written by Richard M. Dolan. This is the second volume of a projected three volume work, following UFO history from 1941 to the present. Dolan is a trained historian, with a master's degree in history as well as a certificate in political theory from Oxford University. His book contains hundreds of UFO sightings from around the world, and Volumes One and Two are necessary reading for anyone who takes UFOs seriously. [See my review of Dolan's book in the December 2009 issue of the *MUFON UFO Journal*. Dolan's list of "Acknowledgements" is a page and a half long, and interestingly, right in the middle, we find this name: Michael Heiser, Ph.D.]

Dolan tells of a UFO case involving two brothers on February 14, 1974, in the state of Nevada. Dolan reports that the brothers were driving a U-haul truck, loaded with their parents' furniture, when they spotted a UFO following them, and then coming at them. "They described feeling as though they had 'been hit by a blast of wind or force field.' The engine lights went out, steering was gone, and— they claimed—the truck floated momentarily, came back down and coasted to a stop." After they stopped, a huge light came toward them. They experienced some kind of strange state for about twenty minutes before they flagged down a car and sought help, since their truck was damaged. "When a tow truck hauled it away, the rear wheels of the damaged truck fell off. Upon examination, it needed new tires, a new rear axle, new outside housing, and gears." (Dolan, op. cit., pp. 29, 30) My question is: if this story is true, what kind of damage might this alien technology do to chariots at the Red Sea? Michael Heiser would say "this is not scientific proof, it is only a story which we cannot check for reliability." I would agree. But we do not really have "scientific proof" that the Red Sea parted. It is a "faith decision" that Heiser and I share that the Red Sea parted, as the Bible describes.

BIBLICAL UFO REVELATIONS

When I raised the issue of UFO propulsion systems, and its relevance to the parting of the Red Sea, here is what Michael Heiser said. "Here's an even better question about the propulsion system, Barry. Since you associate fire (pillar of fire, cloud = smoke) with the UFO propulsion system, how is it that a combustion engine is capable of space travel? Huh? Can you introduce us to an astrophysicist who would affirm that combustion engines are capable of deep space travel? Give me a break."(Blog 5)

I have never said that UFOs operate by a combustion engine, or even like a rocket. I do not know anyone in MUFON who believes UFOs operate by any type of propulsion system that we now understand. In *The Bible and Flying Saucers*, published more than 40 years ago, I speculated, with those like Donald Keyhoe, that UFOs may have some type of anti-gravitational propulsion system. (For an exploration of possible answers concerning UFO propulsion technology, read the book by NASA scientist Paul R. Hill, *Unconventional Flying Objects: A Scientific Analysis*, 1995, especially chapter VII, "Direct Evidence of Force Field Propulsion.")

I have tried to present my case for believing that we need to explore the biblical doctrine of angels, and the Exodus story, in light of our current UFO situation. Michael Heiser believes the way in which I exegete the Bible is false, my work is "nonsense." Even if Heiser were to read the above material he may still believe my views are nonsense. How are we to understand that what is nonsense to Heiser seems plausible to me? It relates to how the issues of faith, science and epistemology relate in the way we do our reasoning. For instance, Heiser brings to the Red Sea story the assumption that the pillar of cloud is not a UFO, and therefore he does not expect any power to come down from above, and lock or break off the wheels of the chariots of the Egyptians. He therefore, like the RSV Bible translators, creates a little mud to "clog" the chariot wheels. But since I believe UFOs are real, and angelic, I look at the pillar of cloud as a UFO which may have some kind of "beam technology" that would produce the signs that the Jews reported. In other words, the previous assumptions Heiser and I bring to the text determine how we interpret the text. I do not think Heiser's "mud" explanation is absurd or nonsense. Mud made sense to the RSV translators. But I think it is wrong, and I think the text says it is wrong. There was no mud. This brings us to our next level of analysis.

II. FAITH, SCIENCE AND EPISTEMOLOGY

Michael Heiser and I are perhaps not too far apart in the way we approach our understanding of the Bible. He says he is not a "fundamentalist to fundamentalists," (Blog 1) and neither am I. He does not insist that the Bible is infallible, especially in scientific matters. He says, "The Bible never claims to be a science book." "It never claims that a round flat earth with a dome is truth that is binding on us. Some of its writers simply presume it because that's what they are. God didn't make them super-humans to avoid such things. I could go on and on here, as this is one of the things that I think the conservative church gets very wrong." "God knew the writers of Scripture didn't know squat about science." (Blog 3) Like Heiser, I do not think there is a dome or "firmament" above the earth. (Gen. 1:6) Heiser accuses me of writing nonsense in my analysis of the Red Sea, but I notice that Heiser does not accuse me of "nonsense" in believing that the Red Sea parted, it is only nonsense that I would say a UFO caused the parting. He says the biblical people can be trusted to report "on the basis of experience" the things they observe. (Blog 3) This is also my view—the biblical people saw the Red Sea part, saw the pillar of cloud, and that is why the story is in the Bible. The church of Christ exists in no small part because of reports such as this, and the faith conclusions about God that follow from this. I presume, therefore, that Heiser believes in the existence of the angelic order that the Bible presents, based on what the biblical people said they saw. How then does our Christian understanding of the angelic order fit in with our modern scientific cosmology? When one of my Princeton Seminary professors denied the Ascension of Jesus because we no longer believe in a three-decker universe, Heiser pronounced this "epistemological garbage." (Blog 3) I agree with Heiser that the biblical people could see Jesus taken up, but not necessarily have an accurate scientific cosmology of "where he was going," or where heaven was. But at the same time, the position taken by my professor is very common now. Many liberal Christians believe that the whole angelic order is mythological, does not exist in any sense. Heiser and I do not think either the parting of the Red Sea, or the angelic order, are mythological. But if the angels are real, and if the biblical people did not "know squat" about science, how are we to understand the angelic order in light of modern science?

Epistemology deals with how we know what we know, or at least how we explain what we think we know. It is part of my epistemology that knowing and believing are not the same thing, but they do have overlap. The main difference between faith and science, from my point of view, is the degree of certainty that science tries to achieve, and perhaps the methodology by which certainty is achieved, and the way evidence is gathered. Let us suppose a scientist wants to know the effect of vitamin B on rats. Several rats can be obtained, two separate cages established, the rats in one cage will be given a diet that includes vitamin B, the other cage will be fed the identical diet, but without vitamin B. Rats in both cages will be examined frequently to establish differences. After the results are established, other scientists are free to follow the same procedure, and either confirm, or deny, the results of the earlier experiment. Notice that the scientist has considerable control over the objects of his (or her) experiment. Heiser sometimes uses the term "hard science," and the above experiment is what I would call an example of hard science.

There are places in life where hard science does not work well, such as the decision that a man and a woman make about getting married. The couple might like to know ahead that the other person will be faithful to them, that if they have children, they will agree on parenting standards, that they will be financially successful together. But each person is in a sense a "free being," they are not rats in a cage, they cannot use "hard science" to decide whether their marriage will succeed. They go ahead with the marriage based on faith. Usually it is not blind faith, it is based on some evidence, the couple usually has dated for a while, they may even have filled out some kind of questionnaire that will reveal their "compatibility." But this kind of pre-marriage evidence is what we might call "soft science." When a man asks a woman to marry him, the woman may expect a little "hard science" as proof of his love in the form of a diamond. Nevertheless, often marriages work, based on faith. And this is understood to be the basis for all who follow the God of the Bible, it is a faith decision based on evidence, but "soft evidence." I cannot "prove" the Red Sea parted, but it is part of my faith. There are many, of course, who do not believe the Red Sea parted, or that Jesus rose from the dead. Faith is the name of what I call "God's Game," and Hebrews chapter 11 spells out the way in which from the time of Abraham, this is a critical dimension of God's will, that we believe by faith, not by sight. "Now faith is the assurance of things hoped for, the conviction of things not seen." (Heb. 11:1) When doubting Thomas believed after touching the resurrected Jesus, he did not receive praise for his faith. Faith involves taking risks that go beyond "hard science." Faith is the way in which we know God indirectly, a way that keeps us from being destroyed by the direct experience of God's power. With these epistemological assumptions in place, I now want to examine some of Heiser's statements about the "nonsense" of my theology.

Heiser says, "We don't know when our interpretation is infallible. But I'd suggest we 'can' know if it's nonsense. For your hermeneutical approach to be reasonable, you need to establish that (a) there really are intelligent aliens and (b) that they came here in antiquity. I suppose you have incontrovertible physical evidence of intelligent alien visitation that would make your interpretative approach reasonable? That would give it a deserved place at the intellectual table? Why don't you turn it over to the dozens of dedicated UFO researchers?" "Problem is, everyone reading this knows that 'hard' scientific proof of ET life and visitation is non-existent, no matter how much we'd like to have it." (Blog 1)

[It is here that Heiser inserts a footnote, saying in effect that believing in God does not require similar hard science evidence, because God is not part of the created order. I would agree, but the parting of the Red Sea is presented as an event in our created order, and therefore is open to scientific investigation. Believing in the parting of the Red Sea is not the same thing as believing in an uncreated God. On what basis does Heiser believe the parting happened? Not hard science I would think. In fact, there are thousands of living witnesses to modern UFO events—not a single living witness to the parting of the Red Sea. UFO science may not be as "hard" as Heiser demands, but it is a lot "harder" than a scientific approach to the issue of the parting of the Red Sea.]

Heiser thus says, if I cannot prove UFOs exist, my theology is nonsense. Here is my response. If Heiser were an atheist, or even a liberal Christian who does not believe angels exist, I would understand why what I have written is "nonsense." But Heiser seems to take the parting of the Red Sea as a literally observed and experienced event, as I do. And he therefore seems committed to the angelic order, which Exodus 14:19-29 says was present and caused the sea to part.

My point is this. I should not have to prove to Heiser that an extraterrestrial reality exists. Any Christian who believes angels are real already believes in extraterrestrial life, and believes extraterrestrial life can come to earth, and be seen by humans. Angels come down from the sky, as did the angel at the empty tomb of Jesus. Where do angels come from? Where is heaven? I do not know, but they come from heaven, not earth. Chapter V in my book, **The Bible and Flying Saucers,** is entitled "Where Is Heaven?" I speculate that heaven may be in another dimension. Could heaven be on another planet? I have no idea, but my point is, any Christian who believes angels are real already believes in extraterrestrial life. Therefore Heiser should not demand that I provide proof that modern aliens exist. Rather, he should see the need to join in this quest: How do we discover whether modern alien reports are or are not sightings of the angels of God? I can understand atheists demanding proof of alien visitation, but I do not understand it from Heiser. Concerning whether or not the pillar of cloud and fire might be a spaceship, since Heiser himself says the biblical people did not know "squat" about science, we should not expect the biblical people to call a spaceship a spaceship, even if they saw one. Thus whether or not the pillar of cloud and fire is a spaceship is a matter to be interpreted in light of what it looks like, and what it does.

From the Christian side, I believe we have an identification problem. Suppose God ordered his angels to fly the pillar of cloud and fire across the United States during one night, maybe at a height of a thousand feet. Suppose Michael Heiser and his friends see it. The next day a United States Air Force spokesman announces that what was seen by thousands was a meteor. Suppose that the pillar of cloud was sent as a sign to the church of Christ to encourage our faith, to fight the atheism of our age. On what basis would Heiser, or any Christians, say to the world: This was not a meteor, our government leaders are lying, this was the pillar of cloud and fire of the Exodus. This is what I mean by an identification problem. When Heiser demands "hard scientific proof" of UFOs, he basically takes himself out of what I call God's Faith Game, and makes fun of me for trying to interpret the signs of our time. Signs are examples of "soft science" given to us to encourage our faith.   In the day of judgment we will be justified by faith, not by hard science.   Conservative Christians who believe UFOs are demonic are at least on target in this sense: they know that UFOs present an identification challenge to the church.   Identification of the nature of UFOs cannot just be left to "hard science."

Furthermore, I am not sure "hard science" can even exist in relation to UFOs. I realize that the general public sees UFOs as a scientific, space age issue. And if we think further, we suppose it is a problem for science and the governments of the world, in case there is danger of an alien invasion, not counting the Second Coming of Christ as an alien invasion, of course. But if we think about the issues here, the techniques of hard science do not apply well.   Let us go back to the vitamin B experiment with rats in the cage. Let us suppose that the rats in the cage have almost human-like intelligence, and start hearing alien stories. "An alien abducted me from the cage. He was funny looking, did not look like a rat. Put a needle in me, then put me back in the cage." Several of these stories start spreading in the rat cage, some rats do not believe the abduction stories, other rats in the cage demand that the government do something about it, carry on a study, get some scientists on it, to solve once and for all the alien rumors.   In the UFO situation we face, it appears that the UFO reality is the scientist, and we are the rats. We are not able to get "control" of that reality, in order to do what Heiser calls "hard science." This is what led me to write the article for the *MUFON UFO Journal,* "The God Hypothesis." (October 1988) UFOs seem to be in a "god like position" in relation to humans. Perhaps one reason UFOs do not "invade" earth and take over is that they may already be in charge, as we might expect the angels of God to already be in charge.

I do not believe it is wise for Christians to sit on our hands waiting for scientists to tell us whether UFOs are real or not.   Scientists are not in charge of UFO science, the governments of the world are.   When I reviewed Richard Dolan's book (referenced above) I said, "Dolan is a trained historian, not a scientist. His point of view as an historian is based on this inconvenient truth: scientists control science, but politicians control scientists, particularly if scientists are doing anything that is of interest to 'the national security state.'" If we suppose that our modern Pharaohs are going to tell us the truth about UFOs, then we have not learned our Bible lessons about the deceptive practices of human leaders.

BIBLICAL UFO REVELATIONS

Heiser suggests that my view that UFOs might relate to the Bible is remotely possible, but so remote as to be ridiculous. He imagines "an ET race of speckled goat-beings" who are very smart, and might have been involved in the development of the human race, an idea which Heiser sees as just as silly as believing UFOs might be real. Timothy Good is a British UFO researcher who published the book, *Above Top Secret: The World Wide UFO Cover-up.* The title of the book is taken from a letter from the late Senator Barry Goldwater, who stated that he was told that UFO information at Wright Patterson Air Force Base is classified "above top secret," and therefore even Senator Goldwater could not have this information. I would say to Michael Heiser: let me know when a United States Senator is told by an Air Force official that information concerning "speckled goat-beings" is classified above top secret. Or when should we expect that Richard Dolan may soon write a book with the title, *Speckled Goat-Beings and the National Security State: The Cover-up Exposed?*

It seems to me that Heiser is very trusting of the way the governments of the world operate, more trusting than Christians ought to be. Heiser says he is kind of for government release of UFO information, unless it is a national security issue. "But for the record, if the government has information that it ought to make public, they should pony up if there is no real national security threat (and I do not believe there is, but I'm not privy to that sort of information), then it's morally wrong to withhold it. I assume Barry would allow that national security caveat as well. You'd have to be loony to think that the government owes us all the information it has on any given subject. " (Blog 4)

Suppose that some Egyptians went to Pharaoh, and said something like this: "Pharaoh, there are rumors that the plague of flies that we just experienced was caused by some kind of extraterrestrial power. We have heard that you have been warned there will be other plagues by some Jewish guy named Moses." And Pharaoh responds, "No comment, this is a national security issue." Is this where it ends? Should the Egyptian shrug his shoulders and say, "I am not privy to national security information?" The arrogance of Pharaoh's national security state will in a few months lead to the death of the first-born sons in every Egyptian home. I worry a lot about the questions Christians are not asking of our modern national security state.

Jesus said we should give to Caesar what is Caesar's, and to God what is God's. The question I am asking is: Do UFOs carry the angels of God? And if they do, then they belong to God, not to Caesar. By surrendering the UFO issue to the national security state, Heiser may be—I say may be, because I do not have proof—surrendering what is God's to Caesar. In any case, I do not think it is "nonsense" from my Christian point of view to be wondering the things I am wondering. Speckled Goat-Beings are not the issue. For Christians right now UFOs are a faith issue founded on "soft science," as faith always is.

Christian Faith in an Age of Scientific Doubt

I am concerned about the signs that the Christian faith is being abandoned in the name of science. Heiser and I are partly in agreement on this, although I think the apostasy of our age is greater than Heiser seems to think. (In fact, the unwillingness of the church to even admit UFOs are a faith challenge is one sign to me of the apostasy of our age. It is as if we have no memory of, or hope for, God's angels being present to our generation.)

Heiser and I agree that Bishop John Shelby Spong represents a serious embarrassment to the Christian faith. I had made a brief negative comment about Spong in my article, and Heiser responded, "For the record, Spong is one of the sloppiest thinkers I've ever read." (Blog 3) I am presenting some material by Spong here because I believe it is significant that a Protestant Bishop can write these things. Spong has written several books, one of which is **Why Christianity Must Change or Die**. In the early part of his book he explains his view of the Apostles' Creed, which begins, "I believe in God the Father Almighty, maker of heaven and earth." He states strongly that he believes in God, although where he got his idea of God is not clear, apparently not from the Bible. Spong goes on to say he objects strongly to calling God "Father," (as Jesus did), this is patriarchal and oppressive, and he does not like the concept of "almighty" either; no serious thinking person today believes God is almighty.

"Other aspects of the almightiness of God found in the Bible are also notably missing from the expectations of people living in this modern world. The Bible suggested that this almighty God had the ability to rain bread called 'manna' from heaven upon the favored people to save them from starvation in the wilderness (Exod. 16). But there appears to be no such divine rescue of starving people in our time; at least no heavenly bread falls upon them. In our generation starving people in Somalia, Rwanda, and in the region of the world known as the sub-Sahara simply die, unless human relief operations are mounted.

This 'almighty' deity also appeared, in the sacred text, to have had a not-so-noble political and moral agenda. The biblical God is portrayed as having had the power to split the Red Sea to allow the chosen ones to walk through on dry land (Exod. 14:1-22) and as stopping the sun in the sky to allow the people of Israel more time to achieve a military victory over the Amorites (Josh. 10:12). But in the same sacred text, that Red Sea was also closed by this God just in time to drown the hated Egyptians (Exod. 14:23-31), and that sun was finally allowed to set as soon as the slaughter of the wicked Amorites was complete (Josh. 10:13). What kind of almighty power is this? Is it even ethical? Is one capable of worshiping so capricious a deity who appears to embody the worst of our tribal and political hatreds? (p. 9)

Spong has described the book of Exodus as a book of superstitions, and a wide range of modern liberal scholarship agrees with him, as I demonstrated in "Hermeneutical Rape." Heiser agrees that there are many who do not even believe the Exodus ever happened, but protests that we should not conclude that "truth is determined by consensus." (Blog 5) But thousands of seminary students are learning from respected professors like Walter Brueggemann who concedes that we want to avoid sounding like "silly supernaturalists." (***Mandate to Difference***, p. 197) What Brueggemann does is go heavy on the poetry of the Old Testament, and light on the historical narrative. This modern mind set has taken its toll. It has taken church members a while to understand that there is little of God's power left in modern liberal Christianity.

My own denomination, the Presbyterian Church (USA) had 4 million members in 1983, it now has 2 million members. Heiser mentions that he does not "affiliate with a Christian denomination." (Blog 3) Perhaps this has helped him avoid the grief of living through the destruction of the church as I have experienced it. My sense has been that no human driven "plan for renewal" would save my church, only a sign from God that would save us from slavery to the scientific skepticism of our age. Perhaps I am wrong that UFOs are that sign, but I have no doubt about the decline of my church.

I was brought up to believe that when the angels of God saved the Jews at the Red Sea, this was a sign of God's saving power, and the manna from the sky was a sign that God could feed us , and sustain us, day by day. This power of God to save is then transferred to Jesus in the New Testament, who saves us from sin on the cross, and from death in the empty tomb. If we trust in Christ, he becomes our manna for our daily journey of faith. (John 6) Does Spong understand that by destroying the God of the Old Testament, he destroys Jesus as savior? Yes he does. Chapter 6 is titled: "Jesus as Rescuer: An Image that Has to Go." (p. 83-99) From my point of view, Spong does not "change" Christianity, he destroys it.

Thus when modern atheists like Richard Dawkins, Sam Harris and Christopher Hitchens condemn the God of the Bible, they have a Christian Bishop cheering for them. Michael Heiser suggested I would feel less bleak about our current situation if I read a book by Alister McGrath (co-authored by Joanna C. McGrath) entitled ***The Dawkins Delusion***. I had actually bought and read this book when I was at Oxford University in England two years ago attending a conference, but I did not find the McGraths' book helpful.

At the beginning of chapter 4 we find this from the McGrath book. "The God that Dawkins does not believe in is 'a petty, unjust, unforgiving control freak;

a vindictive, bloodthirsty ethnic cleanser; a misogynistic, homophobic, racist , infanticidal, genocidal, filicidal, pestilential, megalomaniacal, sadomasochistic, capriciously malevolent bully.' Come to think of it, I don't believe in a God like that either. In fact, I don't know anybody who does." The McGrath book goes on to confess belief in "Gentle Jesus, meek and mild." (p. 46)

This might seem to be a good way to melt the hard atheism of Dawkins except for this. The McGraths did not start the Dawkins quotation at the beginning. The Dawkins quotation begins: "The God of the Old Testament is arguably the most unpleasant character in all fiction: jealous and proud of it; a petty, unjust, unforgiving control-freak; a vindictive........." (Richard Dawkins, *The God Delusion,* p. 31)

What are we to make of this omission: that the McGraths do not believe in the God of the Old Testament? The God of Jesus is the God of the Old Testament. How do the McGraths claim to believe in Jesus, but not the God of Jesus? Or do the McGraths really believe in the God of the Old Testament, but it would have made their book too long to explain why all, or some of the descriptions of the God of the Old Testament made by Dawkins, are not accurate?

In the chapter on "What are the Origins of Religion?" almost all the ideas are taken from psychological theories, and anthropological studies, which perhaps is not surprising, given that Joanna McGrath is a professor of psychology at the University of London. Never in the book is there any hint that the biblical faith might have been influenced by angelic powers, extraterrestrial powers. What we find is the McGraths believe in an ethical Jesus, but not a savior Jesus, not a Jesus with an extraterrestrial identity. My point is this: even those who appear to be defending Christianity are in a nearly hopeless intellectual situation if the assumption is made that the biblical angelic powers are mythological. According to current intellectual theory, all religions are the invention of the human mind and human culture. (I do not consider this an unreasonable point of view, I just don't think it is true.) This is what our children are learning in their "Religious Studies" classes at the university. For modern intellectuals, there is no such thing as "Divine Revelation," which is the core concept of both the Old and New Testament. Jesus as God incarnate is of course the central figure of that revelation in the New Testament.

The Power of Enlightenment Doubt and Our Current Faith Crisis

How did we get to this point? Although enlightenment skepticism was planted in the 1700's, we are now eating the harvest. Only a brief sketch can be attempted here. In the 1800's much doubt developed in the church about the second coming of Christ. It had been hundreds of years since the resurrection, where was the coming, the *parousia*? Albert Schweitzer published a land mark book entitled *The Quest of the Historical Jesus* (1910), which concluded either that the early church, or Jesus, was deluded about his second coming. In so far as the ministry of Jesus was understood to have three main dimensions or offices—prophet, priest and king—the conclusion of Schweitzer, in so far as it was accepted by the liberal church, eliminated the role of Christ as priest and king in any meaningful sense. This left the ethics of Jesus, and his "prophetic" role, as the main religious identity in Jesus that liberals would affirm. The New Testament of course saw the Ascension of Jesus, and his Second Coming, as a single package. As two angels explained at the Ascension, "This Jesus, who was taken up from you into heaven, will come in the same way as you saw him go into heaven." (Acts 1:11)

This meant liberal theology had no eschatology, no hope for the return of Christ, no serious hope for life after death, and hope for the Last Judgment, when the justice of God will be established. Not surprisingly, liberals could not stand the pain of seeing evil in the world, knowing there was no hope for justice after death. It was easy for liberals to borrow from Marxists, who were not waiting for justice in heaven, but were busy liberating the oppressed on earth. Liberal theologians quoted Luke 4:18, in which Jesus, reading from Isaiah, said that he came "to set at liberty those who were oppressed." Although liberation theology began in Latin America, it soon became part of black liberation theology in the United States, followed by feminist and gay liberation theology. Evil was not something individuals did, but rather evil was a class phenomenon. The oppressor class was bad, and the oppressed were good. If you belonged to the oppressed class—blacks, Hispanics, women, gays—you were good, and if you were among the oppressors—usually white heterosexual males—you were bad. Individual morality did not count for much in liberation theology. Justice was based on class analysis, not individual morality. Liberation theology has made life more just for some groups of people, but it is very selective, and creates new stereotypes in the very process of trying to get rid of old ones.

But one of the more important results of modern liberalism is the view that the only just society would be a classless society. Therefore no one should because of race, sex, national origin, or religion, be treated as superior, claim any "exceptionalism," as the term is now used by liberals.

If we apply this concept of justice, then any religion that claims to have more truth than any other religion is in a sense "oppressive" to those whose claims are said to be weaker. How does one establish truth if it is "oppressive" to say that any other religion is false? The answer is you cannot, and should not, because it is argued in our post modern philosophical environment that all truth claims are basically a political power grab. Thus the biblical view that the Jews are "God's chosen people" is itself an evil idea, an example of a power grab. And even worse, the Christian claim that Jesus was God incarnate is a huge act of arrogance on the part of Christians. One of my professors at Princeton Seminary was John Hick, author of the book *The Myth of God Incarnate.* In this book Hick calls on Christians to give up claiming Jesus is God incarnate, for the sake of being able to talk with other religions on an equal basis. This is the classless society and political correctness doing its destructive work on Christian faith. Shame on any religion that thinks its truth claims are true!

[Michael Heiser had recommended that I read Timothy Keller's book *The Reason for God: Belief in an Age of Skepticism.* Keller made note of the danger of Hick's thinking for basic Christian belief. (p. 11) Keller has written an excellent book in the C.S. Lewis tradition, but he may not convert many scientific or liberal skeptics. As Keller points out, "the infallibility of the Bible" is one of the basic doctrines of his church (p. 43), a belief liberal Christians consider another example of making a truth claim that is really a power grab. I can see the liberal point on this, since I also see the Roman Catholic claim for the infallibility of the Pope as a power grab disguised as religious truth.]

Consequently we now live in a scientific culture that is basically godless, which is a good thing from the point of those like Richard Dawkins, something to be accepted in the name of intellectual honesty by religious liberals, and a cause for conservative Christians to retreat into shrink wrapped infallibility (biblical or Papal).

With Jesus as savior drained from our culture, what do we have left? Life that is accidentally caused by the luck of Darwinian evolution, human bodies driven by animal drives for aggressive dominance, vicariously lived out in our sports culture, or in the shopping mall. Without Christ as savior, where is grace, where is forgiveness? Young men come to school or university and start shooting, for no reason, so we are told: unless despair and nihilism are a reason, of course. And then we die, naturally. In losing Christ in western culture, we have lost more than our scientific intellectuals are telling us, more than liberal Christians are telling us. Now what? Has God given us resources to renew hope? Perhaps.

Angels and the Possibility of Extraterrestrial Life

In the Fall of 2009 the Roman Catholic Church sponsored a conference on astrobiology, a fairly new science that explores the possibility, and the meaning, of intelligent life on other planets. Ted Peters is Professor of Theology at Pacific Lutheran Theological Seminary, and editor of the journal *Theology and Science.* Peters has explored questions such as what is proper ethical practice for interaction with an extraterrestrial life form. If we were to have contact with extraterrestrial life, would that life need Christ as savior, would we have to "preach them the gospel," or would they perhaps be unfallen, without sin? The New Testament does not see Jesus as a local savior, rather "He is the image of the invisible God, the first-born of all creation; for in him all things were created, in heaven and on earth, visible and invisible." (Col. 1:15, 16) How would Christ relate to extraterrestrial beings?

The astrobiology conference in Rome was not a UFO conference. The Roman Catholic Church has not taken a public position on UFOs. But Protestants should note this: the Vatican has diplomatic connections that we do not have. I cannot imagine that the higher levels of the Roman Catholic Church have not asked through diplomatic channels: What is the truth about UFOs? The answer from the governments of the world would likely be: UFOs are a highly classified subject, there is some truth to some reports, but no nation plans to make any public announcement in the near future.

The late Roman Catholic theologian Msgr. Corrado Balducci made public statements on Italian television saying he believed UFOs were real, but they came from the "natural order," not the "supernatural order," the order of angels and demons. In other words, UFOs are more an issue for science than for theology, which, of course, is the way the military powers of this world would see it—the way Pharaoh would see it, in case the Vatican should ask. (See my article, "The Balducci Interview and Religious Certainty," *MUFON UFO Journal*, September, 1998.) It seems unlikely Balducci would have made these kinds of public statements without some kind of high level approval from Rome. In my article, I argued that I think it is early in our UFO studies to assume we can make a distinction between the supernatural, and the super technological.

As Michael Heiser has said, the biblical people did not "know squat" about science. Given the non-technological nature of biblical culture, the proper question is: If the biblical people had contact with some type of extraterrestrial power, how might the biblical people explain the nature of this power, and how would we understand that same power now?

Protestant conservatives have studied UFO reports and have come to the opposite conclusion from that of Msgr. Balducci. Some conservative Protestants argue that UFOs are supernatural and demonic, or if not demons, at least fallen angels. (See books by Gary Bates, Timothy Dailey, Chuck Missler, and Mark Eastman that take the demonic or fallen angel point of view, as well as on line articles by those like Lynn Marzulli.)

We come now to the bitter taste of extraterrestrial life and biblical faith. Wormwood falls from the sky like a star (Rev. 8:11) in the person of Eric von Daniken, and for many, I am von Daniken's much less successful brother. Von Daniken is the author of the multimillion best selling book *Chariots of the Gods?*, translated into many languages, originally copyrighted in 1968, the year *The Bible and Flying Saucers* was published. Von Daniken's thesis is that ancient astronauts visited earth thousands of years ago, and caused what we have thought were the many myths of "gods coming down from the sky," but now we in the space age should understand these are not myths, they are reports of extraterrestrial visitation. Von Daniken turns to the Bible as one of his sources of ET visitation. Von Daniken's theories have inspired many television programs, especially on the History Channel, exploring the possibility that ancient ET's inspired the building of the pyramids and ancient temples.

Not surprisingly, von Daniken explores the possibility that the "wheels " of Ezekiel are some type of spaceship. But perhaps his treatment of the story of Sodom better illustrates the conflicting cultural, scientific and theological issues that the space age brings us.

Von Daniken begins exploring the story of Sodom in a chapter titled, "Was God an Astronaut?" He notes how two "angels" came to visit Lot in Sodom, and pleaded with Lot to leave the city quickly, because God planned to destroy it for its wickedness. (Gen. 19:1-28) Sodom seems to have been a city with a little bit of everything. Liberals might see Sodom as the kind of place that would be in favor of gay liberation, and conservatives might understand why the men of Sodom would demonize aliens, except for the bad luck that the aliens turned out to be angels. The angels finally succeed in getting Lot and his family out of the city, fire and brimstone fall from the sky and destroy Sodom; Lot's wife makes the mistake of looking back, and turns into a pillar of salt.

Von Daniken speculates that the "angels" in the story are not really angels under the direction of God at all, but rather a bunch of space guys who for whatever reason favor Lot, but otherwise decide that the people of Sodom are some kind of genetic mistake that needs to be destroyed, perhaps with nuclear weapons, which is why Lot's wife kind of melted when she looked back.

He says, "We may be as religious as our fathers, but we are certainly less credulous. With the best will in the world we cannot imagine an omnipotent, ubiquitous, infinitely good God who is above all concepts of time and yet does not know what is going to happen. God created man and was satisfied with his work. However, he seems to have repented of his deed later, because this same creator decided to destroy mankind. It is also difficult for enlightened children of this age to think of an infinitely good Father who gives preference to 'favorite children,' such as Lot's family, over countless others." (p. 37)

Using Michael Heiser's epistemological concept of "nonsense," here we find two types of nonsense, liberal nonsense and conservative nonsense. Liberals would call it nonsense to take the story of Sodom literally. For liberals, anyone living in our modern age should understand that this is a primitive pre-scientific mythical story. One can imagine Bishop Spong bending over in laughter at the absurdity of von Daniken's book. Spong would suppose that the modern UFO myth, and its cousin the "ancient astronaut" theory, following C.G. Jung (*Flying Saucers: A Modern Myth of Things Seen in the Skies*), are examples of bringing back mythological thinking in a space-age disguise. (This explains the liberal rejection of von Daniken, as well as myself.)

For conservatives, it is "nonsense" to suggest that the angels in the Bible were ancient astronauts. If one holds to a belief in an infallible Bible, this is fairly straight forward. The Bible says they were angels, and therefore they were angels, since the Bible cannot be wrong. But many conservatives have worried. Clifford Wilson worried first by denying that von Daniken had a case in Wilson's book, *Crash Go the Chariots* (1972), but as evidence of the UFO reality grew, Wilson published *The Alien Agenda* (1988), moving to what is now the standard conservative view: if aliens are real, they are demons. It is thought this argument protects the Bible from von Daniken's perversion of angels into ancient astronauts. By suggesting that the "ancient astronauts" were in fact the angels of God, and that they use technology, my own work makes the conservative task more difficult, for which conservatives do not thank me.

What I would say is that von Daniken, like Michael Heiser, does not understand how the Bible eventually separates the concept of God, who cannot be seen in this world, from his angels, who are seen in our physical world. Von Daniken understands that God in his essence is "omnipotent, ubiquitous, infinitely good" and above "concepts of time." How could the timing of the destruction be an issue for such a God? That being the case, the angels are not angels, but rather ancient astronauts, space guys doing scientific stuff, and perhaps using technology to destroy Sodom. This raises the question: even if the "angels" who met Lot are not angels, but rather just space guys, if they are still with us in modern UFOs, might they destroy us if they don't like us? Von Daniken does not explore this question, but it is implied by his logic.

Von Daniken is also offended that any real God would have "favorite children." Bishop Spong would cheer von Daniken at this point, joining together in preaching political correctness, preaching a God who does not discriminate on the basis of anything, especially religion. The Old Testament focuses on God's "chosen people," and it is exactly this offensive God who parts the Red Sea, saving the Jews, and destroying the Egyptians. For Spong only a "capricious deity" would save the Jews, and destroy the Egyptians. This is the liberal moral argument for giving up belief in an "interventionist God." The horror of the Jewish holocaust under Hitler led many Jews and Christians to give up totally on the idea of an interventionist, saving God. (My view of the holocaust is that it proves, like the crucifixion of Jesus, why the human race needs saving.) Liberals suppose a God with real power that could just stand by as the Jews were destroyed in the German ovens could not be loving and almighty. I can certainly sympathize with this liberal sense of moral despair, trying to believe in a God who can save, but chooses not to. Learning to live with a powerless God who loves but cannot do much about it is the point of Rabbi Harold S. Kushner's popular book *When Bad Things Happen to Good People*. Another title for the book might have been: *Learning to Live Without an Interventionist God.*

But the challenges von Daniken raises are mild compared with the direction others have gone. Von Daniken's argument was that the biblical people were too primitive to recognize advanced technology for what it was, and therefore worshipped the beings in spaceships as gods. Now, says von Daniken, we would know better. Thus, in so far as von Daniken is concerned, we have a "mistaken identity" problem to solve in the Bible. If we read "ancient astronauts" for "angels," we will understand the Bible correctly. Von Daniken did not, however, follow through on the implications of treating the pillar of cloud and fire as a spaceship, as I have done. I see the Exodus as a deliberate act by an extraterrestrial power. I am saying that the extraterrestrial power involved in the Exodus, even though it is a technological power, is serving God's purpose. (Modern missionaries fly in planes. That does not deny their God directed mission.)

But others have read the Exodus story in a secular way, concluding that the whole of the Bible is in a sense some kind of extraterrestrial fraud. (See Patrick Cooke's book, *The Greatest Deception: The Bible UFO Connection.*) And in our modern UFO quest, there have been reports from those who say they have inside "classified" UFO information, that the American government has been in contact with the aliens, and the aliens have revealed they have created life on earth, as well as creating many of the world's religions, including the biblical religion. (Richard Dolan, op. cit., p. 477; Linda Moulton Howe, **An Alien Harvest,** p. 188)

There is indeed a lot of Wormwood to deal with as we try to understand the possible implications of extraterrestrial visitation of the earth and the Bible. Is it all "nonsense," or should we be seeking buried treasure here? Is there an underlying divine pattern that makes sense, gives us coherence? It is easy to understand why some Christians suppose the situation is part of a "strong delusion." (2 Thes. 2:11) There are days I would settle for one strong delusion. I see multiple delusions running at once. I have no easy solution other than to do my best to sort out truth from falsehood, God's possibilities from what seems to me to be the dominant atheism of our age. I believe Jesus is the Christ, not just the moral teacher/nice guy of moderate Christian liberalism, or the political revolutionary of radical Christian liberalism. At the same time, although I believe the Bible is a "unique and authoritative witness to Jesus Christ," (a faith statement required of my denomination for all who are ordained), I do not believe the Bible is infallible. Therefore, my faith is based on "soft science," not "hard science." Do modern UFOs relate to the angels of Christ in any way? This is the question I have tried to answer for more than 40 years. Heiser has stressed that he does not find my arguments coherent, they seem to be nonsense to him.

Part of the problem is we have nonsense at several levels. Someone like Bishiop Spong would say the fact that Heiser and I each believe the parting of the Red Sea happened is nonsense. Spong might even say it is immoral for Heiser and me to believe in such a "capricious deity." As far as our believing that Jesus is Lord and Savior, this is "religious imperialism." (Spong, p. 11) Spong's religion, such as it is, is what we have come to call at the secular level political correctness. The sin above all sins according to political correctness is to make an arrogant truth claim like: Jesus is Lord. It is an oppressive statement, a "power grab," from the point of view of those who apply class analysis to "religious studies."

Here is the question for the final section of this article. In answer to Michael Heiser, what kind of coherence do I see between modern UFO behavior, and the angelic reality described in the Bible? My answer is: both the modern UFO reality, and the biblical UFO reality, seem to rule the earth through a technique that could be called "Targeted Intervention."

III. *Targeted Intervention as a Ruling Strategy*

War is *not* targeted intervention. Following the al-Qaida attack on the World Trade Towers and the Pentagon on September 11, 2001, the United States invaded both Afghanistan and Iraq. The purpose of the invasions was and is to totally rule those nations in ways that serve the purposes of America. Anyone who resists our purpose in these nations risks being killed.

The parallel idea to armed invasion in theology is the Second Coming of Christ, and the **Left Behind** series of novels about the end times pictures this type of heavenly invasion when Christ returns in very military terms, which liberals find offensive. But the angels are seen as the army of God in the Bible. Eugene H. Peterson, in his translation of the Bible under the title **The Message**, captures the Old Testament understanding of God very well by calling him "God of the angel armies." This also seems to be the God of Jesus, who could have called on legions of angels to save him, if he asked. (Mt. 26:53)

But when al-Qaida attacked the World Trade Center, this was an example of targeted intervention. No al-Qaida army attacked America, there was no invasion. Rather the Islamic inspired enemy hijacked American planes, and flew them into the Twin Trade Towers, and the Pentagon, killing all on board the planes, including the hijackers.

BIBLICAL UFO REVELATIONS

Although very few al-Qaida lives were lost in the attack, the results have been far reaching. Thousands of American lives have been lost in wars to try to prevent this from happening again, billions of dollars have been spent in the war effort. Although the attack happened almost nine years ago, these were the stories in my local paper on January 3, 2010: the story of a young soldier from our area, shot at Fort Hood on November 5, 2009, now recovering. He was shot by al-Qaida inspired psychiatrist Nidal Malik Hasan, who killed 13 and wounded 30. Another front page story reported President Obama explaining that the al-Qaida agent who tried to blow up a plane near Detroit on Christmas Day was trained in Yemen. On page 11 was the headline: "Iran: We'll Make Nuclear Fuel." (***Binghamton Press and Sun-Bulletin***)

Like dropping a rock in a pond, the ripples of that targeted intervention on September 11, 2001, reach out to every shore. Flying is different now throughout the world. Now major airports are planning to use full body scanners on passengers. A recent cartoon pictured a 747 Airliner in flight with the name of the airline painted on the side: Bare Air. A voice coming from inside the plane was saying, "With heightened security, it was only a matter of time." Targeted intervention is a very powerful way to influence the rule of a society.

Most governments use targeted intervention, not invasion, to rule their populations. Police do not arrest every speeder, but enough so the general population obeys the laws. Traffic police use targeted intervention. The IRS does not audit every tax return, they use targeted intervention, they audit enough to keep the population generally honest. And they also develop "profiles" of those with certain types of employment, or certain types of high tax deductions, to target for audits.

In terms of national defense the CIA has a certain mystique, because we know they operate in some sense outside the law, perhaps sending agents secretly to kill persons in foreign governments that do not do what we believe is in our national interest. James Bond is a fictional character that represents the ideal of "targeted intervention." As a British agent who is licensed to kill, Bond is sent to achieve a difficult mission in a foreign land, usually with the understanding that the British government will deny any knowledge of him, or his mission. In ***The Bible and Flying Saucers*** I suggest that Jesus comes into our world from the heavenly world, like an undercover agent sent to overthrow the evil powers of this world. (pp. 145-148, Lippincott and Marlowe editions)

Targeted Intervention and the Bible

The God of the Bible seems to be able to rule in several ways. God is able to rule nature by natural laws, laws which the sciences of physics, chemistry and biology can discover. These laws seem to be in a way "self governing." This has led to the deistic view of God as the clock maker, who wound up the clock, and now leaves it alone. Since these laws seem to be self regulating, scientists like Richard Dawkins claim they can find no God in nature, or any need for God in nature.

Another level of God's rule is by God's Holy Spirit, which seems to be a separate power from the other two persons of the Trinity, the Father and the Son. In the Old Testament creation story, the Spirit of God moves over the waters, (Gen. 1:2) but also can control human minds in some kind of direct way. (Num. 11:16-30; Acts 2:1-21)

But God's will to control humans is problematic. God's will is to create us in God's own image, and freedom is a key part of God's being. Freedom is required for love to be real, and God is love. The Gospel of Christ giving himself for us is predicated on his being free to give his life, or not. (Jn. 10:17, 18) Grace is not grace unless it is based on God's freedom to give it, and our freedom to receive it, or reject it. If we are to obey God's basic commandments, as Christ summarized them, to love God, and love our neighbor as ourselves, we have to be free, not robots to the power of God.

Thus there is a reluctance on the part of God to force his Holy Spirit on us, though God has the power to do that, as the Pentecost narrative shows. How is God to make God's self known to us in a context of freedom? Targeted Intervention, I believe, helps explain one of the techniques by which God gives us the freedom to know him, and yet the option of rejecting him. The God who creates our world, and then "leaves on a long trip" is illustrated in what I call the "Parable of the Out of Town God." (Mt. 21:33-43) In a sense if we look at life from the point of view of "systems analysis," God's challenge, to create humans in God's own image, requires that we be like God: godless. God has no God. Thus we are created on earth, apparently with no Owner, although there are memories of an Owner who left town. Thus when the religious leaders demand a "sign" from Jesus, and he refuses their demand, Jesus maintains the freedom of the religious leaders to reject him. (Mt. 12:38,39) How God is to use his power in relation to us is the "Catch 22" of divine strategy in relation to humans. If God shows us no power at all, we will not believe in him. No one is interested in a powerless God. But if God overpowers us, then God denies our freedom to reject him, and in denying our freedom, God destroys part of the image of God in us. Targeted Intervention is the technique by which God reveals his power in what might be called in medical terms controlled doses.

The Apostle Paul understood the "paradox of power" that the cross represents. He said, "For Jews demand signs, and Greeks seek wisdom, but we preach Christ crucified, a stumbling block to Jews and folly to the Gentiles, but to those who are called, both Jews and Greeks, Christ the power of God and the wisdom of God." (1 Cor. 1:22-24) When the religious leaders asked for a sign, Jesus responded that no sign would be given except the sign of Jonah, who was in the belly of the whale three days and nights. "Nonsense" is not just an issue in regard to my theology. It is an issue in regard to the gospel—as Paul understood, the Gospel of Christ crucified was a stumbling block to Jews, and a joke to Gentiles. What kind of powerful God would let his son die on a cross?

The cross as a divine symbol of God's power was "nonsense" to both Jew and Greek. As Michael Heiser would ask, "Where is the coherence?" The coherence is in the relation between the two Passovers. In the first story, God can out kill Pharaoh while protecting the Jews who are passed over by the angel of death in Egypt. But on the cross, the killer God becomes the one killed. In Egypt, the power of God is terrifying, and death giving. On the cross, the power of God is subordinated to his love, and love is life giving, not death giving. In the New Passover, Jesus becomes the lamb of God who takes away the sins of the world, and therefore frees us to live without guilt. That is the meaning of the cross, the meaning of Christ as savior, which Bishop Spong wants us to give up. The story of Christ crucified has coherence for those who believe, but not everyone believes, not even bishops.

People near the cross thought they heard Jesus call for Elijah, they speculated that this was a good place for "targeted intervention," (Mt. 27:47-49) if Jesus were the Son of God, how could God not rescue him? No rescue came except at the empty tomb. As the pillar of cloud deliberately led the Jews up to the Red Sea, the Spirit of God led Jesus to the cross. Then the impossible became possible, the sea parted, the tomb emptied. Why was there no intervention for Stephen from stoning (Acts 7), yet Peter was saved from prison? (Acts 12) God saves sometimes, but not other times. This seems like the act of a "capricious deity" to those like Bishop Spong. A good God would not drop manna for the Jews, and let those in Rwanda starve, says the Bishop. But targeted intervention is the way God delivers his message of salvation, but at the same time protects our freedom to reject God's ways, if we desire. This divine pattern of targeted intervention represents "coherence" to me, but obviously, not to everyone.

The parable of the Out of Town God is sure the Owner is coming back. Neither modern science, nor Christians of the Bishop Spong type, believe the Owner is coming back. In the parable the Owner sends "representatives" back to collect the rent, and they are rejected. Eventually the owner sends his Son, and the Son is killed. Sending representatives to the vineyard, from the Heavenly World where the Owner now is, represents "Targeted Intervention," a tactical means to try to get humans, in their freedom, to recognize the freedom and rights of the Owner.

BIBLICAL UFO REVELATIONS

The Bible explains God's targeted intervention strategy from the beginning. God plans to destroy sinful humanity, but targets Noah and his family for salvation. The same theme is found in the story of Sodom; the city is targeted for destruction, Lot and his family were targeted for salvation. But the story of the salvation of the Jews as a nation begins with the Exodus. In the beginning, Moses is targeted as the one to speak for God to Pharaoh. Pharaoh is made to know that a divine power favors Israel over Egypt. Pharaoh in his pride resists (in the best economic interests of the national security state), and plagues follow.

The final plague involves killing the first born males of Egypt (as Pharaoh had earlier killed the sons of Israel), but the Jewish sons will be passed over because the blood of a lamb will be painted on the doorposts of Jewish homes. Death is precisely targeted: on a special day, at midnight, Egyptian males only, first-born only. To the modern mind, this seems cruel, arbitrary, un-god like. Bishop Spong is deeply offended by a God like this. I understand how un-God like this seems to the modern mind. I also worry that modern stories of aliens abducting humans from their beds at night may be true. I worry that our modern UFO reality has the power to do exactly what the Bible says happened at Passover. I worry that our modern Pharaohs may be making decisions that put us, or our families, at risk. And I worry that the modern church seems to have no concern at all about the Power that our modern Pharaohs are dealing with.

Christ could be, should be, the lamb whose blood protects us now. But what kind of church will be protected when its Bishops hate the idea of Christ as savior? We have forgotten the Interventionist God. That God is "out of date, out of fashion." Perhaps. Or perhaps God has only been away on a long trip. And we have ignored the angels who have come to warn us.

It is the signs of God's Targeted Intervention that Bishop Spong hates most. As cited above, parting the Red Sea, dropping manna to feed Israel on their journey, or in the promised land "stopping the sun in the sky. " (Josh. 10:12-14) [I do not believe the sun stood still in the sky, or more accurately, that the earth stopped rotating so that the sun would appear to stand still. Nevertheless, if the angelic power that parted the Red Sea, and led Israel to the promised land, decided to keep a battle field lighted into the night, I believe a way could be found. I believe modern UFOs could light a battle field.]

Modern UFOs and Targeted Intervention

The angels of God did not land on Pharaoh's lawn in Egypt and say, "Take me to your leader," and neither have modern UFOs landed on the White House lawn and said, "Take me to your leader." Many would agree with Michael Heiser that we do not have "hard science" proof of the existence of UFOs. Exactly what that hard science might be, of course, depends on what any individual might demand as proof.

But even without proof of UFO existence, we do have UFO reports, and therefore we can discuss the question: If it should be true that UFOs are real, what do they seem to be doing? The first thing that can be said is they have not invaded earth, as America has invaded Iraq. Hollywood movies have made a lot of money on alien invasion movies such as "Independence Day." But there has been no open invasion. In fact, it is precisely because they seem so shy that those like Heiser can demand "hard science" proof before he will believe.

It appears to me that UFOs, like the angels of God, use targeted intervention as their strategy to achieve their goals. I do not know all of their goals, but one of them seems to be to try to help humanity avoid a nuclear war. In biblical terms, the Owner may have sent agents to keep us from blowing up the vineyard.

UFOs may not exist, but they are classified above top secret by our government. As the result of the efforts of private UFO organizations using the Freedom of Information Act to release UFO documents, the agencies of the government, such as the NSA and CIA eventually demanded that the courts exempt UFO documents from FOIA regulations because UFOs were of high national security concern. The American courts ruled in favor of the government. That is beyond dispute. Now perhaps, if we demanded that the government release all information concerning "an ET race of speckled goat-beings," the request would be denied in the name of national security. However, I do not plan to make such a request in order to find out.

In 1978 an organization called Citizens Against UFO Secrecy was formed; the group "focused on using FOIA lawsuits to obtain UFO documents." (Dolan, p. 161) Attorney Peter Gersten was a key member of this group, and used his legal power to eventually force the government to go to court, and found his effort to release UFO documents defeated by the courts in the name of national security.

Researcher Timothy Good explains the situation clearly. "When researchers such as myself request certain UFO records from the CIA, NSA, DIA, and other agencies, we are often told they are exempt from release due to national security or that 'records cannot be released because they have been destroyed' or that 'the information is properly classified and cannot be released." How curious then, that the official US Air Force position is that 'no UFO reported, investigated, and evaluated by the Air Force has ever given any indication of a threat to our national security." (*Good*, p. 328)

Before the government had the backing of the courts in denying FOIA access, researchers did obtain the release of many formerly classified documents. These documents formed the basis of the book by Lawrence Fawcett and Barry J. Greenwood, *Clear Intent: The Government Coverup of the UFO Experience.*

BIBLICAL UFO REVELATIONS

(1984) Fawcett and Greenwood report a strange UFO encounter occurred in Iran on September 19, 1976. Rumors of the encounter reached UFO researchers, and through persistence they were able to obtain a Defense Intelligence Agency (DIA) report confirming the encounter. A UFO was seen from the ground, an American built F-4 jet was sent by the Iranian Air Force to investigate. As it approached the UFO, it lost all electronic instrumentation, and returned to base. But as it made its turn, its electronics were restored. A second jet was scrambled. As it approached the primary object, a second object emerged from the first UFO, and flew at the jet. The jet pilot was about to "fire an AIM-9 missile at the object but at that instant his weapons control panel went off." (p. 83; quoted from the DIA report) If UFOs exist, they have perhaps through "targeted interventions" such as this sent a message to the military powers of the world: we can control your weapons.

It is likely that an even stronger message has been sent by the aliens to our military powers. An American listening base in the Florida Keys overheard a conversation between the Cuban pilots of two MIG-21 jets which had been sent to investigate a UFO seen on Cuban radar. "Cuban air defense headquarters ordered the flight leader to arm his weapons and destroy the object. The leader reported his radar was locked onto the bogey and his missiles were armed. Seconds later, the wingman screamed to the ground controller that his leader's jet had exploded. When he gained his composure, the wingman radioed there was no smoke or flame, that his leader's MIG-21 had disintegrated." The UFO then accelerated to a height above 98,000 feet. (Fawcett and Greenwood, p. 196) If American jets have been shot down by UFOs, this would certainly qualify as a national security issue, just as Pharaoh would see the destruction of his chariots in the Red Sea as a national security issue. One thing no military power wants to admit is that our enemy is more powerful than we are. And to admit this enemy is extraterrestrial is not something any president would want to announce.

One thing that seems clear is if UFOs exist, "The U.S. nuclear arsenal appeared to be a target of interest, and there was little the Air Force could do about it." (Dolan, 2009, p. 85; also see Terry Hansen, *The Missing Times: News Media Complicity in the UFO Cover-up*, pp. 22-28.) In 1987 at Malmstrom AFB in Montana a glowing UFO had disabled more than twenty ICBM's at two separate sites. On November 7, 1975, a UFO hovered over a missile site designated as K-7. Ground personnel were sent to investigate. When they came within a mile of the site, they refused to go further. "From a safe distance, they noticed it begin to rise. When it reached an altitude of 1,000 feet, it registered on NORAD radar, and F-106 interceptors were promptly scrambled from Malmstrom." (Dolan, p. 95) Later inspection indicated the computer targeting system on the missile had been disabled, and had to be removed.

BIBLICAL UFO REVELATIONS

A major and very complex confrontation between United States military personnel and UFOs at Rendlesham Forest, England, location of USAF Woodbridge. During the last days of December, 1980, a series of sightings occurred in the woods outside the base, but were investigated by base personnel.

Lt. Col. Charles Halt was one of those who investigated the sightings, and over a period of time Halt has become more open about what happened, including a UFO landing in the woods, and being touched by base personnel before flying away. There also seems to have been damage done by some type of beam technology to the nuclear weapons stored at Woodbridge.

Dolan writes, "For years, there were claims that the beams penetrated the Weapons Storage Area at Woodbridge, and even that beams disabled some or all of the nuclear weapons stored there. Given the history of UFOs and their proximity to nuclear weapons, it is certainly plausible." Researcher Peter Robbins says Col. Halt "admitted to them that the beams of light from the UFO somehow penetrated the alternating layers of steel, earth, and concrete of the hardened bunkers. Ultimately they reached the secured areas where the weapons were stored" disabling the firing mechanisms of the weapons. (Dolan, p. 237; also see Larry Warren and Peter Robins, *Left at East Gate: A First-hand Account of the Bentwaters-Woodbridge UFO Incident, Its Cover-Up, and Investigation*; Robbins makes the observation, "National security has become our state religion. Big Brother is watching us, and the situation in both countries [England and the United States] is urgent. There is a pathology at work here; it will not stop itself." p. 418)

If UFOs exist (indeed!), what have they been doing? For one thing, they have carried out acts of "targeted intervention" against military powers throughout the world. We do not know the full scope of these forms of intervention, how many may have led to the death of military personnel, or how many have involved attacks on our nuclear weapons systems. National security regulations keep us from knowing the truth. But my guess is the UFO aliens have sent a message to the nuclear powers of the world that these weapons are not to be used in battle, and they have not been used since the United States dropped two atomic bombs on Japan. There have been nuclear tests, but no weapons used in battle. I suspect we are in debt to the aliens/angels for the fact that there has been no nuclear war on earth yet.

Does this mean that the UFOs would use absolute force to make sure a nuclear war never happens on earth? I do not know. In a way, I see the Jewish holocaust during World War II as the willingness of God to let the human race see clearly how evil it can be. The angels of God did not stop the German Nazi crimes, human armies did. But in regard to nuclear weapons, can we really save ourselves from ourselves? The UFOs have not landed in force, like an invading army.

But they have carried out "targeted intervention" as a kind of shot across the bow of the military powers of the earth. Modern UFOs seem like they could have handled Pharaoh's army at the Red Sea very well.

It also seems possible UFOs have saved us from disasters related to the failure of nuclear power generating plants. One such plant is located at the Indian Point Nuclear Facility in Peekskill, New York. On the night of July 24, 1984, about a dozen plant workers saw a UFO hover over the plant. The UFO was "the size of three football fields." It hovered above Reactor #3, the only reactor operating. The electronic security systems of the plant shut down. The UFO was filmed by a camera for fifteen minutes, and the film turned over to government officials. The director of the plant had planned to order plant personnel to fire on the object, but it flew away before the order was given. The next day all personnel were told that "nothing happened," forget what they saw the night before.

Years later researcher Philip Imbrogno added these points. "He indicated that he had sworn testimony from several plant security personnel that in fact there had been a crack in the wall of Reactor #3, and that they had not only seen an enormous UFO hovering above, but some had seen non-humans walking through the containment wall of the reactor. Apparently, the beings had saved the plant from a nuclear disaster." (Dolan, p. 339)

As part of my own special version of nonsense, I cannot help thinking of Daniel. "Then King Nebuchadnezzar was astonished and rose up in haste. He said to his counselors, 'Did we not cast three men bound into the fire?' They answered the king, 'True, O king.' He answered, 'But I see four men loose, walking in the midst of the fire, and they are not hurt; and the appearance of the fourth is like a son of the gods." (Dan. 3:24, 25)

One can argue that "targeted intervention" is not fair. Bishop Spong might ask, if the angels of God (or UFO aliens) saved many American lives at Indian Point Nuclear facility, why didn't they do the same at Chernobyl? (Dolan says there are reports that a UFO appeared at Chernobyl, and carried out some type of beam activity which lowered the radiation level significantly, or the disaster might have destroyed "half of Europe." p. 366) I cannot fully explain the "ethics" of targeted intervention as those like Bishop Spong seem to demand. But it seems to be very much a pattern of modern UFO reports.

UFOs have not landed on the White House lawn and announced, "We are in charge now." Rather, they have been like traffic cops, making targeted arrests, and sometimes pulling speeding passengers from their own burning car wrecks. Is this demonic activity, as many Conservative Christians argue? It would seem to me that the nuclear powers of the world are the real demons that threaten to blow up God's vineyard, and we all pay taxes so that we may continue to be slaves to the terror of the national security state.

But what about UFO abductions? I don't know what to say about UFO abductions, except they fit the pattern of "targeted intervention." Those abducted seem in some sense to be "chosen people." Abductions make me believe it would be very possible for the angels of the Exodus to kill the first-born of Egypt on Passover night. I am in no position to deny that UFOs might be demons, or fallen angels, at least some of them. But I would ask: are the angels of God more powerful than demons; more powerful than fallen angels? If the answer is "yes," as I believe, then I will go on believing in and hoping for God's mercy. The human race is at risk for destruction every day at our own hands. We do not need any help from demons, or aliens who happen to be fallen angels, to destroy ourselves. We are good at doing our own fallen angel work. I believe in God's love enough to believe God knows that!

A Summary of the Situation from My Biblical Perspective

I believe we have two "contests" going on in our current UFO situation. The first is between the UFOs and the state. As Pharaoh in the Bible held the people of God captive as slaves, so our modern national security state, with the weapons science has built for the state, holding us all hostage to fear of nuclear death every day. I am sure UFO secrecy is motivated for several reasons in the eyes of the state, including fear of "panic" if the truth is released, fear of "religious fanaticism" if the truth is released, fear of "loss of credibility" of world leadership if UFO truth is released. Suddenly the President of the United States, and our military power, our modern Pharaohs, would look very weak and small.

I suspect that in the 1950's the governments of the world worried that we might soon face an alien invasion. But since no invasion has occurred, our human authorities may have concluded the aliens are satisfied to rule the earth through targeted intervention. This means the governments of the world can carry on as usual, with some restrictions. Exactly how these alien ordered restrictions or "Thou shalt nots" have been communicated to human authorities is of course a question we can all wonder about.

The second contest or trial in the wilderness is between UFOs and the church. The state has no trouble knowing that "UFOs are real." The state has taken a punch in the nose from UFO power. But the state has lied to the rest of us, telling us UFOs are a modern mythology, which many religious liberals are only too willing to believe. But the rest of us are caught up in an identification game. The identification game is this: who is lying, the government, or millions of citizens who have seen UFOs? Then on to the next level, if we conclude that UFOs are real, what are they? Just a bunch of space guys from another planet? (Apparent Roman Catholic position.) Or are they demons or fallen angels? (Position of several conservative

Protestants.) Or are they the angels of God, who are technologically savvy? (My position.) Or are they space guys who have deceived us into believing they are gods? (Von Daniken and several of his followers.)

The contest between modern UFOs and Christians is to identify the UFO reality properly, and this is very similar to the situation of the Jewish people when Jesus appeared. Jesus appeared, healed the sick, preached good news to the poor, and demanded identification. Some thought Jesus was demonic, that he healed by the power of the prince of demons. Jesus asked his disciples the critical question, "Who do men say that the Son of man is?" (Mt. 16:13) A variety of answers were given, including Elijah, John the Baptist, or maybe even Jeremiah. But Peter gave the divinely inspired answer, "You are the Christ, the son of the living God." (v. 16) We Christians all agree now: what a crime to crucify the Son of God (our excuse is we did not identify him correctly as the Christ.) Here is our current identification question as Christians: How do we know that UFOs do not carry the angels of God? How can we make the proper identification if our modern Pharaohs lie to us about what is going on? If we do not give the right answer in light of God's will, what might be the penalty? Perhaps God would decide that grafting the Jews back onto the vine is justified. "For if God did not spare the natural branches, neither will he spare you." (Rom. 11:21)

Dr. Barry H. Downing
January 2010

BIBLICAL UFO REVELATIONS

The Editor Red Sea
The Christian Century
October 25, 2010

Sir:

The Colorado team at the National Center for Atmospheric Research supposes a 63 mile per hour wind could part the Red Sea. There have been three traditional explanations for the parting: mythology, the supernatural, or a unique natural event (a 63 mile per hour wind setdown). But the space age has given us a fourth alternative, demanding a meta-narrative reformation.

The main problem with the wind theory is more textual than scientific. The primary power reported at the Red Sea is not an east wind, but rather the "pillar of cloud and fire" which is given credit for what we might call, borrowing from Rick Warren, "the purpose driven Exodus." What is this thing that hovers in the sky, or moves ahead of Israel at will, looks cloud-like during the day, glows in the dark, is cylindrical in shape, and seems to be in frequent voice contact with Moses? (See Ex. 14:19-30)

For more than 50 years, thousands of UFOs have been reported around the world, many cylindrical in shape, some up to a mile long. Former *Boston Globe* writer Leslie Kean, in her book, *UFOs: Generals, Pilots, and Government Officials Go on the Record,* documents how the United States government has led the way in deceiving us about the UFO reality. It turns out modern Pharaohs can't be trusted either.

But should we connect modern and biblical UFOs? Or why shouldn't we? How do we go at these questions?

The text says the Exodus UFO led Israel up to the Red Sea purposefully, suggesting the parting was an escape strategy for Israel. The text says the Lord was the cause of the wind, and the "angel of God" in the pillar of cloud was the center of power at the Red Sea. The Exodus UFO was reported to hover directly over the open sea channel at the time of the parting (v. 24), and when the Egyptians followed Israel into the sea, suddenly the Lord "looked down" on the Egyptians, causing the chariot wheels to come off, or bind up [translation is difficult here]. There is no wind reported, but there is some invisible power at work. Might some type of beam technology cause heat expansion in the axles and hubs of the chariots, locking them up? Suppose some type of beam technology caused the water to part; might the "strong east wind" be only a by product of an extraterrestrial power?

If the United States government either decided, or was forced, to stop lying about UFOs, immediately the larger culture would be asking biblical theologians to explain why the Exodus UFO should, or should not, be connected to our evolving space age perspective. How should we now understand biblical angelology? It may be nearing midnight in Egypt for our theological generation. I do not think we are ready to travel.

Barry H. Downing
Endwell, NY

BIBLICAL UFO REVELATIONS

ARTICLES AND PAPERS BY BARRY H. DOWNING

"Radiation Symptoms in Exodus," Flying Saucer Review, May-June 1972.

"UFOs As a Religious Phenomenon," 1972 MUFON Symposium Proceedings, Quincy, Il.

"Some Questions Concerning Dr. Menzel's Biblical Exegesis," 1973 MUFON Symposium Proceedings, Kansas City, MI.

"Space-Age Spin-Off," Christianity Today, August 31, 1973.

"UFOs and Religion," Skylook, November 1973.

"Religion and UFOs: The Extrasensory Problem," 1974 MUFON Symposium Proceedings, Akron, OH.

"Cult of 'The Two' Composed of Five Elements," Skylook, December, 1975.

"Ufology, Religion and Deception," MUFON UFO Journal, February, 1977.

"UFOs and Religion: Were the Ancient Astronauts Mistaken for Gods?" Ancient Astronauts Magazine, March, 1977.

"Demonic Theory of UFOs," The Encyclopedia of UFOs, ed. Ronald D. Story, Doubleday, 1980.

"Faith, Theory and UFOs," 1981 MUFON Symposium Proceedings, M.I.T., Cambridge, MA.

"Holy Communion," MUFON UFO Journal, April, 1987.

"UFOs and Religion: The French Connection," MUFON UFO Journal, June, 1988.

"UFOs: Four Questions for Theological Seminaries," 1988 MUFON Symposium Proceedings, Lincoln, NE.

"The God Hypothesis," MUFON UFO Journal, October, 1988.

"Strieber and the God Hypothesis," MUFON UFO Journal, November, 1988.

"The Rock of Ages Principle," MUFON UFO Journal, May, 1990.

"ET Contact: The Religious Dimension," 1990 MUFON Symposium Proceedings, Pensacola, FL.

"Did a UFO Part the Red Sea?" UFO Magazine, Vol. 5, No. 2, 1990.

"UFOs and Religion: Of Things Visible and Invisible," 1994 MUFON Conference Proceedings, Austin, TX.

"Exodus as a Paradigm of UFO Strategy," MUFON UFO Journal, October, 1994.

"Light Shining in Darkness," Houston Sky, December 1995-January 1996.

"Cult or Religion? Distinction is Longevity," Binghamton Press and Sun-Bulletin, April 13, 1977, p. E-1.

"The God Hypothesis: A Review," MUFON UFO Journal, April, 1997.

"The Second Coming of Marshall Applewhite," MUFON UFO Journal, May, 1997.

"The Bible and UFO Abductions," MUFON UFO Journal, January, 1998.

"Balducci Interview," MUFON UFO Journal, September, 1998.

"Religion, UFOs, Secrecy and Policy Decisions," MUFON UFO Journal, December, 1999.

"Is UFO Midnight a Possibility?" MUFON UFO Journal, May, 2000.

"UFOs and the Strange Business of Believing," 2001 MUFON Conference Proceedings, LA, CA.

"Biblical Miracles as Super-Technology," The Encyclopedia of Extraterrestrial Encounters, ed. Ronald D. Story, New American Library, 2001.

Review, "The Missing Times," MUFON UFO Journal, September 2001.

"Wormholes, Heaven and the God Hypothesis," MUFON UFO Journal, Part I, November 2001, Part II, December 2001.

Review, "The Hunt for Zero Point," MUFON UFO Journal, October, 2002.

"UFOs, Cults and Cloning," MUFON UFO Journal, February 2003.

Review, "Alien Scriptures: Extraterrestrials in the Holy Bible," MUFON UFO Journal, January, 2006.

Review, "The Lure of the Edge: Scientific Passions, Religious Beliefs, and the Pursuit of UFOs," MUFON UFO Journal, April, 2006.

"UFOs, the Bible, and Targeted Intervention," on line at Strong Delusion—Home, January, 2010,.

"UFOs and the Bible: 7 Theories," On line at Strong Delusion—Home, October, 2010.

"It's High Time for Meta-narrative Reformation," MUFON UFO Journal, October, 2010.

Review: "A.D. After Disclosure," MUFON UFO Journal, May, 2011.

53251678R00110

Made in the USA
Middletown, DE
26 November 2017